IN
COLD
BLOOD

JOHNNY THUNDERS

THE OFFICIAL BIOGRAPHY

JAW
BONE

A Jawbone book
Revised edition 2023
Published in the UK and the USA by
Jawbone Press
Office G1
141–157 Acre Lane
London SW2 5UA
England
www.jawbonepress.com

Published under licence from Jungle Books
(Bravour Ltd t/a)
www.jungle-records.com

ISBN 978-1-911036-11-1

This book is dedicated to the memories
of Johnny Thunders and Jerry Nolan.

Printed by Short Run Press, Exeter, Devon

1 2 3 4 5 27 26 25 24 23

ABOVE Muse and author: Johnny
Thunders and Nina Antonia.
Photo by Jon 'Boogie' Tiberi.

FOREWORD

BY MIKE SCOTT

Johnny symbolises three things: rock'n'roll, looking sharp, and getting out of it. As everyone knows, the third of those eventually outweighed the first two and upturned his musical career. Yet Johnny's preternatural abilities as a rock'n'roller and sharp dresser, even in the depth of his depravities, ensure his legend. If he hadn't been an all-time great rocker or the sharpest dresser of his generation, with a charisma the size of Manhattan, no one would care about him now. He'd be a forgotten junkie who never made it. But the legend lives because Johnny Thunders was the sharpest, slickest guitar-playing stage performer of all time, a larger-than-life cartoon, a streetwise demigod with switchblade moves, drop-dead duds and elegant, contemptuous riffs that sounded like sneers. He had an Italian's style, a New Yorker's sass, and America's eternal youth. No one will ever top him. No one ever did. I saw him once whip a steel comb out of his pocket mid-song, primp his quiff between licks, turn on a dime, and then machine-gun the crowd with his guitar on the return, all in one fabulous movement. The only male performers I can call to mind with a comparably killer blend of moves and artistry are Elvis, James Brown, and Prince. But Johnny was more beautiful than James, more dangerous than Prince, played better guitar than Elvis, and was more reckless than any of them. And more doomed. His story ain't pretty, and his trajectory was laced with calamity, but his natural magic was always present in action or potential. Nina knew Johnny and has observed his life with fandom, understanding, compassion, and detachment. She is more than qualified to capture its dynamics in her well-chosen words and a series of illuminating interviews.

MIKE SCOTT, THE WATERBOYS, DECEMBER 2022

FOREWARNED

Johnny Thunders didn't just flirt with death, he courted it. Even so, his eventual demise in New Orleans on April 23, 1991, still came as a terrible shock. All of the false alarms and embellished whispers of his passing over the years had somehow managed to make Johnny seem both vulnerable and invincible, until the dread inevitable was finally substantiated.

When I first began working on *In Cold Blood* in the early 1980s, Thunders wasn't a memory, and I wrote in the present tense, hope clinging to the ledge, Johnny nine-lives defying the odds. Now it's all consigned to the past.

Johnny Thunders created an almost unique situation in that it was next to impossible to separate the man from his reputation. When reality had finished reporting on drug problems, police busts, and deportations, rumour picked up the story, erasing the fragile line between cold fact and neurotic fantasy. Then you had to separate the man from himself: Johnny Genzale, the shy sweetheart, and Johnny Thunders, the sleepy eyed gutterpunk.

Looked upon as the pale spectre of rock'n'roll immolation, Thunders qualified his image every time he staggered into the mile-high headlines of the press. He lived a dangerous life and eventually came to represent what most people would rather forget when it comes to popular entertainment. Sure, they may want to read William Burroughs or go and see *Trainspotting*, but media tourists rarely want to tangle with the real deal, choosing instead the darkness of the cinema or the printed word, so they can walk the same streets without having to cross through the shadows that exist there. Johnny didn't set out to be a dope-fiend artiste ruling the roost of slum city rock. He wanted to be as great as Presley before the army, or Sinatra in his prime, and sometimes he was.

Sadly, and perhaps obviously, for a great many of Thunders' 'fans', one of the main pulls seemed to be the progression of the guitarist's mental and physical anguish, the tolerance of his body and the levels of his nihilistic, self-destructive motivations. As the condemned man of rock'n'roll, Johnny wasn't always as oblivious as casual observers might have believed, or critics presumed, but he wasn't strong enough to escape, either.

He once said onstage, 'Okay. You got it. I'm gonna die tonight. I'm gonna die up here . . .' and the audience cheered.

In time, the junkie mythology overshadowed Thunders' innate abilities: the unique rock'n'roll sense of finesse, the sharp wit, and a singular guitar style. A legion of musicians has attempted to emulate his stance and attitude but hasn't come close and never will. It's not too hard to play the way that Johnny did, and guitarists have tried and will go on trying, but they can't make it sound the same: a pact between persona, warmth, and power that built to an extraordinary crescendo. When Johnny was on form, he could charm a snake pit of a crowd, snapping out of drugged lethargy to deliver all that rock'n'roll ever promised to be: freedom, subversion, style, release. Johnny Thunders was the last embodiment of a broken perfection that was true rebel culture before commerce overwhelmed creativity. A miniature classic that assumed legendary proportions, he had a way of moving through it all that told you he knew everything, even though there were some things he'd rather forget.

NINA ANTONIA, AUGUST 1999

IN COLD BLOOD

PART ONE

JET BOY

CHAPTER ONE

A JUKEBOX MADE OF CITY

Before the fifties died of an exquisitely painless form of cancer and fear, blood cells tingled to Dion and stolen Lucky Strikes. Leather jackets boasted turf designs stitched on the back like pirate flags, baseball bats swung menacingly in alleyways whilst high above the shadows someone played a Paul & Paula tune. Drive-ins became the official shrines for swift sex, popcorn, and B-movies, and Sal Mineo turned capped sleeved vests into an art form.

On the outskirts of the city, where ivory was still the colour of soap not the polished handle of a switchblade, a little kid with heavy black hair lay in bed listening, when he should have been sleeping, to the music that came dancing across the landing from his sister's room. As he drifted off, the teenage romance and ruin of The Shangri-Las, The Crystals, and The Angels seeped into his dreams: 'I grew up listening to music. My sister Mariann was five and half years older than me and she played all those girl groups, that's how I heard all that stuff.'

John Anthony Genzale was born in Queens, one of New York's outer boroughs, on July 15, 1952, a heady mix of second-generation Neapolitan and Sicilian heritage. His father, Emil, should have been proud, but he was prouder still of his lady-killing charm and good looks, leaving his wife Josephine to fend for the family, as Mariann Bracken recalled:

We lived in East Elmhurst, Queens. It was always just the three of us, my mother, Johnny, and me. My father was a womaniser, and he left when Johnny was an infant. We had little or no contact with him. He never gave my mother any support, financially or otherwise. She had to work at whatever she could, and while she worked I took care of Johnny. We had a hard life but no matter what, Johnny had everything.

Except a guitar. By the time Johnny Genzale was four years old he'd seen Elvis Presley personify what rebellion was on television, and he wanted some. He hadn't had to plead too much for his ma to bring home a plastic guitar from the toy store, and although no melody could be plucked from the strings, it felt right. A year later, Johnny had his first brush with both the law and audience approval, according to Mariann:

> He had to have his tonsils out and he kicked and screamed all the way to the hospital. He wasn't going in. We walked in one door, he ran out the other. A police officer brought him back. Although it was only one night in the hospital and home the next day, we were worried sick. When we went to pick him up, the nurses told us that he had entertained them. He'd been imitating Elvis Presley the whole night!

Although little Johnny Genzale was usually shy outside of his impromptu performances, he was a livewire, and all the esoteric disciplines of the Catholic church and his role as an altar boy did little to curb the wild streak that ran through him. It was baseball that mopped up his energy, hitting the ball as high as the stars, and even though he was kind of petite he was strong enough and fast enough to make the neighbourhood team: 'I used to play baseball from eight in the morning till eight the next night and loved it.' Queens, after all, does boast Shea Stadium, where the legendary Mickey Mantle, the sporting hero of Johnny's childhood, brought the New York Yankees to baseball glory.

If Johnny Genzale progressed through his schooling in a deluge of bad behaviour reports that followed him from Our Lady of Fatima in nearby Jackson Heights to New Town High, his passion for baseball remained a constant feature, something to excel in. Eventually scouted by the Philadelphia Phillies and several other teams including the Boston Red Sox, at the age of thirteen a future in the sport might have been on the cards for Johnny, except for one Little League ruling that insisted upon the presence of the junior hopeful's father. Johnny would later tell journalists that he quit baseball after a coach demanded he cut his hair, evading not the truth but the hurt.

While baseball lost a star in the making, rock'n'roll gained one on the rebound when Johnny traded his bat for a bass guitar, as Mariann Bracken explained:

> After he couldn't play baseball, he really started on his music. He formed a band with a bunch of kids in junior high school. I'd got a job in a small catering firm and they'd play there for bar mitzvahs and things like that. My mother says that at one time Johnny worked in the candy store on the corner, in the ice cream parlour, but the only thing I ever remember him doing was playing music.

Although Johnny & The Jay Walkers originally started out as smart little princelings in their matching nylon no-crease suits, covering the latest chart hits, they would soon abandon the uniformity of both their clothes and their material, evolving into a short-lived rock band called The Reign. Though a minor step in Johnny's story, the band managed to record at least one track with the rather telling title of 'Zippered Up Heart'.

Even though a place at Bryant High, a regular neighbourhood school, awaited Johnny, he managed in what was by all accounts a heartrending turn to persuade his mother that he would be better suited to attending a private, liberal establishment called Quintanos. Tucked behind Carnegie Hall and within easy reach of Central Park, Quintanos aimed to groom its students for success in the performing arts. However, no form of education, no matter how laid back, was going to corral Johnny Genzale, and he bolted at the age of sixteen to play in a city shaped like a million stone jukeboxes. Becoming familiar with the wash of noise and neon, he started hanging out at Nobody's Bar on Bleecker Street, a groupie haunt and pitstop for English bands passing through town and the Fillmore East, renowned for its live rock acts.

It was quite a drive from their respective homes in Long Island, but the journey to New York City signified the start of the weekend for Janis Cafasso and her cousin, Gail Higgins Smith, who explains:

When the Fillmore East opened in New York, we used to go there every Saturday night. In between acts we'd hang out in the lobby, and Johnny was always there with a gang of boys. This was about 1967, when he was living in Jackson Heights. I don't remember how he came up to us but I do remember that by the end of the evening, he and Janis were sitting on the floor talking, which started this great romance.

From that point on we'd go to the Fillmore with Johnny and whoever the boy was that I was seeing. The three of us even visited California together. After that, Janis and I were going to live in San Francisco, but after New York we felt there was no nightlife, so we came back and decided that we would move into the city. We went over to John's house, got the *Village Voice*, and found an apartment in the East Village and the three of us moved in. I took a job at Gimbel's Department store. Was Janis working? Was John working? I can't remember them ever working while we lived there, but we were all chipping in on the rent. I do remember Janis and John fighting, and Janis moving in and out, but, in between the craziness, it was great fun.

We all used to go to our parents and come back with shopping bags full of food. John would bring these big roast beefs from his mother, and we'd cook these huge meals, but we had to eat really fast because John would eat everything that was on the table, so if you didn't eat faster than him, you wouldn't get any. He used to sit in the other room with his bass guitar and try to play and sing. I would scream, 'Give up John, just give up!' The first song he ever wrote was 'Dirty Dusty Dungarees'. We went to Coney Island where they have these little recording booths and we said, 'Let's go in and make a record.' He sung 'Dirty Dusty Dungarees', then we sang 'Duke Of Earl' together.

Costing less than a dollar to make, 'Dirty Dusty Dungarees' has gone the same sad way as the little novelty recording booths, simply vanishing with time. Johnny's future was still misty, but he had already chosen the direction that would engulf him. Gail Higgins Smith sets the scene:

Me, Johnny, and Janis were big rock'n'roll fans. We went anywhere to see a rock'n'roll band and to meet rock'n'roll people. Somehow, because we were brazen, we'd always end up meeting them. When we went to the Newport Jazz Festival, we ended up sitting in a hotel room with Rod Stewart, drinking beer. We met Janis Joplin, and the MC5, who were Johnny's heroes. He was so excited when he met Keith Richards. He would talk about him all the time. We met him at a bar on 5th Avenue and 13th Street. People like Jagger and Lennon used to go there, and one night Keith Richards was there. We sat around this table, having drinks and meeting Keith. Johnny used to say, 'I want to be a pop star, I want to be like Keith Richards.' He even kept Keith's cigarette packet.

In 1969, Johnny and a girlfriend (almost certainly Janis Cafasso) took a three-month trip to London to check out the English music scene. Using a borrowed press pass the young couple hustled their way into a plethora of gigs. One of the highlights of their vacation included seeing Tyrannosaurus Rex at the Roundhouse, in the period when Marc Bolan switched from acoustic to electric guitar. Johnny returned home ready to pursue a future in rock'n'roll. If the finer details of his career were still somewhat vague, he already looked every inch the part with his long dark teased hair, akin to Ronnie Spector donning a tiara of raven's wings. Although his quiet manner ruled out any form of verbal self-promotion, his decorative appearance—which had been further accentuated by Janis, who would find a future in fashion—drew the attention of most of the boys who would become The New York Dolls.

By the end of the 1960s, Central Park was no longer a rallying point for hippie experimentation, and the nudity and headbands were scorned by a new generation of kids who flocked to the park's fountain landmark on Sunday afternoons, dressed to the nines. In July 1991, Jerry Nolan told the *Village Voice*:

> Out of the hundreds and hundreds of people you'd see at the fountain, where everyone was profiling, Johnny and Janis stood out the most. You could see them ten miles away. She looked like a Doll, very heavy rouge, wild socks, platform shoes, lots of colours. He was really young then, fifteen or sixteen. I was older, twenty-two. Janis got Johnny into his look. He was wearing high heels, and you remember that teased-hair look, that Rod Stewart look? Johnny's was like that, but even more dimensionalised and exaggerated, teased all the way up in like a crown. It was so long. He would have a platinum blond streak down the back. He would have a girl's blouse on, and on top of that a sparkling girl's vest. And then maybe a cowboy scarf. Mixing in cowboy stuff with glamorous 40s girls' stuff . . . and he wore makeup, which really set him off.

Originally hailing from Brooklyn, Jerry Nolan had been bounced back and forth between army bases in Oklahoma and Hawaii after his mother, Charlotte, married a military man. At the age of ten, Jerry and his sister went to see Elvis at a local roller-derby arena. Already a little too hep to display outright enthusiasm, Nolan was nonetheless deeply impressed by both Presley's original band and his early sartorial splendour. After being taught to play the drums by a young black soldier, Jerry put into practice all that he had learned at a high school assembly talent contest in Oklahoma. The boy who had such a tough time in class suddenly acquired status in the eyes of his fellow students. 'That changed my whole life. I wasn't ashamed anymore. I could finally do something real good.'

However, when the family moved back to Brooklyn, Nolan found a new status when he joined a gang called The Young Lords. It wasn't morality or cowardice that made him hold back from full-on fighting but the thought of a rumpled suit and the dry-cleaning bill. Violence was a formality but style was everything. It could be said that playing drums eventually got Jerry off the street, but his hard-knock brand of rock'n'roll was not about salvation. Nolan's career had been as choppy as the bumps and grinds of the strippers whose routines he'd backed with a heavy hitting flourish after leaving school. By the time he set eyes on Johnny in Central Park, Jerry had just returned from Detroit, where he'd spent the summer playing in Suzi Quatro's band Cradle. Although Johnny was pretty young, Jerry Nolan could spot rocker credentials from a million miles, and he knew that one day they would be in a band together.

If Jerry Nolan was sure of the future, Arthur Kane, a blonde from the Bronx, and his best buddy, George Fedorcik, were more hopeful than certain but equally impressed by Johnny's sense of style. George:

We used to see Johnny at the Fillmore every time there'd be a British band playing. We were totally into the English scene—the Stones, the Yardbirds. We never really spoke to Johnny, but we'd always say hi because of the way he looked. We thought he was the coolest thing in the world.

The nascent core of The New York Dolls was formed when Johnny started jamming with Sylvain Sylvain (née Mizrahi) and Billy Murcia. It wasn't like Johnny had to audition to play bass with them; Syl and Billy already considered him something of a local legend, as Sylvain explained:

> Now this was the time when *Gimme Shelter* was playing. Me and Billy were in love with that movie and Johnny is in it. He's fooling around with his hair, sitting on one of his friends' shoulders. It's in the sequence when the lights get turned on the audience and Mick Jagger says something like, 'New York, let's look at you, now.' We used to see it every other day and we'd go, 'Hey man, there's that fucking guy we used to go to school with!'

In spite of the fact that all three had been raised in the same neighbourhood and had attended New Town High and Quintano's, it actually took Syl and Billy longer to hook up with Johnny than might have been expected due to a detour into the fashion industry. Sylvain's family had been forced to flee from Egypt during the Suez Canal crisis of 1956, while the Murcia clan made a similarly hasty exit from Colombia after Billy's father got embroiled in a business deal that turned hostile. But both boys looked as if they'd been cut from similar cloth, sharing the same wilful corkscrew curls and slight build. They cemented their friendship after a playground scuffle in junior high and became virtually inseparable.

Billy, who had once been described as 'a cool drink of water with a hot head', started playing drums and Syl reached for the guitar. By 1968 they'd joined forces with an older, more accomplished guitarist called Mike Turby, who had gained neighbourhood notoriety with The Orphans—Queens' retort to The Rolling Stones. Calling themselves The Pox, the trio, whose influences included The Who and the Stooges, cut a demo for Harry Lookofsky, who had been responsible for the grandiose production on The Left Banke's US top ten single 'Walk Away Renee'. Unfortunately, the public remained immune to The Pox, and Turby quit.

Having failed to make a significant gesture with their music, they devoted themselves to what was then rock'n'roll's second in command, fashion. As they began to weave psychedelic sweaters on hand looms, Sylvain learned the details of retail when he started working at a trendy men's boutique called A Different Drummer on Lexington Avenue and 63rd Street. Across the road in an old brownstone building was a hospital, yet no ambulances ever screeched to a halt outside. The victims might have been too small for stretchers, but they were better cared for than the peeling façade above the entrance, which read The New York Doll's Hospital. Billy thought it would make as great a name for a band, as did Sylvain.

As their fashion outlet, Truth & Soul, expanded, orders started coming in from Betsey Johnson's ultra-happening boutique, Paraphernalia, and they began to receive press attention. After being made a lucrative offer by a large knitting mill in Brooklyn, they sold their designs and went to Europe for the best part of a year. Like a down payment on their future, Sylvain purchased an impressive stack of Marshall amps while in London, which were shipped back to New York. Gathering dust in Billy's mom's basement, the amps lay dormant until the dandy duo returned from their travels, nabbed Johnny, and finally activated the Dolls as 1970 drew to a close.

With all the pent-up energy of a freshly lit firecracker, Johnny Genzale was not cut out to be a bass player. Recognising this, Sylvain began to pass on some of Mike Turby's guitar licks:

When it really started between us three, we became like a family. Johnny started coming down to the basement and I taught him all the riffs I had learned from Mike and the things that I had picked up on my own. I basically said, 'Look, if you know those scales and you go like this, instead of doing the whole fucking bar chord, just hold it with two fingers and you make a little power chord.' Johnny took to that, baby! We'd all sit on the bed with these cheap guitars and do Marc Bolan songs, as well as some blues and instrumentals.

However, the opening phase of the Dolls lurched to a full stop when Syl went back to London.

Even if Johnny had in fact closed the door behind him, it always felt like it got slammed in his face when it came to girlfriends. Although he was never short of female attention, his closest relationships were doomed by his volatile neediness, and by the age of nineteen he had already written the song that many consider his finest moment, 'You Can't Put Your Arms Around A Memory'. Inspired by Janis, with whom he was embroiled in a typically intense saga of reunion and despair, the song takes its title from a throwaway line in one of his favourite television shows, Jackie Gleason and *The Honeymooners*, and plumbs the depths of dejection. Eyewitness Gail Higgins Smith:

> Before John started taking drugs, his adrenalin level would make him high. I remember one time he got so crazed because of a fight with Janis, he started banging on this steel door that we'd had built because the flat was on the ground floor. It moved two feet out with the sheer force of him. It was emotional turmoil, not temper that made him like that. The drugs didn't make John crazy, he was like that before he started taking them. He was still insecure.

While they would remain lifelong friends, the overwrought nature of Johnny's relationship with Janis, combined with a disregard for boring stuff like coming up with rent money, led to Gail penning a polite 'Dear John' note in which she asked him to move out.

After finding and losing a place on Avenue A, Johnny resorted to crashing at the Chelsea Hotel before he got back together with Janis. If life wasn't already crazy enough, they turned their new 14th Street apartment into a mini zoo. Aside from Johnny's dogs, Pretty Girl and Onion, they installed a snake and a pet monkey. Mariann, who had married her boyfriend Rusty Bracken and just started a family, got a typically frantic call from her little brother after the monkey escaped. A chase ensued on rooftop and fire escape until the runaway monkey was talked out of doing something desperate by Johnny and Rusty.

With an unruly menagerie to feed, Johnny began making a buck or two selling acid and pot. Knowing that potent hallucinogenics can rip the lid off the insecure, he only occasionally dipped into his stash of LSD. While under the influence however he managed to summon Arthur Kane into his orbit, as Gail Higgins Smith recalled:

> I remember meeting Arthur because Johnny and I were tripping. We'd gone to Nobody's and there was Arthur with these huge platform boots on. He looked like a six-foot-tall blonde Frankenstein. Johnny and I both stared at each other as the same thought crossed our minds: 'Why do they send people like this when you're tripping?!'

Outside of being a surreal figment of acid-tinged reality, Arthur had recently been deported from Amsterdam, where he and George Fedorcik had unsuccessfully attempted to get a band together. Back in the city, Arthur found work at the telephone company while George began a stint at the post office. Before New York got its post wired and its lines mailed, they got serious about their music, Fedorcik reinventing himself as Rick Rivets to denote his rock'n'roll aspirations. Late one evening, in the course of an impromptu attempt to steal a motorbike, they spotted Johnny outside a pizza place on Bleecker Street and decided it was time to get properly acquainted. Arthur:

> We were across the street, and I said, 'Okay, here's that guy, why don't we go over and find out what's going on with him?' I went over and said, 'I hear you play guitar or bass or something, do you want to get together?'

Arthur Kane's indecisive quest to ascertain Johnny's instrument of choice was more prophetic than he could have grasped at the time. Although Johnny turned up for rehearsals with his bass, he was also getting a handle on playing rhythm guitar. After a couple of sessions, Arthur made the crucial decision to swap with him. It was during this period that Johnny Genzale sought a new identity, one that would reflect his transformation as a guitarist. While he couldn't have wished for a first name more loaded with rebel connotations than Johnny, an alter ego was required, something that suited the elemental and distorted quality of his guitar playing. After toying with 'Johnny Volume', he settled on Thunders, after the DC comic book cowboy hero Johnny Thunder—Mystery Rider Of The Wild West. Splendid, childlike, and stormy, Johnny Thunders was created.

With a drummer in tow, they booked some studio time and riffed through a selection of covers including material by The Yardbirds, Chuck Berry, and The Rolling Stones. At Thunders' suggestion, their original sticksman was ousted in favour of Billy, and the band began rehearsing in the Murcia family basement. As Johnny became increasingly adept, Rick Rivets switched to rhythm guitar, allowing Thunders to take over the lead position. His waning enthusiasm for the journey he had to make in from Queens every time the band got together prompted a search for a more central rehearsal space. They found one in the dingy storeroom of a cycle shop off Columbus Avenue and 82nd Street. The owner, Rusty—who the band nicknamed 'Beanie', owing to the funny little knitted caps he always wore—took their money but not their word. Fearing that they would liberate his stock if he allowed them to roam free, Rusty locked them in for the duration of their rehearsals. Faced with nightly incarceration, the band members chose their provisions with care. Arthur and Rick made a ritual out of picking up a quart of vodka, which they shared with Billy while Thunders, who wasn't particularly partial to liquor, supplied downers and pot. He also started to bring in some of his own material.

Although this stage of the Dolls' development is usually referred to as their 'Actress' phase, after a suggestion by Janis Cafasso, the band never officially adopted the title. On October 10, 1971, Rick Rivets captured their unruly blues cacophony when he bought his cassette player down to a rehearsal. The Actress session—released over twenty-five years later as *Dawn Of The Dolls*—is a crucial artefact, almost entirely comprised of Thunders numbers. Unlike the early recordings of most musicians and songwriters, where a glimpse of nascent style might be heard or the glimmer of technique discerned, Johnny is absolutely formed. He is of course very young, and his chewy New York intonation would lessen over the years, but the nasal mewl of his voice would remain just the same. That unique brand of the chaffing married to the melodic already infuses his guitar playing while the core of the songs would be scattered through his repertoire for the majority of his life. 'That's Poison' is an undeveloped blueprint for 'Subway Train'; 'We've Been Through This Before' would eventually metamorphose into the elegiac 'Sad Vacation'; 'I Am Confronted' is a rough sketch for the epic sob story 'So Alone'. Similarly, 'I'm A Boy, I'm A Girl' would also be revived. Perhaps the most staggering aspect of *Dawn Of The Dolls* is the sheer sense of loss in Johnny's material, a motif that would recur throughout his life.

As Thunders was more interested in being the lead guitarist than the frontman, the band started looking for likely candidates and found David Johansen. The product of a working-class Catholic family from Staten Island, presided over by a Norwegian insurance salesman and his Irish wife, David Johansen had grown up with a tantalising view of the New York City skyline that seemed to him like a stage set of miracles. Biding his time, dreaming of a glittering debut, he poured his frustrations into writing poetry and lyrics. These came in useful when he started singing with a local outfit called The Vagabond Missionaries before he made it to the city as part of an art-rock band, Fast Eddie & The Electric Japs, who played around the Greenwich Village area. Quick-witted and fast mouthed, David Johansen combined a love of music with theatrical ambitions and would later tell journalists that he had appeared in a couple of skin flicks prior to joining the Dolls, notably *Bike Boys Go Ape* and *Studs On Main Street*.

While his porno past was just another put-on from his lightning repartee, Johansen landed a walk-on part as a spear carrier in one of Charles

Ludlum's avant-garde Ridiculous Theatre productions. Gravitating to the artistic underground, he met and moved into an apartment on East 6th Street with a former model called Diane Poluski. Part of the Andy Warhol scene, Poluski had played Holly Woodlawn's pregnant sister in *Trash* and introduced David to some of the participants in the world of Warhol—all of which put him in good stead when Billy and Arthur made a house call, as David would recollect:

> There was a Colombian guy who lived in my building, and he was friends with Billy and me. He told me that he knew these guys who were looking for a singer in their band. One day Billy and Arthur came to my door. I'm kind of exaggerating here, but Billy was like four feet tall and Arthur was eight feet tall and they both had these really high boots on and were kind of dressed like Marc Bolan. I just saw them standing there and liked them right away. I thought, *Oh God, this is great, what a pair of lunatics!*

Possessing a voice that could sandblast a city and a rootsy harmonica technique, Johansen passed his audition and brought to the band a flagrantly dramatic edge partially copped from Warhol's drag queen muses, Candy Darling, Jackie Curtis, and Holly Woodlawn. When she later described the essence of drag as 'It's not a man or a woman, it's fabulous', Woodlawn could have been introducing The New York Dolls.

The band finally reactivated the Dolls' moniker as the end of 1971 loomed, Arthur tagging on the 'New York' prefix:

> I wanted to add the 'New York' because in New York you would always be hearing on the radio and television like . . . New York Jets, New York Yankees, New York Vets, New York this and that . . . and I thought we'd get an immediate local following if we called ourselves The New York Dolls, and also it sounded like something from a 1930s Broadway show.

When Sylvain returned from Europe, he was understandably piqued, for not only were the band up and running without him but they were also using the name he'd originally suggested. Fortunately, harmony was restored with heels, as Sylvain would note:

> I'd come back from London with all these boots from Johnson & Johnson. There was one particular pair, knee-high maroon suede lace-ups with a layered leather platform heel. Johnny went nuts for them. They were a little bit small, but he traded half his house for those fucking shoes. Whenever Johnny would move into a new apartment, which he seemed to do all the time, me and Billy would help him, 'cos we had a car. He had so many clothes; it would be like a party.

One party that Syl missed out on was the Dolls' debut at a city-sponsored beggar's banquet. The welfare workers in charge of the Endicott Hotel, a crumbling refuge for the homeless across the street from Rusty Beanies, had been left high and dry when the group they had booked to play at the residents' Christmas bash, reneged on their promise. Unable to miss the nightly racket issuing from the cycle shop, one of the welfare workers approached the band. On Christmas Eve, The New York Dolls got a bedraggled crowd up and dancing to a fine selection of R&B covers. However, their official launch was not enough to keep the necessary momentum going for Rivets, who had begun to slack off. The situation was remedied almost instantly, according to Johnny: 'Rick Rivets started fucking around, coming to practise late and stuff like that, so we canned him and got Sylvain in.'

CHAPTER TWO

CURSED, POISONED, CONDEMNED

Freed from the restraints of reality or inhibition, The New York Dolls became their own fantasy of how they imagined life in a band would be: a fabulous delirium where the music never stopped, the joints 'n' pills 'n' liquor 'n' sex were always in plentiful supply, and the purgatory of morning was banished forever.

Extravagantly erotic, the Dolls projected their dream world in a neon-coloured thrift shop burlesque, wearing clothes that looked best after midnight and tawdry in natural light, a hybrid of straight-baiting semi-transvestism. Although their shimmering plumage and high heels, which lent a tottering feminine gait to the proceedings, were a terrifying violation of natural order to most hetero males, the boys in the band knew that girls liked nothing better than to play with Dolls.

Everything was exaggerated: the gesture, the drama, the lyrics, the dirty R&B throb that kept the momentum in their music. As estranged from convention as The New York Dolls were, they retained all the best traditions of rock'n'roll and reinvented whatever they couldn't quite grasp, creating a uniquely dyslexic approximation of the Stones, Bo Diddley, and The Shangri-Las, combined with their own highly idiosyncratic style. What the Dolls lacked in refinement they made up for with a streetwise sophistication, yet they remained tenderly oblivious to just how subversive they were until they tried to transcend their immediate domain.

In their gestation phase, The New York Dolls got further acquainted with playing live in front of a small crowd at their loft on 119 Chrystie Street. Situated above a Chinese noodle factory, the loft became the band's central HQ after Johnny, Janis, Billy, and Sylvain moved in. Mainly surviving on shoplifting sprees, the band threw parties whenever the rent was due. Sylvain:

> One of Johnny's friends would be at the door collecting two dollars from each person that arrived. Janis was in charge of the lights. We performed in the kitchen area, 'cos it was a step or two up. Behind us was the refrigerator and the sink. There would be guys selling drugs and girls selling sex and we'd play rock'n'roll. 'Human Being' and 'Frankenstein' came from one of those long, rent-party nights.

Mindful of their fabulous destiny, and living in almost continuous performance, The New York Dolls quickly developed a set list. Aside from the grotesque glory of 'Frankenstein' and the wry assessment of mortal frailty that is 'Human Being', 'Jet Boy' also took its first steps in the Chrystie Street loft, as Sylvain recalled: 'Johnny was playing the opening riff and I said, Wait a minute, and did my little baby chords, which was a D and a G. We jammed it at rehearsal, and David said he had some great lyrics for it. Then we added the background oohs and ahhs.' The Dolls were all Jet Boys, cartoon kids of the jet age flying around New York, and by the spring of 1972 they were ready to descend on the city.

Before The New York Dolls even had a reputation, they managed to confound the critics when they played their second gig on May 29, in the Palm Room of the Diplomat Hotel. Running adjacent to the X-rated crossroads that was then Times Square, the Diplomat was a suitably seedy setting for an 'Invitation Beyond The Valley' that also featured Jackie Curtis (who would subsequently be immortalised by Lou Reed in 'Walk On The Wild Side') and a band called Shaker, whose drummer Jerry Nolan particularly impressed Billy Murcia.

If Jackie Curtis and Shaker were at the opposite ends of the spectrum, the Dolls were less easy to define and garnered a couple of lousy write-ups by local journalists who couldn't quite decide whether they were a theatrical turn or a rock act, or both. The response of the patrons at a bathhouse in Brooklyn where the Dolls played their next two dates, again with Jackie Curtis, might have erred toward the pernickety, but the band eventually won out, according to Arthur Kane:

> It was like there was no audience because all the guys stayed in their cubicles having sex with someone, so we didn't know what to do. Everyone in the group had taken MDA; I think I was selling it at the time. It was kind of like LSD without the heavy thinking, but it makes you stumble around, hallucinating. We weren't sure how to dress for the bathhouse, so the first night we went feminine—I wore hot pants. They didn't seem to appreciate the femme look, although we had a lot of fun on the MDA. The next night we came back in leather and chains and got more interest. Everyone came out of their little cubicles to watch us.

What the Dolls wanted was to get the whole glittering island of Manhattan out of their little cubicles and dancing, but oddly enough there were very few venues where they could start to establish some sort of following. Many of the clubs that had flourished in the previous decade had fallen into dereliction, and although Max's Kansas City would have been an appropriate place to start, The New York Dolls were initially considered to be upstart urchins in the hierarchy of the underground firmament that gathered there. Like most innovators, the Dolls were left to blaze their own trail, a journey that led them to a theatre complex one block west of Broadway called the Mercer Arts Center.

Attached to the crumbling Broadway Central Hotel, the Mercer Arts Center was a contemporary venue that housed several different sized theatres named after various authors and playwrights. The Dolls might have been considered a little freaky by the Center's booking agent, but

CURSED, POISONED, CONDEMNED

he agreed to let them play there, designating a tiny room in the back of the complex so they wouldn't scare off the regular patrons of the arts. Used to the language of the theatre, the Mercer Arts Center advertised the forthcoming gig as 'The Dolls Of NY', which sounded more like a Busby Berkeley musical than a rock band.

In readiness for the big night, the band put in some extra practice. It wasn't a question of perfection, they just honed what they did best: alienated rock'n'roll roughly punctuated by 'Killer' Kane's cavernous-sounding bass lines and the Flintstone shudder of Murcia's drumming. Probably the most accomplished musician of the bunch, Sylvain constantly resuscitated the faint melody under Thunders' fractured, squawking riffs while David Jo's full-strength unfiltered vocals flayed the lyrics. As the band developed, Johansen and Thunders emerged as the main songwriting team, penning the profoundly sexy 'Bad Girl' just before they began their legendary residency at the Mercer Arts Center, the lead singer's astute mini melodramas in a turbulent alliance with Johnny's wildly careening guitar maulings.

Tired of the lock-ins at Rusty Beanies, the Dolls moved to Talent–Recon, a more accessible rehearsal space run by a fire-eater called Satan. In the less obscure location, they came into further contact with Shaker, who also rehearsed there and managed to inspire a denim clad cowboy band who plugged away night after night in another room. Knowing they could never be as pretty or provocative as The New York Dolls, the cowboy band eventually took the guise of glam animals and emerged as KISS. However, the group with the highest local profile at Talent–Recon was Eric Emerson and The Magic Tramps, their frontman having once shared a scene in *Chelsea Girls* with Nico and danced in Andy Warhol's live multimedia event, The Exploding Plastic Inevitable.

When The New York Dolls finally made their debut at the Mercer Arts Center, it was as support to The Magic Tramps (minus Emerson) and Satan. Perhaps it was a Busby Berkeley musical after all, the one where the little-known starlets unexpectedly dazzle the audience. As David Johansen later told *Circus* magazine, 'It all came together at the Mercer Arts Center.

We were opening for The Magic Tramps, but we were so good that they booed the Tramps offstage, so we opened and closed the concert.' After the resounding success of their opening night, the band were given access to the larger Oscar Wilde Room. While the staff at the Arts Center were unused to dealing with the mutant Mardi Gras that started to turn out in force for the Dolls' shows, they drank like a return to prohibition was imminent and tripled the bar profits.

On June 13, 1972, The New York Dolls kicked off a seventeen-week Tuesday-night residency in the Oscar Wilde Room. With several floor-to-ceiling mirrors that reflected the Dolls from all angles, the two hundred-capacity theatre became a narcissistic playroom, the crowd almost as much of an event as the band. The Dolls' seduction of New York's decadent demimonde was swift, melting ice and hearts into one glorious pink cocktail; they quickly became the toast of the town.

Suddenly everyone had an opinion on The New York Dolls. Lou Reed thought they were cute, while some wry social observers christened them The Velveteens, the junior oracles of Manhattan poised to take the baton from Reed's former band. Andy Warhol came a-courting, and David Bowie infiltrated their scene, then staggered away with a harder look, higher heels, and a rockier sound. At each successive gig, the celebrity guest list expanded. Alice Cooper checked them out; his girlfriend, model Cindy Lang, began an affair with Thunders, while Cooper's manager, Shep Gordon, showed an interest in the Dolls' career. Rod Stewart's manager, Billy Gaff, also made a business overture to the band, but all bets were cancelled after he got them a gig supporting Long John Baldry out on Long Island. Although Gaff supplied a limousine to take the Dolls to the club, they had spent the day snacking on a cheap form of powdered acid that was rolled up in a cigarette paper then guzzled down with a liquor chaser and arrived too late and too addled to go on.

News of the Dolls started to filter into the local press, and this time there were no misunderstandings over where they were coming from, as Ed McCormack noticed for Andy Warhol's *Interview*:

anything to say, although he was the funniest of all of them and probably the most intelligent. Billy and Sylvain were bubbly and extroverted, full of life, interested in bedding down as many women as they could and looking great in as many clothes as they could buy. None of them had any knowledge of the music business and nor did they care—they were really quite naive about all of that. They just seized on the possibilities of getting a manager, playing around the world, and becoming rock stars.

So smitten was he by the Dolls that Thau scrapped the flimsy proposition of a one-off single deal and became their personal manager instead. While he appeared to have all the trappings of success, Marty lacked the kind of funds it would take to hoist the Dolls' star into a prominent position, but he did have the phone number of Steve Leber and David Krebs, two booking agents from the powerful William Morris agency who had set up on their own. A business alliance had been mooted by Leber and Krebs during Thau's stint at Paramount, and now it was time to call them on it. After Marty invited them to see the band, they joined forces. It was a fairly unusual setup, Thau taking a paternal role to Leber and Krebs' traditional suits, as Dolls soundman Peter Jordan explained: 'Leber and Krebs were strictly attracted to one thing, the potential for lucre. I got along with Leber and Krebs, but they are both sharks in the true showbiz sense. Marty isn't a shark, he's more like a dolphin.'

Of the three, Krebs had the least input in the Dolls' career, spending most of his time with their other new act, Aerosmith. Later, when the managerial trinity split back into its original factions, it would be alleged that The New York Dolls and Aerosmith had been pitted against one another as part of a boardroom wager. However, when the Dolls signed on the dotted line in the summer of '72, they were tipped as the hot favourites. If being in love means never having to say you're sorry, then 'In Perpetuity' means having to say you're sorry forever, but the nuances of business eluded the NY Dolls.

Before the contracts were sealed and delivered, Marty Thau whisked the band into Blue Rock Studios for an evening. While the Dolls knew how to move, preening and teasing like the fairest of them all in front of the mirrors in the Oscar Wilde Room, they hadn't had the same chance to reflect on their music in such detail. Although the Blue Rock recording was never meant to be anything other than a test run for the band, it was later released as *The Mercer St. Sessions* and reveals them in confident mood.

Aside from nailing gritty versions of 'Bad Girl', 'Jet Boy', 'Human Being', and 'Frankenstein', the Dolls laid down 'Looking For A Kiss', a grimy revamp of Marc Bolan's 'Get It On' that pitches desire against drugged doom. Who wants to waste time waiting for the man when you can have a kiss instead of a fix? If only the band had taken their own advice. They also recorded 'Personality Crisis', a wonderful portrayal of social disintegration that captures their fetchingly awkward musical dexterity, each instrument seemingly on the verge of collision yet managing to swerve away just in time.

It's often been said that The New York Dolls didn't play so great at first, but they never aspired to being polished or polite, which aided their affinity for raw rhythm and blues. Right from the start, the band incorporated cover versions in their repertoire. Accordingly, the Blue Rock session would not have been complete without souped-up revisions of Bo Diddley's 'Pills', Sonny Boy Williamson's 'Don't Start Me Talking', and Parker, Floyd, and Cropper's 'Don't Mess With Cupid'.

* * *

As the summer gave in to autumn, the Dolls continued to put the life back into the nights of a devoted coterie of followers. Aside from regularly playing at the Mercer Arts Center and Max's Kansas City, they also put Kenny's Castaways on the Upper East Side of Manhattan and the Coventry in Queens on the map, establishing a rock'n'roll circuit that many other bands, including KISS, would traverse in their wake. Despite the ensuing furore that the Dolls' gigs generated, the record companies failed to take the bait, as Johnny T noted in an interview with journalist Lisa Robinson: 'The record company people who have come to see us have been freaked out, and we're not really doing anything except standing there playing.' Following on from Thunders' comment, David Jo concluded, 'I think we turn them on. Their wives get drunk and start dancing and they go crazy. But then they think about their kids … you know … and that's what stops them.'

The Dolls were undeniably popular, but the conservative core at the heart of the industry would not yield to the band's charms. Marty Thau:

A&R people would come to see them, but they couldn't see past the Dolls' exterior. They were such repressed times, people today wouldn't believe it. You couldn't even say 'Goddamn' on television. The issues of women's rights and gay and lesbian liberation had been put on the table, but they weren't put into practice. The music business perceived the Dolls as a bunch of degenerate queers. It was all down to homophobia.

One man, however, rallied to the Dolls' cause and became their dedicated champion. Had it not been for the noble Paul Nelson, The New York Dolls may well have been doomed to notoriety and little else. Having landed a position in A&R at Mercury Records, the former rock journalist began a solo campaign to get the band signed, which included deploying a small squadron of company scouts to Dolls' gigs between August and mid-October. The subsequent feedback was rarely unanimous or flattering, and on one particularly spectacular night, when the band were only an hour late for their scheduled appearance at the Mercer Arts Center, Johnny Thunders in his platform basketball shoes managed to kick holes in the stage and Arthur Kane failed to notice that his bass had come unplugged for four songs.

While Nelson prevailed and Mercury prevaricated, The New York Dolls' managerial trinity changed tactics, according to Steve Leber: 'The Dolls' time had not yet arrived here, so therefore we decided to go to England in order to get a record deal. We thought that the timing, their image and the excitement they could create would be incredible. I paid for the entire group to go.' Assisted by Roy Fischer, a London-based promoter, Leber organised a handful of dates for the band. The crowning glory of their campaign came when they got the Dolls a support slot to Rod Stewart and The Faces at the eight-thousand-seater Wembley Pool. In return for Fischer's services, it was agreed that the band would record a couple of songs on his behalf once they arrived in England.

Roy Fischer, who had a thing for transport stunts and had orchestrated a car smash in a shop-window lark for Alice Cooper, arranged for a horse and carriage to collect The New York Dolls from Heathrow airport. Hung-over and jet-lagged, the band perched as prettily as they could for a small group of photographers before giving way to nausea, the antique wheels of the carriage amplifying every bump in the road. Eventually they were ushered into a Mercedes and driven to Escape Studios in Kent.

Quarantined in the former oast house, which had been converted into a studio with accommodation, the Dolls recorded new versions of 'Personality Crisis', 'Looking For A Kiss', and 'Bad Girl'. The old Actress number 'That's Poison', which had been reincarnated as 'Subway Train', was also captured. Like the Flying Dutchman transported on to the IRT, the lovelorn protagonist of the song can't understand why he has been 'Cursed, poisoned and condemned' and is fated to ride on a subway train, the screeching crescendo of guitars like failing brakes.

After fulfilling their obligations to Fischer, the band headed for London. Steve Leber had already settled into his suite at the Dorchester while the Dolls and Marty Thau had reservations at a somewhat less salubrious hotel in Holborn. The New York Dolls made their UK debut at the Speakeasy—as starry in its own way as Max's Kansas City—but their performance was hampered by an inadequate PA system.

On October 26, the Dolls supported The Groundhogs at the Alhambra

Rock in Birmingham. Before going onstage, the band were presented with a couple of crates of Newcastle Brown Ale, most of which Billy Murcia violently regurgitated during their set. It was nothing unusual; Murcia didn't have the hardiest of constitutions, especially when it came to alcohol. Unfortunately, while in London, the drummer had also got his mitts on some Mandrax (aka 'Mandies', a barbiturate-like sedative especially potent when mixed with booze) courtesy of a model called Marilyn, whom he'd met at the Speakeasy. It was just another rock'n'roll transaction, but one that was to have tragic consequences.

On Sunday October 29, The New York Dolls played the biggest gig of their entire career at the Wembley Festival Of Music. After the confines of the Mercer Arts Center, the stage at Wembley looked bigger than an airport runway, but they created their own little maelstrom, refusing to yield to the collective smirk of a largely hostile crowd. Journalist Mark Plummer captured the moment for *Melody Maker*:

> The New York Dolls played what was possibly one of the worst sets I've seen. Their glamour bit brought wolf whistles and shouts to go before a note had been played, and by the time a string had broken on Johnny Thunders' Plexiglas guitar they had lost what audience sympathy they had. Musically their set was dire and failed to gel, their two guitarists play all the old tired licks. And who really wants to know about 'Pill City'? Wembley didn't, for sure.

One artful kid who had broken into the venue to see The Faces and the Dolls disagreed vehemently with Plummer's dour assessment. Future Sex Pistol Steve Jones:

> The Dolls played rock'n'roll music how I liked to hear it, kinda sloppy. I was a real big fan of the Faces, but they were a bit more controlled, more like good-time music but the Dolls were seriously crazy and I'd never seen anything like that. I don't think anyone

had. The audience hated them and started slinging shit at them but they kept on playing. They were great, wild.

As a special treat for the band after their appearance at Wembley, Kit Lambert, The Who's manager and the boss of Track Records, hired out an expensive restaurant for their use only. Of all the Dolls' potential suitors, Kit Lambert was the keenest: he wooed them from the moment they set foot on British soil, inviting them to party with The Who and introducing them to a social circle where the aristocracy mingled with new rock money. Aside from Lambert, representatives from Virgin and Charisma Records also made their interest known, as well as Mick Jagger, who flew in from Ireland to see the Dolls when they played at Imperial College with Status Quo and Capability Brown. Although it was never official, The New York Dolls were effectively auditioning for Rolling Stone Records, and while Jagger deigned to talk to them after the gig, he later told the press 'Yeah, I've seen The New York Dolls. We were almost going to sign 'em up at one point. I went down to the Imperial College gig and—uh, their lead singer—I saw 'er and I just didn't think much of it all.'

On November 4, The New York Dolls opened for Argent at the Mile End Sundown in East London before travelling to Liverpool, where they had a support slot to Lou Reed at a former boxing ring called the Stadium. The Dolls didn't even make it as far as round one, Reed sending a message to their dressing room threatening to cancel if they set foot on the stage. Suddenly Uncle Lou didn't think they were so cute anymore. Rebuked by the main draw, the dejected Dolls left the venue. Returning to London, the band made good use of their free time before the next date on their itinerary, November 9, with Roxy Music at Manchester's Hardrock. Steve Leber and Marty Thau continued to negotiate with Kit Lambert, drawing ever closer to a deal with Track Records, but on the evening of Tuesday, November 7, everything changed.

Nearly three decades later, the memories of the surviving protagonists from the Dolls' camp had faded, like the ink on the death certificate, while the outside catalysts remained silent. What is irrefutable is that Billy Murcia died sometime between the hours of 8pm and 11pm at Brompton Lodge on the Cromwell Road. Marty Thau always maintained that Billy met his fate because of a telephone coincidence. Lounging in his room, Murcia apparently took a call from a wrong number but got talking anyway, and, after admitting to being a NY Doll, was invited to a party. Before leaving, he picked up some pocket money from Marty, who suggested he get a lift in the chauffeur-driven managerial limousine that was waiting outside the hotel. Once the hired limo returned from dropping Billy at Brompton Lodge, Steve Leber and Marty Thau sped off to impresario Danny Secunda's apartment, where Kit Lambert and his business partner Chris Stamp awaited them. Several hours later, and a breath away from signing the band to Track Records for £100,000, the meeting was interrupted by a phone call for Marty. The caller, whose identity has never been revealed, told Thau that Billy Murcia was dead. Steve Leber, however, recalled being at the Dorchester when Scotland Yard contacted him and broke the news. Leber then dashed over to the Dolls' hotel, filled them in on what little details he had been able to glean, and told them to ditch any drugs in their possession. Unable to register what was happening but wanting to be near their friend, the band quickly made their way to the Cromwell Road, where Marty Thau had already fulfilled the unhappy task of identifying the body.

The following day, the stricken band members were sent home on the next available flight while Leber and Thau stayed in London to help the police with their enquiries. Needless to say, negotiations with Track were never resumed, and aside from letting the music papers know that the band would no longer be supporting Roxy Music and had left the country due to the demise of their drummer, Marty engineered a press blackout:

> I suspected that this could grow into a big rock'n'roll scandal. It was certain to be ammunition for *Melody Maker* and *NME*, and I wanted to spare the band and the Murcia family, more than anyone,

the pain and the anguish. Their son was dead and he died under such a grey cloud, or at least that would be the way it would be manipulated and portrayed.

At the inquest, held on November 24, 1972, in West London, it was revealed that Billy Murcia had in fact called Speakeasy Marilyn and been invited to her apartment on the Cromwell Road. In a statement to the coroner, Marilyn Woolhead claimed that he arrived in a reasonable condition: 'He didn't seem absolutely sober, but he didn't seem that drunk.' Also at the flat were two of Woolhead's friends, James Owen and Malcolm Raines. Raines went out for a short while as James, Marilyn, and Billy shared a bottle of champagne. Unfortunately, the drummer had also been taking Mandrax, which caused him to pass out on the bed. By the time Raines returned to the flat, Owen and Woolhead were in a state of panic, unable to bring Murcia round. At this point, an ambulance should have been called, but instead the two men employed second-hand drug folklore in an effort to revive their guest. Submerging Murcia in a cold bath, they simultaneously held ice against the back of his neck while feeding him black coffee. Both denied that Billy's head had tilted back into the water. A verdict of accidental death was recorded, caused by drowning in a domestic bath while under the influence of alcohol and Methaqualone (Mandrax).

In the immediate aftermath, The New York Dolls retreated to mourn their friend. Beyond the funeral, they had no plans. A badly shaken Johnny Thunders would later admit, 'I just couldn't describe how I felt about Billy dying, how I still feel. He was a close friend, and you never get over a thing like that.' When the Grim Reaper sneaks up on a band, the gravity of the situation imbues a fatalistic authenticity. Suddenly, The New York Dolls were taken more seriously than ever before.

Eventually they started auditions for a new drummer. Disbanding would have been akin to a second death for Billy Murcia, but the tragic implications of his passing haunted the next phase of The New York Dolls, as photographer Leee Black Childers explained: 'Instead of sobering them

CURSED, POISONED, CONDEMNED

up it made them crazier. It affected Johnny a whole lot. He'd had a real innocence about him, but when Billy died, he started to plunge into self-destruction.'

The only real contender as new drummer was Jerry Nolan. He already knew the guys and had even lent his kit to Billy a couple of times. After Shaker, he'd notched up some gigs with Wayne County's group, Queen Elizabeth, playing the same circuit as the Dolls. The beat of the city was in the fabric of Jerry Nolan's soul. Much as he wanted to join the NY Dolls, he kept his customary cool at the audition:

> I respected the Dolls' ideas very highly. They didn't play so well and, being a little older, I was more advanced as a musician, so a lot of my friends would say, 'How can you play with those guys? They don't play so good.' I said, 'Hey man, you're missing the whole point. Nobody plays so good at first. What they've got, what I see in their approach and music, is magic.'

Following the audition, Jerry was welcomed into the Dolls over a round of drinks at Max's. Early the next morning, Johnny met Nolan on the corner of 14th Street and 3rd Avenue and took him up to the apartment he now shared with Sylvain to present the new drummer with some assorted Dolly finery from the communal wardrobe.

Jerry Nolan made his live debut with The New York Dolls on December 19, 1972, at the Sean O'Casey Theater, one of the largest rooms in the Mercer Arts Center. Unfortunately, the gig was more like a record industry convention. David Johansen recalled the night for *Creem* magazine:

> Someone had invited down Ahmet Ertegun, Clive Davis, Joe Polydor, and these other crazy people. Out of an audience of five hundred, there were maybe twenty real kids who were there to rock. The rest of 'em were record company people, and if you mess up ... well, goodbye, and the trap door opens and you fall into the snake

pit. We came onstage and all we could see were these balding old relics with their polished heads, snorting coke and thinking that they're so outasite. And I'm supposed to get a record contract out of these people?

The top brass went home disgruntled; hadn't those boys learned to mind their manners yet? Others shook with rage. Or was it excitement? Clive Davis, the president of CBS at the time, was rumoured to have said that if you wanted to keep working in the music business you didn't admit to having seen the Dolls. Such a faux pas was likely to bring one's sexuality into disrepute. Nothing had changed within the industry, and that included Mercury, who still couldn't make up their minds. Ever loyal, Paul Nelson put his career on the line as he continued to petition the company to sign them. Eventually he succeeded, and on March 20, 1973, The New York Dolls were officially taken on by Mercury for a two-album deal. It was a daring move for the conservative second-rung label whose biggest-selling act was Rod Stewart minus The Faces. However, just because the Dolls were now onboard, it didn't mean that their detractors within the company were willing to throw them a life raft.

The hunt began for an appropriate producer to work on the Dolls' all-important debut album. Phil Spector was briefly considered, while David Bowie declined their advances. Todd Rundgren wasn't an initial choice, but he was accessible and had plenty of prior studio experience. Peter Jordan:

There was a lot of oddball ideas as to who should produce. We wanted to try and get Roy Wood—Wizzard were brilliant and Wood could duplicate the style of Dion or The Ronettes. He had pink hair and a two-necked guitar and was pretty crazy—well, too crazy actually, because it turned out he was having a nervous breakdown, so we nixed him. Leiber and Stoller, who wrote 'Jailhouse Rock' and had worked with The Coasters and produced some great records, didn't like us. The reason why we got Todd Rundgren was because, apart from producing The Band and Badfinger, he was available, lived in New York, and was young. Although he looked pretty outrageous and had a large purple streak in his hair, he was a very straight guy.

According to an interview he gave *Creem* magazine, Todd Rundgren's decision to produce the Dolls was based on geography rather than musical compatibility:

> The only person who can logically produce a New York City record is someone who lives in New York. I live here and I recognise all the things about New York that the Dolls recognise in their music. It doesn't necessarily mean that I testify to that stuff; it doesn't even mean that the Dolls' music testifies to that stuff. The only thing that it testifies to is that they're punks!

The divisions between Todd, who looked the part but wasn't, and the Dolls became apparent once recording started in Studio B at the Record Plant on 44th Street. Rundgren was a remote taskmaster. The band larked around with their entourage and girlfriends between takes, extending their seven-day weekend ethic to the maximum, which is roughly how long it took to make the album. For those familiar with the Dolls' live sets, there were no surprises when it came to the choice of material, 'Jet Boy', 'Frankenstein', and 'Bad Girl' rowdily jostling for attention alongside the adorable confusion of 'Trash', Johansen's voice in direct competition with the seismic drumming and jarring guitars. The only vaguely gentle number, 'Lonely Planet Boy', has all the restless containment of a noisy, fidgety child who has just been told to hush up.

In spite of the disparities between the band and Todd Rundgren, he managed to capture the frantic rush of the Dolls' music and also emphasised their backing vocals, which recalled the glory days of the 60s girl groups from The Shangri-Las to The Dixie Cups. Unfortunately, Mercury unduly hastened the mixing process, while Rundgren's production didn't endear him to Johnny Thunders and Jerry Nolan. Later that year, Johnny told the *NME*'s Nick Kent, 'He [Rundgren] screwed up the mix really bad. Every time we go on the radio to do an interview we always dedicate "Your Mama Don't Dance And Your Daddy Don't Rock'n'roll" to Todd.' Thunders and Nolan's disillusionment with the recording process set a precedent that would reoccur over the years.

The New York Dolls' eponymously titled debut album was released in the US on July 27, 1973, to a typically mixed reception. Most of the critics gave it a standing ovation, including Kent, who wrote, 'The New York Dolls are trash, they play rock'n'roll like sluts and they've just a released a record that can proudly stand beside Iggy & The Stooges' stupendous *Raw Power* as the only album so far to fully define just exactly where 1970s rock should be coming from.'

Outside of their own realm, the legendary 'kids' that David Johansen had predicted would love the band turned the other way and bought The Rolling Stone's lukewarm *Goats Head Soup* instead. Paul Nelson addressed the issue eloquently in the *Village Voice*:

> They [the Dolls] were unquestionably brilliant, but finally too spare, too restricted, to reach the hidden places in suburban, smalltown hearts. In the end, they rode on real rather than symbolic subway trains to specific rather than universal places, played for an audience of intellectuals or kids even further out than they were: and when they eventually met the youth of the country, that youth seemed even more confused than captivated by them.

The record's infamous drag cover proved even more contentious than the music. Some were intimidated by it, others were repulsed; too few understood the sense of humour beneath the lipstick and mascara and took it at face value.

Between picking up bouquets and dodging missiles, The New York Dolls stepped out on their first American tour, sharing a couple of the dates with Mott The Hoople. While they were away, the Mercer Arts Center collapsed when the adjoining hotel fell down. The incident occurred during the day, causing only one fatality. The Mercer's unfortunate finale was a seismic blow for the city's counterculture. The venue had been an important steppingstone for the Dolls en route to playing more established venues.

Prior to commencing a weeklong residency at Max's Kansas City, Sylvain invited Johnny, David, and Arthur to a fashion fair. At one of the more outrageous stands, Syl introduced them to Vivienne Westwood and Malcolm McLaren, whom he had met during his solo trip to London, back when the Dolls were just getting started. McLaren was immediately intrigued, perceiving them as the very essence of NY's seamy allure, but he didn't fall head over heels until he listened to the album:

I thought, *My God, this is so bad, how could they make a record like that?* I was absolutely shocked and it made me laugh. It made me laugh so much that I suddenly thought you can be brilliant at being bad and there were people loving them for it. I loved them from that moment on. I was sold hook, line, and sinker, and I loved the photograph of them on the album cover, sitting on the couch. I loved that asexual or bisexual look, which in many ways had a direct correlation with much of what had happened in English pop, but Vivienne and I liked it much better because we thought it was somewhat cruder and tougher. They were in many respects inspiring for us.

Following the block booking at Max's, the band had two days off before they were due to fly out to Los Angeles for a five-night stint at the Whisky A Go Go. Things should have been peachy but, miffed at being told she couldn't go to LA for financial reasons, Arthur's Amazonian girlfriend, Connie Gripp, went for him with a kitchen knife. While trying to disarm her, Kane got his hand filleted. The incident left the bass player in plaster and unable to play for the next two months. Although Peter Jordan deputised, Arthur was still taken on tour. Left to his own devices, Kane's unstable lifestyle and alcoholic tendencies put him at risk. After Billy Murcia, no one was taking any chances.

The New York Dolls' run of gigs at the Whisky became the stuff of legend and would have a lasting impact on the LA rock scene. The English musicians who had once reigned supreme on Sunset Strip were well and truly trounced by the Dolls. Finally, Tinseltown started living up to its reputation. In *Creem* magazine, Lisa Robinson reported what happened when New York trash met Hollywood sleaze:

> The line at the Whisky A Go Go is, indeed, up the block. Kids who can't be more than twelve years old, boys with lipstick smeared on their faces, girls with all those kitschy, clutzy shoes, hot pants and feathers. Like some kind of fungus, it's slowly creeping across the country, but it's at its best in LA. I'm talking about sleeeeze. Sabel Starr is there of course, the undisputed Queen of the Strip—and she's holding on tightly to Johnny Thunders.

Within days of meeting Johnny T, the beauteous Miss Starr (née Shields) announced her retirement from groupiedom. One of LA's most celebrated rock courtesans had found true love at last. Hailing from the exclusive neighbourhood of Palos Verdes, Sabel and her sister Corel had canoodled with a string of bands until Corel started going steady with Iggy Pop. After seeing a picture of the Dolls in *Creem*, Sabel set her sights on Johnny Thunders. When the band finally rolled into town, Sabel was waiting for them at their hotel, but her heart was reserved for Johnny. It was valentines all around once he took her up to his room. Janis Cafasso had faded from the scene after Thunders' insecurity spilled over into unpredictability, but, to the besotted Miss Starr, the Dolls' cute lead guitarist was the embodiment of all her rock'n'roll fantasies. If The New York Dolls really were the junior Stones, as some of their more affable critics reckoned, then Johnny and Sabel became teen world's Keith and Anita, exuding a damaged glamour.

Aside from the gigs, Miss Starr and Mr Thunders spent every waking and sleeping moment together, Johnny phoning home to tell his mom he'd just met the girl he was going to marry. Naturally, they started hanging out with Corel and Iggy, but the innocence of double dating evaporated when Pop found an initiate in Thunders, as Sylvain recalled:

> Johnny was a big Iggy Pop fan and the four of them were always together, and one thing led to another. Johnny's the kind of guy, you turn him on to one joint and the next day he's got a whole pound, so they fix together, and that's when that started. Johnny began using—not regularly at first, just a little bit here and a little bit there. It turned out to be the worst thing you could ever introduce Johnny to.

Before the band headed down south, Johnny packed Sabel off to New York for safekeeping but, unbeknown to Miss Starr, her mother had called out the National Guard. In the confusion, David Johansen's pretty blonde girlfriend, Cyrinda Foxe, was mistakenly apprehended by the Texas Rangers while she waited for the Dolls at the next stop on the tour. As Sabel recounted, 'Marty Thau was outraged when Johnny sent me back to New York to wait for him on my own for the next three weeks. I'd just turned sixteen but I was very mature for my age. When I realised what my mom had done, I phoned her and told her to call off the police, 'cos it really was quite scandalous.'

Further castigation awaited the Dolls when they hit Memphis with Iggy Pop. Despite warnings from the local police department, who had been whipped into a frenzy by a group of moral vigilantes known as the Mothers Of Memphis, the band went ahead with their gig at the Ellis Auditorium. The rioting began when a boy broke through the police cordon around the stage and planted a kiss on David Johansen. As the cops started beating up the kids in the crowd, the Dolls' frontman attempted to calm the situation but was hauled offstage and charged with inciting a riot, which was later bolstered by a 'lewd behaviour' rap. After an uncomfortable night in the slammer, David Jo was bailed out and the band beat a hasty trail to Detroit.

The tour climaxed on their home turf with a Halloween bash in the Grand Ballroom of the Waldorf Astoria. It was the major event of NYC's autumn season, featuring a fancy-dress competition. The winner could look forward to a night on the town with The New York Dolls; second and third prizes were a weekend for three at the Newark Motor Inn in New Jersey and a bottle of New York State Champagne. However, the band's characteristically late arrival and the Waldorf's reticence to open the ballroom doors to the children of the night, who had shown up in force, resulted in fractious scenes with some two thousand party goers turned away. Although the Dolls missed their midnight stage cue by two hours, they swiftly revived any flagging spirits in the audience. But as the *New Yorker*'s Ellen Willis noted:

> To know the Dolls' repertoire is to love it, but I've already heard it live half a dozen times and some fresh material would have been nice. The Dolls' next album according to Johansen is tentatively titled *Too Much Too Soon*. I hope so, but one new song per set is more like too little too late.

Since Billy Murcia's demise, allegiances within the band had changed. While Syl and Johnny had been very close, Jerry Nolan now became a profound influence on the lead guitarist. Older and more streetwise, Nolan knew how to handle the diminutive firebrand:

> The first time we went on tour together, we got into a big fistfight in the back of the limousine, and I kicked the shit out of him. Ever since that day, Johnny was like my son. He loved me for it. Every once in a while, he would push and I would let it get so far then I'd say, 'No more, boy, no more.' For some reason I happened to know Johnny real well; I knew his type. Maybe it was the neighbourhood

I grew up in. I taught Johnny everything he knows, he got the blame for it all, but I actually did it all.

Independently of Johnny, the drummer had started chipping away at heroin—not so much that it would detract from his playing, for Nolan was a stickler when it came to professionalism—and the gradual alignment of their habits became a further bond. However, at the halfway mark of the Dolls' short career, Johnny was still more partial to heroin's opposite number, speed.

When Syl and David buddied up, Arthur Kane was left out on a limb. The knock-on effect of the new loyalties estranged the band's main songwriting team, who'd never been that prolific in the first place. 'Babylon', the Dolls' sprawling answer to 'New York, New York', didn't really qualify as a new number, given that it had nearly made it on to their debut platter, while 'Who Are The Mystery Girls?' had also been kicking around for some time. Aside from the camp and catchy 'Lone Star Queen' and the rollicking 'Puss 'N' Boots', which considers the plight of a shoe fetishist, there wasn't much evidence of fresh material for the second album. Matters were not helped by an extensive touring schedule that took them right up to the end of the year.

On November 20, 1973, The New York Dolls returned to England. Apart from a couple of university gigs, the first key moment of their trip came when they appeared on *The Old Grey Whistle Test*, a television programme that took its music seriously and expected the bands to do the same. The Dolls' inclusion on the show was a miraculous aberration. When Bob Harris, the *Whistle Test's* presenter, mocked their brilliantly gauche performance of 'Jet Boy' and 'Looking For A Kiss', he earned the collective wrath of the upcoming punk generation. Sex Pistols drummer Paul Cook later told authors Fred and Judy Vermorel:

I saw them [the Dolls] on the telly and I was fucking knocked out by them. It was mainly their attitude . . . I couldn't believe it, they was just all falling about all over the place, all their hair down, all knocking into each other. Had these great big platform boots on. Tripping over. They was really funny and they just didn't give a shit, you know. And Bob Harris at the end of it went: 'Tut, tut, tut, tut, mock rock' . . . just cast it off in two words.

Up in Manchester, Steven Morrissey was so galvanised by the Dolls that he wrote to Leber-Krebs' office letting them know of his intentions to start a fan club for the band.

The live high point of The New York Dolls' English jaunt came when they played two nights in the Rainbow Room, a huge art-deco lounge and bar on the sixth floor of Biba, the most decadent department store that London had ever known. Unfortunately, Arthur Kane was nabbed by security when he switched the price tag on a jacket he wanted but couldn't afford. Barbara Hulanicki, the shop's creator, recounted the incident in her autobiography, *From A To Biba*:

> The day they were due to appear we were watching their roadies setting up the equipment when the head of our security arrived, gripping two bedraggled looking creatures who had been caught shoplifting dresses and who claimed to work for us. They were part of the group and reluctantly we had to let off. The Dolls did not go down very well with our audience either.

Like a crowd scene from *The Great Gatsby*, a gathering of sultry sirens and lounge lizards sipped their cocktails while pretending not to look at the assembled celebrities, who included Paul McCartney, Brian Eno, and Elton John. Whatever they were expecting from the band, it wasn't what happened. Melody and harmony flew out the window as the Dolls tore into their set, breaking the sound barrier and the audience's ear drums. It had not been a good idea to borrow The Rolling Stones' PA system, which was intended for stadium use. On each consecutive night, only the die-hards like Malcolm McLaren stuck it out until the end: 'It was fantastic. They were like the worst striptease rock act you can imagine. I loved their awkward, trashy vibe. We became a part of their entourage and like groupies we followed them to Paris.'

The Dolls' arrival in France became infamous, Johnny taking over from the late Billy Murcia when it came to throwing up in public, but the assembled ladies and gentlemen of the press were not amused, and neither were the European representatives of Mercury. Only the *NME*'s Nick Kent, no stranger to decadence himself, failed to take umbrage:

> Five minutes off the plane in Paris, walking up toward the airport entrance, and Johnny Thunders throws up. Bl-a-a-a-g-h-h! God know how many photographers are there: *Paris Match*, *Stern* magazine—all the European rock press and the nationals. The record company folks have arranged a special little welcome. Bl-a-a-a-g-g-h-h! The members of the band look stone-faced and wasted, wondering if he's maybe going to fall into his vomit.

Aside from being sick, Thunders and Nolan seemed to be sharing the same malady, according to Peter Jordan:

> I noticed that Johnny and Jerry were acting a little funny. That was the first time I became aware of their abuse of narcotics. When Jerry joined the Dolls, he didn't even smoke cigarettes, he didn't do any kind of drugs, he didn't drink. If he did go out and have something to drink, it'd be something really corny, like whisky and soda.
>
> It was a surprise to me that either of them had gotten into heroin. Johnny was a hip guy and he'd been around the block, even though he was very young. Frankly, there was enough aggravation already going on, so the last thing I expected anyone to do was to get strung out on heroin.

The next day, the band had a chance to make up for lost ground at a press conference in the bar of the Ambassador Hotel. Unfortunately, the question-and-answer routine was supposed to start at twelve noon, normally the time the band would just be tumbling in or out of bed. While a harassed Marty Thau attempted to round up his unruly charges, the foyer started to fill up with journalists. Attempting to stave off any ill feeling over the band's tardiness, Thau threw the bar open. As the day turned to dusk, The New York Dolls finally assembled and the interviews began. While Marty's cordiality eased the situation, Mercury subsequently railed against the $8,000 bar tab run up by the press.

Later that evening, the Dolls went off to play a live concert at Radio Luxembourg. Sozzled to the point of near collapse, only Nolan's hard-hitting backbeat kept them buoyant. The broadcast was later released as *Paris Burning* or *Paris Le Trash*. Sylvain: 'If you listen to that recording you can hear what condition David was in. He was a drunken mess. His ego had gone completely overboard and he couldn't do no wrong in his own eyes. He was trying to talk in French, and he was so out of it.'

Contrary to the expectations of their newfound foes at the French branch of Mercury, The New York Dolls rose early the following morning and arrived on time at the prestigious Olympia Theatre for a matinee show. Once again, Nick Kent was in attendance:

The Dolls troop onstage at the Paris Olympia at 3:30pm, suitably bedraggled. Johansen decked out in bastardised evening dress with various badges and emblems strategically placed on his costume ('for political purposes, I mean the leftists will get off on my Mao button and . . .') commandeers proceedings, but the band are immediately dogged by a PA failure which totals the electricity for five minutes. Once underway the sound is distorted and falls like lead inside the hall, pinpointing the already cacophonous sound to a slightly less-than-comfortable degree. And there are other . . . uh . . . problems. Johnny Thunders looks about as well as his guitar is in tune. He staggers around the stage in obvious pain, attempting to motivate himself and the band simultaneously and succeeding only in beating his instrument into an ever-more horrendous stage of tunelessness.

The last gig on the Dolls' French itinerary assured Thunders' legend in Paris for years to come. It was without doubt the birth of punk, but for Johnny it was a matter of honour and survival. Situated on the Rue Voltaire, the Bataclan was a functional venue that had sold out well in advance. Once the band hit the stage, trouble started brewing in Thunders' corner when a couple of guys in the audience began spitting at him. The guitarist retaliated in kind. A few well-aimed kicks followed. The guitarist retaliated in kind. When a volley of flying objects was lobbed in his direction, Thunders picked up a microphone stand and sent it spinning, like a weighted frisbee, at the perpetrators. The gig was aborted after the perps stormed the stage, baying for blood.

On December 4, The New York Dolls bade a fond farewell to France before continuing their European jaunt, returning home in time for Christmas. Ensconced in New York, Johnny and Sabel cozied up in their new apartment on West 24th Street. As Sabel recalled, it was a short-lived idyll:

Everything was so good those first few months, like a dream come true. We were going to get married. Johnny was like a child; he'd bring me sweet little gifts, cute little notes and he was so gorgeous. The first Christmas we had together was so sweet. He bought me an Irish setter puppy and he took me to Central Park for a buggy ride. There was this innocence about Johnny but then he turned so hardcore. There was always speed and tons of marijuana. He'd smoke about twenty joints a day; if there was opium, he'd swallow that. He started getting crazy, any weird thing would trigger him, and he'd get in these jealous rages.

Johnny and Sabel's relationship spiralled out of control along with the fortunes of The New York Dolls. The year 1973 had faded, but there was no real reason for the band to do the same. However, Mercury were becoming agitated; although the Dolls' debut LP had fared well, racking up sales of 110,000, the record company had expected it to go gold and was becoming less tolerant of the band's transgressions. Redemption, it was hoped, would come with their second album. However, since the Todd Rundgren experience, the subject of a compatible producer had become rather thorny. Bob Ezrin, who worked with Alice Cooper, was given the once over, but ultimately the prize went to George 'Shadow' Morton, the mentor and producer of The New York Dolls' soul sisters, The Shangri-Las. The delinquent faction of the girl groups, The Shangri-Las gave their all to a divinely dysfunctional street opera populated by bad boys and ill-fated runaways. Tough yet vulnerable, the girls notched up four top twenty hit singles between September 1964 and November 1965, including 'Give Him A Great Big Kiss', which the Dolls often covered in their live shows, addressed to the feminine.

Shadow Morton also thought he would be addressing the feminine the first time he met the Dolls. Surprisingly, in spite of an apparent camaraderie with the band, Morton lacked empathy with their material. Whether the difficult years since his platinum paradise lost with The Shangri-La's had taken their toll, we'll never know. Unfortunately, the dramatic sweep and fraught intensity that he had once conjured in the studio failed to flourish in the Dolls' domain. Rather than setting their torrid visions aflame, he succeeded only in dampening their spirits. If the Dolls' debut album could be construed as their NY epic, *Too Much Too Soon* carries shades of Los Angeles, a cinematic landscape at once tawdry, glamorous, and perverse.

In comparison with the opening track, 'Babylon', which still pulls a punch, 'Stranded In The Jungle', which the Dolls normally performed with a raw bravura, was tenderised under Morton's auspices. 'Who Are The Mystery Girls?' makes a stab at brassy liberation, but Gamble & Huff's '(There's Gonna Be A) Showdown'—the second of four covers on the album—sounds more like a number from a big budget musical than the rocking rumble it ought to be. 'It's Too Late', one of the finest moments on *Too Much Too Soon*, manages to overcome Shadow's restraining order, although the harmonica is overused in places.

The album finally transcends the producer's boundaries on Johnny T's 'Chatterbox'. Dating back to the earliest inception of the band, the track, which evolved from 'The Milk Man' aka 'Milk Me', marks Thunders' hard-won campaign to sing his own composition and the budding, if hesitant, desire to take centre stage. As journalist Ron Ross observed in *Phonograph Record*, 'Johnny's double-tracked vocals make him sound like the beehive brunette from Queens we always knew he was.' In the stampede of guitars Morton loses the reins and 'Chatterbox' runs wild.

Prior to the release of *Too Much Too Soon*, The New York Dolls made their last great extravagant gesture when they staged a St Valentine's Massacre at the Academy Of Music. In conjunction with photographer Bob Gruen, the band created a spoof movie in which they starred as the Lipstick Killers—the gang who couldn't do a job without their lipstick on—as Gruen recounted:

We decided we'd make a newsreel of them as 1930s type gangsters as part of the Academy of Music show. The film ends with them riding up 14th Street firing off machine guns, then running into the theatre. Then they would suddenly appear for real, running down the aisles wearing the same gangster costumes, shooting the audience. Now for some people in the audience who were on the right drugs and peaking at the right time, this worked amazingly well. I know some people for whom this was the experience of a lifetime!

For the next six months, the Dolls gigged solidly across the States and back again; best that they should keep moving as the critical backlash commenced. Nick Kent summarised the situation in the *NME*:

The overall impression though is that this album is messy and shot through with unfulfilled potential. It's exactly the wrong sort of product to launch on a public, liberally weighed out with folk only too ready to pull the whole 'I told you so' number at the Dolls' expense.

Mercury had their hands firmly on their holsters, ready to take aim, while Leber-Krebs began to regard the band as yesterday's affair; fun while it lasted, but maybe it was time to settle down with the less challenging Aerosmith. More readily accessible and a great deal less exotic, Aerosmith translated The New York Dolls for the mainstream market. Marty Thau:

> Krebs was very quietly handling their management roster. Later on it seemed to me that he was watching the whole Dolls thing, and when he or Aerosmith saw something they could take from the Dolls, in terms of style, showmanship and musical riffs, they would. I've had my suspicions that Leber and Krebs wanted to keep the Dolls down 'cos Aerosmith were moving up and CBS was backing them.

In mid-April, the Dolls began what they described as a miniature world tour comprising a week's worth of small club dates in Manhattan. A step backward disguised as a cute move. Many of the larger promoters had begun to distance themselves from the band, wary of the high-spirited crowds they attracted and the Dolls' habitual lateness. The high point of their hometown odyssey was a show at the 82 Club, one of NY's most famous drag venues. Of course, they lived up to the occasion, save for Johnny, who steadfastly refused to wear a dress.

Hot on the heels of the 82 gig, the Dolls began a hectic three-month cross country trek to push *Too Much Too Soon*, which had got off to an even more uncertain start than their debut album. The confusion that the band generated was ably illustrated when *Creem* magazine voted them both the best and worst new group in May '74. On the downside, the Dolls were considered to be even more horrendous than The Osmonds, Grand Funk Railroad, Slade, and Dawn. However, they were also deemed to be better than Queen, Aerosmith, and Lynyrd Skynyrd.

Midway through their touring schedule, Johnny Thunders managed to get his mitts on some uncut methamphetamine when the band arrived in Canada. Never one to moderate his intake, Johnny binged on the pure speed to the point of psychosis, clawing the walls and anyone who came near him. Paranoid and distraught, he refused to go onstage unless Sabel came to Toronto. She finally caught up with the band in Montreal, but no amount of gentle persuasion could talk Johnny down from the ledge inside his mind. Eventually he collapsed and had to be taken on board a plane to the next gig in a wheelchair.

The episode was a prelude to a string of calamities for the band. A trip to England in July was pulled, and when the Dolls got to New Orleans they found the venue had burned down. From Fayetteville the band travelled to Los Angeles, where they had a four-night stand at the Roxy Theater. Owned by the influential music business entrepreneur Lou Adler, the Roxy was also hosting performances of *The Rocky Horror Show*, a project seemingly dear to his heart, for when the musical was made into a movie, Adler was the executive producer.

While trying to set up the Dolls' equipment, some of their roadies removed the actors' tape markers. When the cast complained, the Dolls were banished from the venue after only one gig. The incident proved a major irritant to Steve Leber, but the band rallied for a great in-concert performance on *The Don Kirshner Show*, a nationally syndicated TV programme. However, when the Dolls returned home, they got a stormy reception. Against Marty Thau's wishes, Steve Leber decided to minimise the band's activities, further devaluing their reputation by booking them into smaller and smaller venues.

Johnny, meanwhile, polished off the rest of the methamphetamine with disastrous consequences, according to Sabel:

He really got crazy and started hitting me in front of the band, one night when we were in Chinatown. I slit my wrists and Syl had to take me to Bellevue. The doctor said, 'I won't send you to the psychiatric wing, but I want you to get the first plane home.' I did.

Left distraught by Miss Starr's departure, Thunders began an ardent campaign to win her back. Done with the brutality of speed, he turned with increasing frequency to the numbing embrace of heroin. Nothing was ever half-hearted with Johnny Thunders, from baseball to learning the guitar. So sad then that he should apply the same concerted effort to junk. If self-destruction and addiction are different sides of the same theme, they were both playing loud and clear for Johnny.

On October 11, 1974, the Dolls made their way to LA for the last time, to take part in the Hollywood Street Revival & Dance. Something has to be over for it to feel like a reunion, and a sense of nostalgia permeated the event, which also featured Iggy Pop and a selection of rock'n'roll riffraff, including the remnants of Silverhead and The GTOs. Journalist Richard Cromelin delivered a premature obituary for The New York Dolls:

> More than any of the other acts at the Trash Dance, the Dolls are hooked to a time that's inexorably rolling away, and their only redeeming feature is the perversely fascinating way they suicidally cling to their path to oblivion.

At least the gig was a triumph for Johnny, who made up with Sabel Starr. An item once more, they returned to New York together, only for their second honeymoon to flicker out with the dying light of the Dolls.

Even though *Too Much Too Soon* had sold marginally less than the Dolls' debut offering, Mercury granted a stay of execution when they opted for a third album. A series of meetings began between the band and their managers, Steve Leber adding the incentive of a trip to Japan if they cleaned up their act and said goodbye to Marty.

The Dolls were in no fit state to negotiate the managerial tug-of-war that had developed between Leber and Thau. Regretfully, Marty walked of his own accord, citing Leber's decision to put the band on the club circuit as one of the main reasons for his departure. Jerry Nolan remembered, 'Marty Thau fought for us against two guys that didn't believe in us, but it was a losing battle.' If the Dolls couldn't look to their managers for stability, they certainly weren't going to be able to find it within themselves.

Between the loucheness of alcohol and the anaesthesia of heroin and all the other personal complications, Johansen and Thunders had drifted apart as a creative team, but the Dolls were not a spent force. Sylvain and David collaborated on 'Red Patent Leather' while Johnny, growing ever more confident as a solo songwriter, delivered 'Pirate Love'. They had the material for a third album, but there was an irreparable rift within the band, as Peter Jordan acknowledged:

I would wind up rehearsing all this material with Johnny, some which would turn up with the Heartbreakers, like 'Pirate Love', but a lot of it disappeared. By then, everyone had their own agenda, their own lives. David and Johnny became so fucking alienated they wouldn't work with each other, but the real pain in the ass was David wouldn't work with Jerry if you gave him a million dollars. The other thing was, Johnny had songs he wanted to do and David said to me one time, 'What am I supposed to do while he does his songs, play tambourine? I'm not going to do that.'

Matters were taken out of the group's hands when Irwin Steinberg, the big boss at Mercury, retracted the offer of a third album and demanded repayment of losses and loans. The bitter seasoning at the close of business at the end of 1974 came when Leber-Krebs withdrew all financial support from the band. Like Cinderella, the Dolls were reduced to standing in line for welfare and playing dingy clubs, as the careers of Aerosmith and KISS were taking off.

It was Malcolm McLaren, newly arrived in NYC, who came to the rescue, just as his beloved Dolls were buckling under. He couldn't free them from their ties to Mercury and Leber-Krebs, but he could at least get them functioning again. While McLaren's intentions might have been good, his reasoning wasn't entirely altruistic. Regardless of the band's predicaments, any association with them bestowed a certain tarnished frisson, and McLaren benefited from letting people know he had managed The New York Dolls, especially once he returned to England. However, Malcolm's official position was never clarified, as the ever-pithy David Johansen quipped: 'I know he says he was our manager, but he wasn't really. He was our haberdasher.' Nonetheless, McLaren was dedicated in his endeavours. Enabling them to continue rehearsing, he rented a loft for the band, which they shared with an outfit called The Demons. Malcolm then addressed the Dolls' personal habits; Arthur Kane was packed off to Smithers, a top-of-the-line rehab, and, although they took some persuading, Johnny and Jerry saw a doctor.

Compounding their problems, The New York Dolls were now in a cultural void. Although they were being hailed as royalty on the burgeoning CBGB's scene and were no older than any of the punk bands that played there, the Dolls' music was rooted in a different time; you could jostle to the Ramones or twitch to Television, but you couldn't dance anymore.

Seeking to kill off the Dolls' old image, McLaren took his cue from 'Red Patent Leather' and sent some preliminary ideas to Vivienne Westwood, who produced five varying outfits in the same garish ketchup hue. Of all the associations in the spectrum of red—blood, lipstick, passion, danger—Malcolm chose to politicise the tone. When he relaunched the band like the rent-boy regiment of the Red Guard with a hammer-and-sickle backdrop, McLaren saw only the artistic aesthetic and not the context. The Vietnam War was still raging. The New York Dolls had already assailed the senses of the moral majority and suffered for it, but taking the commie route was creative suicide. The Dolls became McLaren's crash test dummies, prototypes for his next project: the Sex Pistols. According to the formidable Jerry Nolan, 'Malcolm's just a parasite. He observed the Dolls and what they were up to, and he was smart enough to know what they had, what sold, what kind of potential we had, and he used up everything he learned off us to put his own group together.'

The Dolls unveiled their new look and set list over four shows at the Little Hippodrome in New York between February 28 and March 2, 1975, with Television and Pure Hell in support. Aside from a dedicated contingent, reactions to the red regime were as critical as Rhett Butler's parting words to Scarlett, 'Frankly my dear, I don't give a damn.'

Rather than stay home and wallow in the critical barbs, the band set off on a tour of Florida accompanied by Malcolm. Careening through backwater towns and staving off the attention of *Deliverance*-style locals, the Dolls' last dates descended into a B-movie morality tale as the band drifted from hotels to motels, finally running aground in a neglected trailer park owned by Jerry Nolan's stepfather. Ensconced in the rusting carcasses of yesteryear's mobile dream-home, Johnny and Jerry started to get sick. Junk sick and heartsick, as Thunders admitted:

> We told David we were sick of the Dolls and that we were going back to New York to start again, and he said, 'Anyone in this band can be replaced.' But when we left, that was the end of the Dolls, the ONLY Dolls.

For Johnny and Jerry, it was indeed the end of the band. Tamper with the alchemy of any great line-up and what is left is at best a facsimile of the original. After Florida, David Johansen and Sylvain enlisted Peter Jordan for The Dollettes, aka The new New York Dolls, and toured Japan before embarking on separate careers. Arthur Kane high-tailed it to LA for the best part of a year. He never truly recovered from the demise of the Dolls and spent his life yearning for what once had been.

Malcolm McLaren eventually returned to the UK, where he combined The New York Dolls' attitude and misadventures with Richard Hell's look and launched the Sex Pistols. Although Thunders and Nolan would remain wary of him, Malcolm was to play a crucial role in the next stage of their journey.

The last word on the original New York Dolls should go to their great and often forgotten champion, Paul Nelson, whose moving lament on their demise appeared in the *Village Voice* after the Florida finale:

> The Dolls went out with their high-heeled boots on. They did it their way and got carried out dead, but with their pride intact. True, they did not grow old with the country, but that's probably the country's loss, not theirs. Corporation rock'n'roll, wherein musicians like Bachman-Turner Overdrive are more gray-flanneled than the businessmen who kow-tow to them, is so formularized, homogenised, and impersonal it must surely cause the death of anything that is all out-of-bounds, mythopoeic, and rebellious. The Dolls were alive. Perhaps it killed them not to become stars, darkened their personalities, drove some of them into private worlds; but at least they had the courage to become figments of their own imaginations.

CHAPTER THREE

MALICIOUS ROMANCE

D
one with the decadent tawdriness that The New York Dolls now represented, Johnny Thunders and Jerry Nolan returned to their rock'n'roll roots, reinventing themselves as The Heartbreakers. With a new flag to fly, Johnny explained The Heartbreakers' rationale: 'It's like the kids that never did anything right; everyone they touch goes out of their minds—like someone who comes along and burns down your house—that's breaking your heart.' It was to prove something of a prophetic statement.

Back on their home turf, Thunders and Nolan hit the ground running and swiftly nabbed bassist Richard Hell on his departure from Television. Unlike Johnny and Jerry, however, Richard aspired to a more literary remit and had commenced his creative life with a poetry magazine entitled *Genesis Grasp*. He then collaborated with his high-school friend Tom Verlaine on a collection of verse called *Wanna Go Out?* under the shared *nom de plume* of Theresa Stern. After the demise of their first band, The Neon Boys, Hell and Verlaine formed Television as an equal partnership. However, when Verlaine started to edit Hell's songs from their set list, he quit.

If Hell's bass playing erred to the angular rather than the refined, his immortality had been assured as the man who inspired the gaunt NY punk look. A rare combo of Rimbaud and Jacques Dutronc, the bassist was an engaging presence with an armoury of lethal tunes, which made him a desirable contender as far as Mr Thunders was concerned. Richard Hell spills the beans:

The reason Johnny wanted me in The Heartbreakers was because
he liked my songs and he liked the way I looked onstage. We
essentially had the same agreement as Television, but I came into
The Heartbreakers with many more songs than Johnny, 'cos I
bought with me all the songs I had written in Television.

The line-up was finalised with guitarist Walter Lure, formerly of The
Demons, who used to share the Dolls' rehearsal space. Once a student of
pharmacology, Lure was a fine guitarist and ace foil for Thunders, as Jerry
Nolan expounded: 'Walter was just a kid from Brooklyn that always wanted
to be in the Dolls. I just knew he was the right guy for The Heartbreakers.'
    In their first months as a unit, the band nailed a sound doused in
50s minimalism harking back to Eddie Cochran and Chuck Berry, with
a lethal hit of The Yardbirds via Alphabet City, courtesy of their own
dissolute talent. Symbolically aligning himself to The Heartbreakers'
stark ethic, Johnny Thunders got his hair cut, adopting a classic *West Side
Story* hoodlum look a million light years away from his former Dollish
incarnation. The Heartbreakers were in business.
    In an attempt to break away from the regimes they had all previously
played under, Thunders and company moved along more shared lines
with each to his own song. From the last days of the Dolls, Thunders
introduced 'Pirate Love' and a new tune, 'Goin' Steady', which confirmed
the guitarist as an old fashioned romantic. Richard Hell hit the target with
'Blank Generation', 'Love Comes In Spurts', and 'You Gotta Lose', while
Walter Lure brought along 'Flight'. Even Jerry Nolan got in on the act with
the existential rocker 'Can't Keep My Eyes On You'. Then, of course, there
was the highly contested 'Chinese Rocks', ostensibly written by Dee Dee
Ramone but occasionally attributed to Richard Hell. The Heartbreakers
adopted the song as their own; after all, they were now living the junk
life that 'Chinese Rocks' portrays so concisely. In less than three minutes,
the number summarises the entire remit of the heroin experience from
poverty, pawnshops, co-dependent relationships, and chemical desire. For

Johnny Thunders and Jerry Nolan, it was all too real. As Jerry explained, however, there was still plenty that the guitarist had yet to learn:

> When I told Johnny how to get an advance, boy that was the fucking biggest gift, like handing over a scroll. I said, 'Johnny, c'mere, I'll show you how we'll get high. We got a job at Max's. Right, come with me.' He came upstairs with me to talk to the manager, Tommy. I said, 'Listen, Tommy, we got a gig, you know how much money we make, I want half of it right now.' We got that half and spent it in five minutes, shooting up heroin. Ever since that day, Johnny knew what it was like to get an advance.

The local circuit on which The Heartbreakers emerged was seething with a new generation's ambitions; hometown contenders like Blondie, the Ramones, Talking Heads, and Television, all fighting for record deals and recognition. In terms of crowd pulling, The Heartbreakers were a big draw. Any band featuring two ex-Dolls was always going to generate interest, but Thunders and Nolan now suffered infamy's bitter consequences. Many unfairly pinned the demise of the Dolls on them, and the industry steered clear. As Jerry noted, they also had detractors within the scene itself: 'A lot of bands at the time felt me and Johnny didn't deserve a second chance. We fucked up the Dolls so we shouldn't be around anymore—that dumb number. They really hated us for getting a band together so quick and making it pretty successful too.'

Writing for the *NME* in March '76, Nick Kent sensed the band's plight:

> The Heartbreakers are ready to break out of their tightly bounded Lower West Side pitch and with some decent hard-sell record company back-up, combat the garish, synthesised likes of KISS and Aerosmith with a vengeance. Only thing is, the big uptown wheeler-dealers aren't biting on the bait—yet. Hell, for example is glumly resigned to a further 6 months in limbo before a halfway

decent offer comes the way of the band. Meanwhile, they become easy prey for a whole battalion of sycophantic incompetents offering two-bit management deals and the like. It's all very sad and frustrating.

Attempting to break the deadlock, Johnny Thunders approached the debonair Leee Black Childers to manage The Heartbreakers. Daring and astute, Childers was probably the only man in New York with enough vision to actively capitalise on the band's nihilistic tendencies. Aside from being a dazzling raconteur and photographer, Childers was no stranger to the rock business. As the former vice-president of David Bowie's MainMan company, Leee had taken care of Iggy Pop during his most self-destructive period—and lived to tell the story. When Johnny made his request, however, Leee was less than certain:

> I'd sworn that I would never get involved with management again. I didn't wanna die young, but I really liked the Heartbreakers. I loved their songs and I loved their music. I loved the presentation. It was everything I thought rock'n'roll should be, and so I realised I had victimised myself back into it again.

Under Leee's auspices, Richard Hell's photographer girlfriend, Roberta Bayley, orchestrated a memorable shoot with the band in which they all appear to have been mortally wounded. The blood was in fact melted Hershey Bars, but it looked convincing enough. Under the heading 'Catch Them While They're Still Alive', the image of the wounded Heartbreakers was used to advertise gigs—but was it also playing to fate?

As far as getting a deal was concerned, The Heartbreakers were already dead in the water, stateside. Aside from recording some demos at SBS Studios in Yonkers, they made little headway, as Walter Lure concurred: 'Well, we played CBGB's and then we played Max's, and then we played CBGB's and then we played Max's again . . . and it went on and on for fuckin' ages. Once in a while we'd go out of town to Boston or a new club would open up and we'd open it.' While Patti Smith, the Ramones, and The Dead Boys secured deals, The Heartbreakers were left out in the cold, but this wasn't about talent, it was about fear. Yet despite the wall of nervous abstinence, Johnny had no desire to play up the past. He told *Punk* magazine:

> The Dolls? I never heard about the Dolls . . . who were the Dolls? I wanna make a record 'cos I never really made one yet. When we were the Dolls we never made a good record. We always had too many hands in the cookie jar. Now we're gonna produce ourselves, The Heartbreakers, you know? We're the kinda band that has no fuckin' gimmicks. What we're doing now is more to what Jerry likes. Jerry's my inspiration. Me and Jerry are like Moe, Larry, and Curly—in two.

Slow death sets in when a band waits to long for their reward. Whether ultimately frustrated by lack of progress or tempted by promises of a deal from Marty Thau's new company Instant, Richard Hell made an unexpected move to usurp Johnny Thunders. Jerry Nolan took immediate action: 'Richard wanted to do all the singing himself, and he figured he'd get rid of Johnny; but little did he know—we got rid of him. He was a little shaken, his ego wasn't sure of that, he thought we'd listen to him and get rid of Johnny, which was a big mistake.'

Richard's sudden departure finally pushed Johnny to the centre of the stage. His days of waiting to take his turn were over:

> It was great when it first started [The Heartbreakers] but, you know, when Richard was in Television, Tom Verlaine wanted to sing every song, and that's what Richard did to us; I could sing one song out of ten, and Walter could sing one song a night. Naww, I didn't wanna back up a lead singer; I'd done that for too long.

Hell went on to form The Voidoids, and despite his hasty exit from The Heartbreakers, he had the grace to look back with a raw fondness at his time with Thunders & co. 'It was a good experience for me, because without that I could never have started this band.'

Richard's replacement was Boston born Billy Rath. Unlike his ambitious predecessor, Rath was a no-frills contender and powerful bassist, as Jerry Nolan explained: 'Well, obviously, we didn't want anyone who was on any sort of trip after Richard, and Billy was just perfect. He's just a bass player who loves playing rock'n'roll. He ain't worried about bein' a star. No way.'

The 'Breakers' first gig with their new bassist was given a rave review in *New York Rocker* on July 23, 1976. The writer was one Nancy Spungen. Hailing from Philadelphia, Nancy, a former Dolls fan, had relocated to New York and pinned her hopes on landing a job in the music industry. She also pinned her heart on Jerry Nolan, but despite the distractions turned in a competent overview of the band at Max's Kansas City:

> The band were amazingly tight for a first performance. Jerry's already fine drumming sounded twice as good with a great bass player. Finally, Johnny and Walter were riffing off each other; both taking leads; both providing interspersing rhythms. All four members together created a perfect chemistry, a certain magic, if you will, and the audience sure knew it. They didn't seem to mind the loss of Richard Hell at all, receiving the familiar tunes with joyful fervour and accepting the new ones as if they were old favourites. They went beyond all expectations and certainly erased any doubts that anyone may have had.

With Hell's departure, the 'Breakers had been forced to rebuild their repertoire, filtering out the nihilistic angst in favour of a more classic appeal that included the triumphant battle-cry of life on a downward slope that is Thunders' 'Born To Lose', Lure and Nolan's mischievous 'Get Off The Phone', the moody swagger of 'It's Not Enough', and 'Baby Talk', which cops its explosive central riff from The Yardbirds' 'I've Been Wrong', plus Nolan's solo stab at romance, 'Take A Chance With Me', and a cover of The Contours' 'Do You Love Me'.

The Heartbreakers continued to play every corner of Manhattan but the music industry remained immune for the same tired reasons. Walter Lure: 'We were drawing a big following, always capacity. New York was such a dead scene though. Record companies didn't want to know because of our and the Dolls' reputation. Talk about uncontrollability, drugs, et cetera...much exaggerated.'

Virtually every piece of press The Heartbreakers received in 1976 charted their hometown hurt. In the midst of a gold rush they were mining rocks. Salvation came from an unexpected quarter when Leee Black Childers received a phone call from Malcolm McLaren, inviting the 'Breakers to join the Anarchy Tour alongside the Sex Pistols, The Clash, and The Damned. It made perfect sense, McLaren upping the ante by importing two former New York Dolls.

In Blighty, the Dolls' legend burned brightly, and the addition of The Heartbreakers to the Anarchy line-up furthered the tour's risky frisson. Thunders, a man of few words, would describe Malcolm as 'the greatest con-man I've ever met'. He was an adroit media manipulator and yet over in New York, little had filtered back about London's burgeoning punk scene.

With only the vaguest idea of what was brewing on the other side of the Atlantic, The Heartbreakers prepared to embark for the UK. After all, what did they have to lose? Or as Childers quipped, 'We would have toured with anybody, even Barry Manilow!' It probably would have been a lot less hassle. On December 1, 1976, The Heartbreakers touched down at Heathrow airport. The same evening, the Sex Pistols fired their warning shot at Bill Grundy, the normally staid host of Thames TV's *Today* show. Goaded by Grundy on prime-time television, the Pistols and their entourage got into a little minor-league swearing, the kind of surly comments that can be heard in any pub in England when last orders are called. It was enough to get the punk bandwagon rolling at full speed.

The Fleet Street rags were hysterical at this unexpected Christmas gift, churning out horrified headlines and outraged quotes:

'The FILTH our children have to watch.'
'When will it end?'
'Not fit for the eyes and ears of a dog.'
'Wash their mouths out with soap.'
'Don't they have parents?'

Malcolm was delighted. The public reaction was a thousand times greater than he could have wished for. James Holmes, a forty-seven-year-old lorry driver, proudly informed the *Daily Mirror* that he had been 'so disgusted with this filth that I took a swing with my boot. It blew up and I was knocked backward.'

In a blaze of Punk! Rock! Shock! News, the Anarchy Tour got underway. Sort of. Out of a possible nineteen dates, only three went ahead. Local MPs formed watchdog committees to vet each band, while the powerful Rank Group gave the thumbs down to the possibility of any punk acts playing in their many venues. Johnny Thunders was amazed:

They're all fuckin' assholes. They don't know anything. They're full of shit. When we went on tour with the Pistols, we had all these people outside singing Christmas carols. There's more of them outside than at the gigs. In Cardiff they even had these priests with microphones screaming 'The Devil's in there ... the Devil's music' Nowhere in America would they do that. Sure, in the Midwest they'd come and break your head but they wouldn't come and pray at you first.

With cancellations running across England at the speed of the Black Death, it was a surprise in itself that the 'liberal' student body at Leeds Polytechnic got their chance to throw beer cans.

Pete Silverton reviewed The Heartbreakers in the December 18 edition of *Sounds*:

> The Heartbreakers have THE best drummer in former NY Doll Jerry Nolan, and the craziest-looking bassist in Billy Rath, who could've stepped out of *West Side Story* . . . they also have a great song about a telephone conversation which ends with one of the parties hanging themselves on the phone flex.

On December 22, the Anarchy Tour swerved to a halt. Childers had understandably presumed that cancellations or not, his band would receive some financial compensation. He was mistaken, and The Heartbreakers were left to starve in splendour through the Christmas period, as Childers explained:

> We were staying with Sebastian Conran (the ergonomic designer and son of Sir Terence Conran), bless his heart—he took a shine to us and of course he had more money than he could possibly deal with and a fabulous house on Regents Park. So we were staying there. We had a place to live but he didn't feel compelled to feed us, and I was really freaking out, 'cos I had these starving people who were my dependants!

The band were itching to return home where life's necessities—steady drug connections, food, and girlfriends—awaited them, but Childers insisted they could make history if they stayed on, and initially it appeared that he was correct:

> The first gig we did in London was at Dingwalls, and it was magnificent. You couldn't have got another person in there with a crowbar! It was so packed. I thought, *Oh boy, we're gonna be the*

next Beatles, we're gonna be so-o-o rich. Of course, the last Beatles weren't wildly self-destructive junkies, which sort of created a bit of a problem in terms of our success. Our next gig was at the Roxy.

Tucked away in Covent Garden, Andrew Czezowski's Roxy Club was at the forefront of the punk movement. The Heartbreakers became its overseas VIPs, ensuring a sardined safety-pinned crowd at every gig, as Czezowski acknowledged: 'Knowing how desperate The Heartbreakers were to do something, we booked them. They went down a storm and drew more than anyone else.'

Although The Heartbreakers were a classic rock'n'roll act, their inclusion on the Anarchy Tour had propelled them into punk's inner circle, and every show they played at the Roxy was sold out. Whilst the English punks adopted dangerous imagery, aside from Sid Vicious, the scene was largely an art school construct populated by suburban kids. The Heartbreakers, however, walked it liked they talked it, as guitarist Marco Pirroni recalled:

> I met The Heartbreakers outside the Sex Pistol's rehearsal room on Denmark Street. I only twigged this was Johnny Thunders when he introduced himself. I was well impressed. I'd never seen him in the flesh before; all I'd seen was The New York Dolls on TV and in photos. I didn't realise how little he was without all the high hair and platform boots. I saw every gig that The Heartbreakers did at the Roxy. I loved them. They came across as being incredibly slick compared to the English bands. They could start and finish a song at the same time, which the other bands couldn't do. My theory is that the punks didn't really wear leather motorcycle jackets before The Heartbreakers arrived. They also didn't do heroin.

Eventually, Johnny & co—along with Nancy Spungen, who followed them over in hot pursuit of Jerry Nolan—would be held responsible by certain parties for introducing heroin to the English punks, as Jerry Nolan told the *Village Voice*:

> We hung out a lot with the Sex Pistols. I was the first guy to turn John Rotten on to heroin, the first guy to shoot him up. I'm not proud of that, and I learned a lesson. I didn't like the feeling I got from it, and I changed my mind about turning people on to drugs. I didn't do it anymore after that. Nancy, who I introduced to Sid, was the first to turn Sid on.

Despite Nolan's honesty, Vicious always denied that Nancy was the first to introduce him to heroin. The unfortunate accolade undoubtedly goes to his mother, Anne, who was an addict. Any child growing up in a household where drugs are openly used, as was the case with Sid, is naturalised to substance misuse. While The Heartbreakers made no secret about their drug use it's also foolish to presume that there was no heroin culture in the UK before they arrived. Besides, initiates to the land of nod have to study hard before the drugs take a hold—but there's no denying the influence the band exerted.

* * *

Before The Heartbreakers' reputation caught up with them, Leee endeavoured to get them a deal. Always a *tour de force* live, there was no shortage of industry suitors. The French label Skydog was interested, as were EMI, but having been burned in their dealings with the Pistols, they were only prepared to offer a single deal to start with. Arista was enthusiastic and CBS ready to talk, but it was the old team at Track Records, headed by Kit Lambert and Chris Stamp, who were the most persistent. Having lost the Dolls, they weren't about to let The Heartbreakers slip through their fingers. Leaving Leee to sift through the offers, the band split back to Manhattan for ten days. Thunders return was delayed by a twenty-four-hour stay in a police cell for possession of a small quantity hashish. He was fined £15.

Back in London, John Genzale aka Johnny Thunders, Gerard Nolan aka Jerry Nolan, Walter Luhr aka Walter Lure, and William Wrath aka Billy Rath gave their legally binding autographs to Track as The Chris Stamp Band Ltd., an indication that all was not what it seemed within the company. The provision was made that if CSB Ltd. was to go bankrupt, all the tapes would revert back to Heartbreakers Inc., a condition inserted into the agreement by Leee Black Childers and business manager Peter Gerber. The Heartbreakers may have thought they'd hit the big time with the promise of a £50,000 advance but they'd merely taken a short lease. As they settled into London life, Johnny's fiancée, Julie Jordan, toddler Johnny Jr, and baby Vito flew over and moved into The Heartbreakers' communal base.

Unlike Walter and Billy, who grudgingly put up with the ensuing domestic chaos, Jerry Nolan relocated, as he told the *Village Voice*:

I was able to move out of The Heartbreakers' house, which was just madness with Johnny's wife and kids. So I moved out to Harrow on the Hill. My methadone doctor—he was Keith Richard's doctor too—got me my own home, a beautiful apartment. That's how great they treat you over there, how good they are. American methadone programs treat you like shit.

All the starry trappings that had been withheld from the band in New York started to come their way but, like the deal with Track, the payoff was always partially obscured for one reason or another. Julian Temple's footage of the Anarchy Tour was shelved, although Roxy club DJ Don Letts filmed The Heartbreakers for his *Punk Rock Movie*. Meanwhile the press reported that Johnny T. would be appearing in The Who's movie *Quadrophenia*. However, as The Who were legally detaching from their management team at Track, it was nothing but a long shot disguised as publicity.

For a while, the 'Breakers became press darlings, and all those tales they drawled about gang warfare, homemade zip guns, and scoring smack were lapped up like tutti-frutti until the flavour wore thin. On one occasion, an interview with Tony Parsons for the *NME* captured nothing but the sounds of Thunders' throwing up into the tape recorder. Instead of musical CVs, the band's history was presented like a trailer for a Martin Scorsese movie. Walter Lure:

> We all come from New York gangs. Each one is made up of lower middle-class kids who think they're in a band or something. Sure, we had street corner fights all the time. Something to do, you know. Sure we used weapons: Zip guns, car aerials … whip someone in the face with one of those, boy, and he's scarred for life. Rumbles useta start real easy, but I never broke nobody's neck.

Especially once he started studying pharmacology.

Jerry Nolan—the only member of the band with any real gang affiliation—stated:

> Gangs tended to be run on almost military lines. You had officers, vice presidents, presidents and the like . . . there was a lot of discipline involved. A lot of gangs were more powerful because they had better strategy. But fights between rival gangs were often very heavy … killings sometimes, stabbings … a lot of serious injury. It's even more frightening to look back on it now.

In their press kit, Nolan claimed previous membership in the Ellery Bops, Master Chaplains, and the Young Lords (the junior branch of the Phantom Lords), while Walter Lure (allegedly) flew the flag for the Green Dogs. Lacking any gang credentials, Billy Rath earned his stripes 'fessing up to having spent an entire weekend with a Girl Guide troop, while Johnny reckoned he'd run with the 90th Street Fast Boys. Later, Thunders retracted his involvement, stating that he preferred 'hanging out in parks'. His baseball bat really had been for sport, not cracking heads.

Continuing with the gang theme, the band announced that they were going to call their long-awaited debut album *L.A.M.F.*—'Like A Mother Fucker' being a spray-can warning to keep off gang turf. If one mob decided to muscle in on another's territory, they'd prefix the opposing team's Mother Fucking tag with 'D.T.K.' ('Down To Kill'). Unfortunately, when Tom Petty trod on the toes of their shiny buckled boots and called his band The Heartbreakers, he had corporate protection. Seizing the moment, Johnny & co considered a new moniker guaranteed to boost healthy interest.

THUNDERS I think we should change our name to The Junkies.

NOLAN Yep, he's right.

PRESS But you'd never get any airplay with a name like that.

THUNDERS Who fuckin' needs it. The name will provoke a reaction.

NOLAN Walter's seen Tom Petty's Heartbreakers.

LURE They're a bunch of pigs.

NOLAN Yeah ... but dead. Tom Petty: born to be punched.

THUNDERS We don't wave flags for or against drugs. Imagine how young kids are gonna get off telling their parents they're going out to see a band called The Junkies.

Aside from using Track's badge-machine to run up some 'Junkies' badges, the name passed into the annals of 'What Might Have Been'—the most likely outcome being commercial suicide.

Preparations for *L.A.M.F.* began when the band booked Essex Studios from February 20 to 22, 1977, and recorded four demo tracks: 'Let Go', Thunders and Nolan's revved-up line to an inhibited chick; the gleeful pessimism of 'Born To Lose'; a grinding 'Chinese Rocks' complete with drooling, junk-hungry 'oooh' and 'ahhh' backing vocals; plus Waldo and Jerry's study of introspection, 'All By Myself'. It was all so promising. The following month, Track taped two of their live shows at the Speakeasy, the performances intended as a warm-up for the album.

Through March, The Heartbreakers set to work on their debut platter, returning to Essex, where they laid down 'All By Myself', 'Let Go', 'Get Off The Phone', 'I Wanna Be Loved', 'Can't Keep My Eyes On You', and 'I Love You'—a perfect rundown of The Heartbreakers' low-life cynicism bouncing off Thunders' penchant for rock'n'roll valentines. Rather than using an outside producer, Track associates Speedy Keen and Danny Secunda sat in behind the mixing desk. The action then switched to The Who's studio, Ramport in Battersea, where the band recorded eight more tracks: 'Goin' Steady', 'Baby Talk', 'Do You Love Me', 'Born To Lose', 'Chinese Rocks', 'Pirate Love', 'It's Not Enough', and 'One Track Mind'.

It was with the release of 'Chinese Rocks' / 'Born To Lose' on May 20, 1977, that the fun began. Somewhere between the studio and the manufacturing plant the sound got dragged through mud, as Walter Lure recollected:

> The record wasn't really up to par, production-wise. Somebody said the voice is too loud, so Johnny said to have it different. We forgot that when you get it out of a studio and put it on a record the sound changes. No one heard it before it was finally released, and the voice was too low.

Problems also arose with the twelve-inch version of the single, owing to an excess of vinyl on the disc. Despite the setbacks, within a week of its release 'Chinese Rocks' had sold twenty thousand copies and sailed to the number one spot in the alternative charts, briefly outpacing the Pistols' 'God Save The Queen'.

For a first outing, 'Chinese Rocks' was a bold if reckless statement that drew ire from certain quarters, including *NME*'s Charles Shaar Murray, who commented, 'Anyone who sings *I'm living on a Chinese Rock* deserves to be marooned on one . . . you cool fool!' Thunders spat back the critical venom when he announced, 'They can hate fuckin' heroin and still like Chinese Rocks, either they like it or they don't fugginlahkit.'

Track's publicity department flooded the market with 'Chinese Rocks' T-shirts and badges, and Johnny explained the dedication to 'the boys on Norfolk St' (which appears on the back of the record sleeve) to anyone brave enough to ask:

> It's a street of closed-up buildings, boarded-up windows, and nailed-up doorways, basement clubs, Puerto Ricans and black guys, very heavy junkies. It's a very heavy area to be in. Any white boy in the neighbourhood is definitely there for one reason. It's not easy to walk down that street. You've got to know how to take care of yourself if you live in New York.

Before setting off on the extensive Chinese Rocks tour, the band tried to fix the sound on the rest of the tracks at different studios but mixed nothing but trouble for themselves. At Olympic, one harassed engineer marked the tape boxes as '2 downers before the overdubs'. As Walter Lure said, 'It sounded great in the studio, but as soon as it went on record it sounded fucked up. We couldn't get around that, every time we gave them a tape it sounded screwed up.'

The Heartbreakers started bickering among themselves, growing ever more agitated. Given the way Thunders and Nolan had felt regarding the production of the Dolls' two albums, the possibility of a reprise was almost too much to contemplate, and they sought in vain to rectify the situation before *L.A.M.F.* was unleashed on the public. As tapes later found from the sessions testify, the Heartbreakers played their parts brilliantly, and Keen and Secunda did no wrong. Therefore, the problem was either down to the cutting process or the manufacturing. Although their record company was entering its twilight, Track had a history of quality releases from Jimi Hendrix to The Who, yet none of its personnel was able to unravel The Heartbreakers' mix mess.

Escaping from the insanity of the studio, the band made ready to go on the road, accompanied by their new tour manager, the exuberant Gail

Higgins Smith. Meanwhile, the music papers announced the forthcoming Chinese Rocks dates:

> Johnny Thunders and The Heartbreakers set out next week on a twenty-four-venue tour extending until the end of June. The dates are split into two legs to allow for a four-week TV and promotional visit to Europe starting in mid-May; taking in Holland, Belgium, and France.

Petrol fumes, hitchers, a million greasy spoons, and a hostage situation. Who could have asked for more? On June 3, prior to The Heartbreakers' concert at Leeds Polytechnic, a gun-toting stranger prowled the corridors of the Wesley Hotel, where the band were staying. Gail Higgins Smith:

> We were in our hotel room. Johnny and Julie were travelling separately and hadn't got there yet. A guy knocked on our door and said, 'Could you please keep the noise down?' We weren't making that much noise, but he came back five minutes later with the same request, then pointed a gun at me and said, 'Get in the room, I'm from the secret service.'
>
> Inside there was some of the support band, Slaughter & The Dogs, a roadie, and Billy and Jerry. He told us that the hotel was surrounded and there was a man on the roof with a shotgun trying to kill us, and that he'd been sent to protect us. We didn't know if this was true or if he was just a madman. He kept going out into the hall, saying, 'I'm just checking with the rest of the secret service about the situation, you can't leave yet.' We were going, 'We have a soundcheck to do.' He was going, 'You can't leave, it's too dangerous.'
>
> This went on for about four hours, everyone was getting bored and pissed off. Then the phone rang and it was Walter from downstairs, asking me to come and buy him lunch. I was thinking

about how do they do this in the movies, to warn someone that they're in trouble? In the end he came up and the gunman opened the door, pointed the gun at him, and said, 'Shut up and get inside.' Now we're all in this room except Johnny and starting to get convinced that he'd set this up as some sort of joke, 'cos he was the only one not there.

Finally, the gunman goes out into the hall and says, 'My superiors says you can leave now, the coast is clear, but because I'm in the secret service, if you call the police, they'll deny I exist.' I called the police anyway. They came along and had to fingerprint all of us because they had to take prints from the whole room, to see if there were any of the gunman's. Johnny still hadn't arrived, and the fingerprints on the back of *L.A.M.F.* are mine, not Johnny's.

If nothing else, at least the sleeve artwork for the album was coming together! DS Lorriman of the Leeds police commented at the time, 'We are treating the matter very seriously and are making further inquiries, including running a check on The Heartbreakers.' Any suspicions the local constabulary may have had about the band were confirmed when certain parties smashed up a payphone trying to get at the change inside. As for the gunman, he was picked up three weeks later, trying to steal a car. A plastic replica of a gun was found on his person.

In between all the dramas, the tour continued, audiences wooed by The Heartbreakers' brand of malicious charm. Writing for *Record Mirror*, Barry Cain laid on the praise:

'You asked for it,' warns Johnny, 'If you wanna pass the hat around all donations will be accepted . . .' and cracks into 'Do You Love Me'. Nolan is a blur, Rath cruises, Lure sings/plays like there's no next second, let alone tomorrow. Second encore: 'Take A Chance' and a stroke-of-genius 'Chinese Rocks' reprisal. It's so good it hurts. That's no joke.

Noticing Thunders and Nolan's growing status in the UK, Mercury Records saw a chance to recoup by reissuing the Dolls' albums as a single package, piously trumpeting in the advertising blurb, 'Before anyone discovered New Wave Rock, the Dolls were inventing it'. Still, it gave all those who had thought the Dolls were an offshoot of Max Factor the opportunity to listen and learn, but Thunders and Nolan weren't to be placated.

THUNDERS They gonna put out the two Dolls albums in a double package next month, even the record companies can see the Dolls influence now.

NOLAN They should remix the fuckin' albums an' not just re-release them. Hey, we gonna get any money outta that deal?

Nolan had little time to reassess the royalty situation when a more pressing situation arose concerning The Heartbreakers' work visas. Following an investigation into the band's paperwork (or lack of), the Home Office issued a letter ordering them out of England within twenty-four hours. The trouble dated back to the band's original entry for the Anarchy Tour, when they had showed up without work permits. Track Records had rectified this, once the group signed with them, as spokesman Alan Edwards told the press: 'As far as we know the band have their work permits in order, and their exchange permit has been ok'd by both the English and American Musicians Unions.'

In spite of this, the Home Office removed their passports, and the band's gigs became open to speculation. Leee Black Childers lodged an appeal and was told the decision would be handed down on July 4— American Independence Day. The Heartbreakers had been planning to hoist the star-spangled banner over Hyde Park with a concert and a thousand pounds worth of fireworks to celebrate both the date and the success of their single, but the dour Greater London Council turned down the application.

Making the most of a temporary reprieve by the Home Office, The

Heartbreakers appeared at the Vortex Club in Wardour Street. However, as Walter explained, the event was soured by the headlining band:

> The Buzzcocks didn't want us to steal their fucking show. They wouldn't let us have our gear in the place until they had finished. The club owner told them about it. It was their show and we were going to do a special set after but then they wanted us to go on before them at about fuckin two in the afternoon. It was a pity all the shit started creeping into the scene . . .

Regardless of the fun and games, the night belonged to The Heartbreakers. As this was to be their last gig for the time being, the audience swelled to include various members of Generation X, The Damned, and The Clash.

Grown desperate for legal grounds to keep the band in England, Track suggested they marry the secretarial staff from their Carnaby Street offices. A spokesman from the company with all the wit of The Heartbreakers' manager sneered, 'If it was Peggy Lee, I'm sure they'd find a way round the problem.'

Anxious to keep his charges in the UK, Leee knew that a protracted absence would be a crucial setback as the release date for the band's forthcoming album loomed. Back home, there was little to sustain The Heartbreakers, save for gigging in small venues. In the words of the formidable Leee Black Childers, 'Rock'n'roll hasn't taken off there yet. You've got CBGB's and Madison Square Garden and nothing in between.'

LEEE BLACK CHILDERS INTERVIEW

NINA When did you start managing The Heartbreakers?

LEEE In the fall of '76. They talked to me then about managing them
'cos they needed some sort of management and someone to get 'em a
record deal. They also talked to Tony Zanetta about managing them
at the same time, and then they talked about us doing them together.
I begged Ze, Tony Zanetta, to join with me, but at the last minute
he backed out, said he couldn't deal with it. While this was going on,
Richard Hell decided to quit. I talked to him and I tried to reason
with him and get him to stay. Basically, I think it was just a big ego
conflict. Half of the audience would be watching Richard Hell and
the other half would be watching Johnny Thunders. There were these
constant arguments. Richard left, and then there was a period of
looking for a bass player, and that was when I first started working
with them. Once we found Billy, the first gigs we did were two nights
at Max's. We placed this full-page ad in the *Village Voice*, which was
a huge picture, and at the bottom it said, 'Plus Friday The Vest, plus
Saturday Blondie' in little bitty letters, and Blondie were furious at
us. I remember they all went nuts, screaming about how their name
was so little, and I had to tell them that it was because it was such
a privilege to support The Heartbreakers. Subsequently they all
became millionaires, which serves me right! But the shows went down
fabulously, lines around the block. That was the beginning.

NINA There was a problem, wasn't there, about getting them a record
deal?

LEEE Yeah, well, I'm sure you know the reputation that the Dolls had
gotten? Some of which was deserved. Some of which was hysteria on
the part of the record companies. Businessmen don't want to deal
with personalities of any kind; much less strong, heavily destructive
personalities. The record companies just didn't want to know. There

was a lot of gossip, it may have been some direct information fed from the previous people that had worked with the Dolls. Partly it was drugs, but mostly the big problem that I ran into when I talked to the record companies was that they had gained a reputation of not showing up for gigs. Or showing up in the town but not going on for one reason or another. Or doing two songs and storming off the stage and throwing things. Of course this was pre-punk, so it was totally unheard of that anyone could act like that and expect to sell records. I didn't really have much argument for American record companies, because it was before the Sex Pistols. I couldn't very well say, 'Oh, but that's good that Johnny calls the audience motherfuckers and they spit at the audience and walk off stage after two songs and curse.' There was no precedent to prove to anyone that anyone would want to buy records from someone that horrible. I was just stonewalled. Even companies like Sire, and Terry Ork who had this little independent label, didn't want to get involved—particularly with Johnny. He had the real bad-boy reputation. He had taken, I think not entirely deservedly, most of the bad publicity from the Dolls.

NINA Was he a real 'bad boy'?

LEEE Yeah. Oh, he *is* a real bad boy. So is Nolan. After the Dolls, Nolan got away pretty well. Everyone still thought he was such a nice guy and everyone thought David Johansen was a nice guy, and everyone thought Johnny was the problem. I soon learned who the *real* problem was, but whenever Johnny's name was mentioned the American record companies didn't want to know. That call from Malcolm McLaren was a lifesaver as far as I was concerned, 'cos I wasn't getting anywhere and they couldn't just sit around in New York playing Max's Kansas City and CBGB's for the rest of their lives—even if no one expected their lives would be that long anyway.

NINA You shared an office with McLaren, didn't you?

LEEE Yeah. When he called me in New York and asked me if we wanted to come along on the Anarchy tour, I didn't even know who the Sex

Pistols were. I asked Johnny and he thought he'd heard something about them, but he wasn't sure. He thought they copied Richard Hell's look. Off we went to England without any promise of any salary. When we got to Heathrow Airport—Malcolm had sent us one-way tickets—we had no work permits, nothing had been arranged of any kind … so you can imagine! They wouldn't let us in. We had to beg and plead. On the other side, Malcolm McLaren was begging for them to let us in. If we'd come *one* day later, we'd never have gotten in the country.

The next day was when all the newspaper headlines came out about the Bill Grundy thing, Malcolm couldn't have got us in 'cos he was the biggest villain in the UK then. The next morning, we still really didn't know who they were. They took us out to the Great American Disaster, a hamburger restaurant on the Fulham Road, then we went back to this little bed and breakfast place Malcolm had put us up in. We said, 'What are they? They don't look so weird. They look okay.' Nils Stephenson, who went on to manage Siouxsie & The Banshees, poor little thing, he had spiky hair and one of those big fluffy sweaters, and in America only girls wore big fluffy sweaters. I'd previously been talking to Malcolm's secretary, Sophie, on the phone, so when I met Nils, I kept calling him Sophie, and he kept looking at me real funny.

The next morning, Nolan, who *never* sleeps and had been wandering the streets of London all night, picked up the morning papers. He came in and woke me and threw 'em down on the bed and said, 'THIS is what we're involved in now. What are we gonna do about this?' I said, 'I dunno. I guess you're gonna have to shoot the queen for you to get in the papers now.'

NINA When did Track Records first approach you? Jerry Nolan said EMI offered a one-single deal?

LEEE EMI? Well, Mike Thorne was a producer, and he came along. There had been all this publicity because of the Anarchy Tour; all the record companies were sending their people up. The Clash got a lot of attention and we got a lot of attention. Mike Thorne really loved the band and he wanted to do a deal, but EMI had, of course, just been through the Pistols thing, and they were very reluctant to get involved with anybody again; and I think that's about as far as he got. He could offer a definite one-single deal—with all those options to blah blah blah—but it would mean they wouldn't give us a huge advance. Arista were very interested and CBS was talking to us, but then I ran into Julian Kraker. His sister used to do makeup for David Bowie. He suggested Track Records, because he said they were friends of his, and he took me down there.

Track Records was very weird. They had very large offices but they didn't have any acts to speak of. They had Shakin' Stevens but they weren't doing a thing with him. They had The Who and all that, but that was all gone. They were very rich and they had a lot of money. It was very weird, very laid back; Chris Stamp was really crazy, and Kit Lambert was wandering blindly in and out in those days. Stamp was nuts, and so was Danny Secunda. They became really interested in the music that was happening on the new scene. They didn't like the straight record industry either. They just loved the idea of shocking the pants off it and doing awful things. They'd had Arthur Brown, who used to set his head on fire. And The Who, in their day, had been very shocking. Danny Secunda said, 'Sure. We'll sign The Heartbreakers up', without even seeing them!

NINA Was it true that it was just some sort of weird business setup?

LEEE Yeah. We weren't really signed to Track Records, although the label on the records said 'Track'. We were on something called 'Chris Stamp Band'. They were going through lawsuits to try and keep the catalogue they had, and to try to get royalties from *Tommy*. They had to be a real, functioning record company putting out records, but they didn't sign us directly to Track, because if they had then the money they promised us in the contract would be guaranteed by The

Who's back catalogue. They signed us to this 'Chris Stamp Band' thing and promised us what was a huge advance for those days. Then, when they didn't pay it off, which they didn't, they just let the 'Chris Stamp Band' go bankrupt, and we couldn't really do anything.

Fortunately, we had a genius of a business manager named Peter Gerber, who has since died, who asked Stamp to personally guarantee the money with his own fortune—I mean, his name was on it—and Stamp wouldn't do it. Peter said, 'In that case, if you go bankrupt, we want a clause in the contract that we get all of our tapes back.' In other words, the receiver won't get them. Stamp was furious. How dare we insult him? That a company with his name on it would ever be allowed to go bankrupt, blah blah blah.

As it turned out, the best we can figure is that was always his intention, to use us as long as they could. The way it worked was, Mathalda Hall, who was the only honest one, really—she was a well-respected director who had come from Arista, and she really worked. Chris Stamp said to her, 'Listen, you need a holiday. Go away to Africa for two weeks,' so off she went. During that time, Stamp cut off everyone's funds—no one could get any money. He was insulting to everyone, and then he just said, 'The party's over—hit the road.' As far as I know, Mathalda was furious when she got back, but by then there was nothing she could do, he had already closed up shop.

Did you hear how we got the tapes? The receivers came and started noting everything down; Jan Stevens, the secretary, was there, and they told her, 'You're being made bankrupt. Get out.' Jan ran to a telephone and called me. By the time I got down there, everything was closed. The doors were sealed and padlocked, and the tapes were inside. The next day was a Saturday—I was with my friend, Mrs Simpson, who had been my high school sweetheart, and she was visiting with her teenage son and her teenage boyfriend. We all piled into her little Morris Minor and went down to Carnaby Street. We had the boyfriend and the son climb up the wall and break in through a window. They found a service door that wasn't padlocked and let us in. Then we had to break into the tape vault. The whole time I'm on to my lawyer, going, 'Am I doing anything illegal or what?' He was saying, 'Take only what's yours.' There were all the Who tapes, Marc Bolan tapes, Jimi Hendrix tapes, and I was thinking, *Ahhhh, I want those.* But he's saying, 'Take only what's yours and you're fine. You haven't broken any law.' So we did. We found some paint, we wanted to paint 'L.A.M.F.' real big on the walls, and my lawyer said, 'No. You can't do that. That would be vandalism.' So we found this huge bit of canvas and painted 'L.A.M.F.' on that and tacked that up on the walls, and that was all right. Then we left. It was weeks before anyone realised all The Heartbreakers' tapes had vanished, and they were hidden for years.

NINA Did Johnny have Julie and the children with him?

LEEE He had little Johnny and Vito, who we called the Sprog. Poor little thing was always on the floor, kind of crawling around on its back. They lived with us in a house in Islington, but not Jerry. Jerry refused to live with them. We had to get Jerry a separate place in Pinner. Walter and Billy and Julie and Johnny and Sprog all lived together in Chelsea in one of those luxury service flats, it cost a fortune and they all fought constantly, hated each other and threw things and broke things. The phone used to ring continuously in the middle of the night with one of them screaming about another one. It went on and on and on. Of course, Walter and Billy weren't allowed to have girlfriends in because it made Julie crazy to have 'groupies' around. They [Johnny & co] came to live with me, and then I understood everything. I was going crazy. I loved the kids, but they were just . . . I mean, you don't want to have little kids around all the time, it drives you nuts. Then Johnny went to live in Soho and around that time I stopped working for them.

NINA Do you think there could have been any way to avoid The Heartbreakers' disintegration?

LEEE No, not at that time. Besides themselves, there was a lot of outside destructive influences. Whispers in the ear, you know? Destructive people, somebody whispering in Jerry's ear that he wasn't getting fair treatment, that Johnny was being treated as *the* star. Oh, they always, always complained about it whenever they were billed as Johnny Thunders' Heartbreakers, even though there were other Heartbreakers in America that they could have been confused with. They couldn't stand it! Particularly Jerry Nolan ... but they all hated it.

NINA Jerry said, in the press, that he left because of the bad mix on *L.A.M.F.*

LEEE Darling, first of all, this was supposed to be raw rock'n'roll, right? First they went into Essex Studios and recorded 'Chinese Rocks' and 'Born To Lose', and they did a mix with some inexperienced engineer and the whole thing sounded raw. I thought it sounded wonderful; that was what they wanted. But Jerry didn't like it: and in those days, what Jerry didn't like, Johnny didn't like—and that was the end of it. So, they had to get a more expensive studio.

They were all sort of unsuccessful con artists. I love a *good* con artist who can do a big, million-dollar con. I think that's wonderful, but to do little cons like, 'We can't be at Essex Studios because we've heard about a studio that costs more', and that was really what everything was built upon—what it cost. As if there weren't gonna be any money the next day. As it turned out they were right, there wasn't gonna be any money the next day. But I just don't think that's the way you can keep on going. We ended up in this studio across the river that was The Who's studio, and it did cost a fortune. The engineers, although undoubtedly very good, were used to all this older type rock'n'roll stuff. The mixing sessions began, and if you just keep mixing and adding on, and mixing and adding on and getting stoneder and mixing some more, you end up with mud. So we had mud. Jerry Nolan threatened to quit the band unless he alone was allowed to re-mix. This was his big ace in the hole, every time he wanted his way: 'I'll quit the band, I'll get a divorce.' So he was brought ahead, secretly, of the other band members.

NINA This was when they'd all been deported?

LEEE Yeah. Everyone was back in America, and Mathalda Hall said, 'Listen, we have those awful mixes.' There's nothing I hate more than sitting around in a studio while people mix the same song over and over, but I had to sit there otherwise they wouldn't have mixed at all, they would have just drunk brandy all night. So I sat there and I saw who was twiddling the knobs and was screaming and demanding more and demanding more. It was the blonde one, not the brunette! I knew good and well who'd created the mud in the first place. So Mathalda said, 'Bring him back. It can't get any worse.'

He arrived on his own at Heathrow Airport, eating an apple and carrying *two* valid American passports, which is against international law. He gave them both to the immigration guy. They called me and said that not only were they not going to let him in the country but they were also going put him in prison. I went down to Heathrow and I begged and I cried. Fortunately, I can cry on cue, so I begged and told them how much loss to the British revenue would happen if this album didn't come out and they relented and forced him to destroy or made him promise to destroy one of the passports. At great expense, we got him into the studio. There was just no point in throwing good money after bad, at that point. The only thing that could have been done would have been to shoot Jerry Nolan and put the rest of them back in the studio from scratch—with a drum machine. Then, maybe, they could have gotten something out of it.

NINA Everything just disintegrated then?

LEEE Yeah. Jerry went away waving his arms and screaming that he'd been screwed! Johnny at that time was very emotionally dependent on Jerry and didn't know what to do, which way to turn. I think the other two were just tired. It had been a long haul. They had worked very hard over two years; almost constant touring, recording, doing something. The whole time just on survival money. I mean, very few luxuries, very few relaxing moments when they could just let their hair down and have a party. Clearly, Walter and Billy got back to work with Johnny, so it wasn't anything personal—everyone had to just stop. I know I did. I didn't know which other way to go. I had fought and clawed and lied and cheated and done everything I could do to keep them working as a band. I couldn't think of what the next move should be. I was exhausted too.

CHAPTER FOUR

SO MANY STAINS AND WISHES

The Heartbreakers' return to New York coincided with a major power outage, the wonderful hieroglyphics of Manhattan's neon vanishing in sequence under the heel of a blackout. Once electricity was restored, they discovered that little had changed in their absence. The same bands played the same clubs to the same audience, while CBGB's remained the centre of NY's punk universe; but it was a much smaller scene than the one The Heartbreakers had gotten used to in the UK.

NEW YORK ROCKER How does it feel to be back in New York, Johnny?
THUNDERS I hate it . . . its SOOOOO baw-ring.

In *Sounds* magazine, October 1977, Jon Savage asked if their look drew stares in New York. Walter Lure replied:

> They couldn't figure it out. 'Why, they're wearing ties with no collars, clothes that made no sense, weird looking hair.' Y'see, the punk thing hasn't hit there nationally, just underground.

While the band got their bearings, Johnny met up with his family and told them that he was going to do the decent thing. Anyone who could turn out the sort of love songs that Thunders did had to be the marrying kind, as his sister, Mariann Bracken, concurred:

When Johnny originally met Julie, she was about three months pregnant. Johnny knew he wasn't the father. She had the baby and they named him Johnny. When Vito came along they decided to get married in a civil ceremony. We hoped that this was a good move for them. On the way home from the wedding reception, it was announced on the radio that Elvis was dead. It was August 16, 1977.

Ill omens seemed to plague The Heartbreakers, but once the confetti had been brushed away they made the most of their enforced exile by rehearsing and working on new material. Any plans to play live were initially sketchy. 'Not unless,' quoth Walter Lure, 'we arrange some sort of special gig.' The special gig turned out to be a three-night stand at the Village Gate. *New York Rocker*'s Roy Traikin made it backstage for the second show:

The dressing room was a scene of utter chaos, as Leee Black Childers would poke his head in every few minutes and inquire ever so demurely, 'Ready in five minutes, boys?' No reaction. He smiled slightly and left. Johnny had strapped on his guitar (he somehow looks as if he is missing an arm when he doesn't have it on) and began lazily strumming. Interviewing became impossible. Childers leaned in again and tried to get someone's, anyone's attention. 'Anarchy In The UK' blared out of the juke box. The boys were oblivious. 'After Anarchy, okay, boys?' Walter took the initiative. He blinked his eyes nervously and spit it out, 'Let's go, Johnny.' They hit the stage . . .

Saturday is the last gig in what's been a sell-out run to an avid crowd, with a finale comprising of guests Sylvain Sylvain and Robert Gordon, who joined the band for an encore of 'Jailhouse Rock'. Richard Hell stood smiling by the bar in certain approval of the events, Thunders got a kiss from Debbie Harry, and even David Johansen turned up to pay his respects, causing *New York Rocker* to ask Johnny if he'd ever play with Johansen again. Thunders: 'Sure, yeah. I'd fool around with him in a studio—but I'd NEVER be in the same band as him again.' Walter Lure, while apparently having enjoyed the Village Gate shows, remained somewhat cynical: 'Sure, it was good. It was the best New York audience we'd seen. They must have been educated the six months we went away but they danced to us. They at least got the energy from somewhere, but they were doing the Hustle. They were STILL doing that, man, jumping up and down, the whole number.'

Even if 'Chinese Rocks' had slipped by the tall dame with the torch and was now available on import, the band still had no concrete deal for the US release of their first album. The two main contenders seemed to be Ork Records (Terry Ork having eased up on his view of Thunders 'reputation') and Marty Thau, who apparently wanted them for his own Johnny Records.

NEW YORK ROCKER Would you consider cutting 'Chinese Rocks' or something for Ork?

THUNDERS Would you cut off your head and eat it?

With the release of *L.A.M.F.* bearing down on them, Johnny & co figured they should at least have the front cover ready. With Roberta Bayley in tow, the band set off on a trip down every backstreet the guidebooks tell you to avoid, before finally winding up in SoHo (south of Houston Street). Using some grievously worn brickwork as a backdrop, the band lined up (or rather leaned in line) for Bayley, whose photograph managed to capture the atmosphere of the surroundings as well as The Heartbreakers, who looked every mean inch a part of them. Walter Lure: 'We went out one night and took some pictures and sent them over to England. They liked the one they used, and anyway they were so tired of us fighting [over the sleeve] that they put it out.'

It was then that Jerry Nolan left for England, to try to remix the album. Billy and Walter had their own suspicions and returned to London not long after the drummer. Thunders, of course, missed his flight, and it wasn't until September that the band put the finishing touches to their pre-album EP: 'One Track Mind' / 'Can't Keep My Eyes On You' / 'Do You Love Me'. It seemed the chance to move out of the forever-dimming cult spotlight was within easy grasp at last. A major UK tour was planned to coincide with the October 3 release of *L.A.M.F.* but unfortunately, like their record company, The Heartbreakers' days were already numbered. Knowing full well that the tide was about to take everything away, Track threw a pre-release album party in their Carnaby Street office.

Working against the clock and each other, the band tried to salvage *L.A.M.F.* Jerry Nolan claimed he remixed a total of nine tracks, pressurised all the while by the record company's promotion squad with their 'fixed schedules to meet' and the ever popular 'Look, we've booked advertising for certain dates.' Even before the album came out, Nolan felt that principle was going to force him to leave the band:

Track said, 'Okay, Jerry, tell you what, let the first five thousand go out and then we'll use your mix.' That's when I knew it was over. That first five thousand were gonna go out to the fans and the press, they're gonna judge us by that, right? So I told 'em they could shove the five thousand up their ass, and split.

If only someone had pinpointed the source of the problem. Every time the master tapes left the studio, the process faltered. Why Track didn't advise the band to attend the cutting process will remain a mystery, like most of their manoeuvres. Maybe they were too besieged by their own problems to pay attention. Johnny's take on the situation appeared in an October 1977 issue of *Melody Maker*:

What happened was, we mixed it, right? And everybody liked the mix. Then Jerry Nolan went back to London ahead of us while we were still in NY. We'd heard a test pressing and liked it, and then he (Nolan) started remixing the album. I was still in NY and didn't even hear what went down until the album was out. You know, he started screwing up all the mixes and so it sounded the way it did. Jerry didn't want the album to come out then, 'cos he knew it was fucked up. Walter and Billy wanted it out 'cos it was due three months before, and they ... ah ... forced it out. Then Jerry quit the band. I didn't know what was happening.

When interviewed for this book years after the episode, however, Johnny wasn't quite as certain who did the damage:

Jerry Nolan and Walter Lure didn't get along too well, and, uh, we mixed the album, right ... and still liked it and split back to New York and Walter was still here and he fucked around and fucked the album up and mixed ... then Jerry went in and remixed it again ... and between those two they had it out and then Jerry quit.

Track Records decided to play down whatever internal problems the band might have been having with an off-handed comment from spokesman Alan Edwards, The Heartbreakers' publicist: 'Jerry leaves every two weeks, so why should this be any different?' One interviewer asked Johnny if he was happy with *L.A.M.F.*'s production job. His response was ever candid.

THUNDERS Well ... lemme put it this way ... I wouldn't put it out in the States.

INTERVIEWER So you treat us as inferiors?

THUNDERS America's a bigger market ...

Critics who disliked the band harked on about the murky mix, while those that liked them blamed the production. Curiously, the cassette release of

L.A.M.F. was far superior to the LP version, testifying to a repeated cutting or mastering fault. It would take until the twenty-first century to finally resolve the curse of *L.A.M.F.*, following Jungle Records' release first of a four-disc *Definitive Edition* in 2013 and then of *The Found '77 Master* in 2021, the latter taken from a copy belonging to Danny Secunda.

* * *

With Paul Cook sitting in for the departed Nolan, The Heartbreakers kicked off their autumn tour at Bristol Polytechnic. Steve Jones also climbed onstage for part of the set, picking up a few tips from Johnny. The gig was reviewed in the October 8 edition of *Sounds*:

> Rock'n'roll The Heartbreakers are through and through. Punk really isn't it at all—even if they did have half the Sex Pistols playing. It's broader and more mature; doing stuff like The Monkees' 'Steppin' Stone', 'Do You Love Me', and 'Sweet Little Rock'n'roller'. They cross barriers that other new wavers wouldn't dare to for fear of losing face. The Heartbreakers are great, hot and anybody's. All you need is a pair of ears and an open mind.

Just when it seemed the band would be doomed to a series of temporary drummers for the duration of the tour, Track issued a press statement.

> Jerry Nolan is no longer a member of The Heartbreakers, but a hired musician. He will be performing with the band for all the British dates through to the Croydon Greyhound on November 6. Jerry Nolan added, 'That's because Johnny asked me to do it, for old time's sake; so I said sure, I'll do that, I'll even train their new drummer for them.'

To their audiences, at least, the band were as good as ever, but Johnny and Jerry were hurting. Nolan had co-founded The Heartbreakers, and whatever casual remarks he issued to the press, the symptoms of suddenly finding himself a hired hand may have eaten into him deeper than even he knew.

Away from the stage, Nolan seemed to take his new role to heart, showing little interest in interviews and keeping to himself for most of the tour. Thunders, never one to wallow in tact at the best of times, responded to a journalist who asked him if he was happy: 'Happy? Naw, I ain't all that happy at the moment. Christ, I'm lookin' for a drummer . . .'

Rumour had it that The Damned's Rat Scabies was up for the post. Thunders: 'It's not gonna be Rat Scabies. We already tried that. He's a great guy, but his style is totally different. Like sixties heavy metal . . .'

Nolan seemed almost on the verge of paranoia when he decided there were other factors, apart from the infamous mix, behind his reasons for quitting, as he explained to Barry Cain from the *Record Mirror* in a particularly cryptic interview:

> There's one guy in this band I don't like. I've discovered he's a coward, and I can't work with cowards. He's done things behind my back, he gave in to allow the album to be released. He's only interested in reading about himself in the papers. I can't live with that. There's also another guy in the Heartbreakers setup who acts more like a middleman in a drugs deal rather concentrating on what he should be doing. The whole thing's a joke and I want out.

On Thursday, October 20, the tour climaxed with a show at the Rainbow featuring Siouxsie & The Banshees, plus The Models in support. As the lights dimmed, masking the theatre's decomposing grandeur, spotlights were trained on an impressive painted backdrop of a street scene featuring a pawnshop to match a line from a certain song. Following a searing blast of the Heartbreakers' intro music—which comprised an alarming collage of sounds including police sirens, falling bombs, traffic horns, and the heavy tread of jackboots—the band commenced their set. Some witnesses claimed that Johnny Thunders threw a brick at the illustrated pawnshop window.

From the opening number it was apparent that The Heartbreakers were at their very best. It was also apparent that the bouncers were at their musclebound worst, taking great delight in clubbing anyone in their way and throwing them out of the hall with a kick for a memory. After Johnny stopped the set long enough to comment on the antics of the 'red-shirted fuckers', the bouncers pulled back, but their overly heavy manners had angered both the band and audience alike. The tense situation was further heightened by the arrest of Banshees drummer Kenny Morris after the concert. He was later fined for that trusty legal standby, 'obstruction'. Nobody ever said of what.

The tour was not a happy one, as evidenced by a despondent Thunders, who told one journalist, 'I don't have enough money; I don't have a private island and I don't have a jet.' He didn't have a drummer, either. By November, Nolan had left with plans to form a band of his own, The Idols.

The Heartbreakers were now a trio looking for a replacement, but Jerry Nolan was an impossible act to follow, as Walter Lure admitted in the music press: 'It's going to be hard to find someone. For a lot of the drummers on the punk scene, Jerry's their idol so we should find someone with the right style soon. It's probably better. He's a great drummer and he has a lot of good ideas, but he created a lot of problems. He's the main reason we haven't rehearsed once in the last year.'

The original drummer for The Clash, Terry Chimes, played one out-of-town date with the band and met with their approval. With Chimes in tow, they began working on a couple of new songs, 'Too Much Junkie Business' and 'Laughing At You', apparently written about Nolan's departure. The final line reads, 'There'll never be no one like me and you.'

By playing two nights at the Vortex, The Heartbreakers got the chance to break in their new boy and, as Johnny told the press, the opportunity 'to remove some of the bad feeling caused by overzealous bouncers at the

Rainbow'. But the band seemed to have an albatross circling over them. No sooner had they found a replacement drummer than Track shut up shop. Walter Lure:

> We didn't know at the time there was a whole lot of politics behind the scenes. Track really didn't give a shit about us at all. They were just trying to present us as a Track band because they were trying to get all this money from *Tommy* from The Who and there was this big lawsuit going on, 'cos The Who didn't want them to get it, because they said they weren't helping them out, weren't managing whatever for them. Track had to show to them and the lawyers that they had a record, and they were working with people, so they just used us as a front.

At first, Track clammed up, then decided that The Heartbreakers owed them £100,000. Before the fight got real dirty, the company was declared bankrupt. The group's last single on the label, 'It's Not Enough' / 'Let Go', was recalled shortly after its release. In some confusion, Thunders related to the press that he didn't anticipate any trouble with Track as no deal had been signed and negotiations were already underway with CBS.

On December 13 (probably a Friday), the Mk. 3 Heartbreakers entered Riverside Studios to record a trio of tracks: 'London Boys', a retort to Johnny Rotten's anti-Dolls diatribe 'New York'; 'Too Much Junkie Business', a knockabout slice of street farce composed by Lure and Thunders; and a cover of The Shangri-Las' 'Great Big Kiss'. Whether the Riverside demos were intended as an incentive for CBS will never be known, but any further negotiations with the company petered out like the band's career in London. By Christmas it was black curtains in the Heartbreakers camp. Walter Lure and Billy Rath returned to New York, where Jerry Nolan was busy working with The Idols, while Leee Black Childers issued a terse 'no comment' to anyone left interested in a four-way divorce and drugs story. Of the band, only Johnny remained in London.

The two shows that The Heartbreakers played at the Vortex were destined to be the last England would see of them as a unit for almost a decade. Jane Suck, writing for the December 3 issue of *Sounds*, gave them quite a send-off:

Heartbreakers: Born to lose / Baby I was born to lose: but for the fact I love Leee Childers and don't want him to take the first plane back to NY, I'd let fly ... like, why are The Heartbreakers back in the Vortex? That ain't cool, that's dumb ... and, ah, why is Thunders the most arrogant slob to ever stumble across a stage? Sure, we love The New York Dolls, but ... 1977 / hope I go to heaven: You won't get past the pearly gates, Johnny, not unless you drop the 'Look, Ma, I'm a star' jive. We're all jizbags in London, after all. Nice rock'n'roll / the same old Heartbreakers set: 'Chinese Rocks', 'Get Off The Phone', and, oh dear, 'Too Much Monkey Business'—scars, scars / the stars and the bars, my Carmen—you get what you deserve, Heartbreakers, last week's laundry.

CHAPTER FIVE

NIGHT OF THE LIVING DEAD

T he slate-grey shroud of winter folded itself around England's capital. Punk hysteria of the Fleet Street brand was old news and 1978 crept in like an afterthought. Save for Julie and the children, Johnny was left without the support of either band or management and facing a pile of growing debts which he was ill-equipped to deal with, as Nick Kent reported in *NME*:

> The band remains in the same no record-company limbo caused by the Track break-off, and their former publicist Alan Edwards has been relieved of his duties. More to the point, both bassist Billy Rath and guitarist Walter Lure are still ensconced in their native Manhattan, where they returned for a brief Christmas holiday two months ago. Only the band's communal pad in Chelsea is still operative, though the phone has been disconnected through lack of payment, various other amenities are in jeopardy, and important bills have apparently still not been paid.

And yet all was not lost. Leaving the mail to pile up and the apartment to gather dust, Thunders and family moved to a new flat in the seedy heart of Soho, above a massage parlour. Their new abode on D'Arblay Street was in walking distance of the office of Real Records impresario Dave Hill, who also managed The Pretenders. Citing Thunders as a rock'n'roll hero, Hill began to pull strings on the guitarist's behalf.

The first stirrings of activity commenced at Island studios in Hammersmith, with Eddie & The Hot Rods bassist Paul Gray, drummer Steve Nicol and fledgling producer Steve Lillywhite. Gray, who had been photographed in a 'Chinese Rocks' T-shirt the previous year and was a Thunders aficionado, recalled:

> J.T. liked the way me and Steve [Nicol] played together, so we got asked down to Island Studios. It was very loose, a few tracks turned into a few more. There was precious little direction. Johnny would just pick up his guitar and Steve and I would jam along until we were ready to tape it. He probably let us know if he didn't like something or other when he was awake, but my main recollection was that it was down to Steve Lillywhite to decide what was working or not. Johnny did get quite precious about timings, but then he'd go and play the same song completely differently the next time, so you never really know where you were. J.T.'s songs were great to play to, lotsa space and great melodies to bounce off.

The Thunders/Rods combo was an invigorating booster for the guitarist during an uncertain time and paved the way for his next venture, a louche revue entitled The Living Dead who played a residency at the legendary Speakeasy. Although The Living Dead's line-up was liable to change from week to week, depending on the participants' touring schedules, the main habitués included Snatch chanteuse Patti Palladin, French teenager Henri-Paul (formerly of The Maniacs), Paul Gray and Steve Nicol, plus Mike Kellie and Peter Perrett from The Only Ones.

For Peter Perrett, the raffish frontman of The Only Ones, a chance to play with Thunders in a more casual setting had an insolent appeal. He had first met Johnny at the Speakeasy in 1977, where they shared an instant, chemical camaraderie. Thunders was so enamoured of Perrett's songwriting he eventually suggested that the two of them should team up on a musical venture, but Peter was otherwise engaged: 'Johnny wanted to form a band with me. I was happy with the way The Only Ones was going, but I liked playing with Johnny, I liked playing his music, it was a diversion and it was fun not being the frontman.'

* * *

Saturday night at the Speakeasy. The Living Dead haunt the shadows around the stage while a twenty-four-year-old Thunders prowls across to the microphone. He looks so anaemic it's impossible. A shark's tooth earring hangs from one lobe and he glares out at the audience with a permanent expression of near total apathy on his angular face. His eyes bore into the spotlights, hooded, like a set of ruthless wet stones. Beyond the stage, Sid Vicious desperately tries to catch his hero's attention ...

After several weeks of petitioning Thunders to allow him to join The Living Dead, Sid's wish would finally be granted, as Peter Perrett explained:

> Because Johnny was his hero, he really wanted to play with him. I think Sid used to get stoned with Johnny and he promised Sid that he could play this one gig. We did a soundcheck and he was meant to be learning the songs—one of which was 'Stepping Stone', which the Pistols sometimes used to do—but he was totally hopeless. Maybe they played it in a different key. I said to Sid, 'Just play E.' He didn't know where E was on the bass guitar. To try and teach him, I put his finger on the fret and moved it about, but it didn't seem to sink in. After the soundcheck, Johnny said, 'He's too useless, I'm not going to let him play.'

Johnny relented after Perrett pleaded for clemency on the hapless Pistol's behalf but, when it came to the gig, his bass was discreetly unplugged by a roadie. Less discreet was Sid's other half, Nancy Spungen, who bounced onstage semi *au-naturel* to present the band. Peter Perrett:

> For a laugh, Johnny told her it would be really good if she went

out topless and introduced the group. Johnny probably didn't even notice, but Sid was really hurt by it, which was ironic because half the world had probably already seen her like that. She went out topless, introduced it, then said all our names. For the first three or four songs, Sid got really into it. He was jumping up and down, posing. Then I think he must have listened out for what sort of noise he was making, 'cos all of a sudden he realised that nothing was coming out of his amp. He thought that somehow it was broken, I don't know if he realised it was sabotage. He started calling out for a roadie to fix it, but Johnny walked up to the mic and said, 'Thanks very much, Sid, now we've got Henri-Paul coming up to play.' Sid slinked off the stage. It was like he'd been substituted and thrown off.

A small contingent of The Living Dead flew over to Paris at the invitation of Gibus club manager Bernard Torrent to play three shows in the first week of March. The dates got a varied response, and Thunders was kicked out of two hotels for making too much noise.

Despite the rock'n'roll antics, by April 1978 the news broke in the music press that Johnny had a new manager in the form of legendary PR man B.P. Fallon, who had worked with Led Zeppelin, T. Rex, and The Boomtown Rats. Meanwhile, Dave Hill offered Johnny a deal with Real Records. Thanks to the innovative Hill, creative salvation loomed at last, and Thunders was reborn as a solo artist, signing to Real for a one-off album deal. While Johnny now had a supportive network around him, he decided to call the album *So Alone*. The title could be taken as ironic and yet a sense of loss was innate to Thunders' character, as Paul Gray observed: 'It was difficult to get near to J.T.. I always felt an air of sadness and loneliness about him. He seemed to be very on his own . . . preoccupied. Perhaps if I'd have indulged in the same drugs as him, it would have been a different matter.'

The contractual details of the forthcoming album and the pledge of a £10,000 advance had been mapped out by Xena Perrett, Peter's wife and the manager of The Only Ones, on Johnny's behalf. However, need eclipsed rationale when Thunders traded the advance for a handful of ready cash. Peter:

> Xena was furious, and I was really pissed off with him. He'd gone out and bought either a quarter ounce or a half ounce of coke or smack, but he hadn't even got a good deal. Whenever he gave you drugs, he was really pleased, because normally he was broke and on the scrounge, so when he was the person to give it to you, it made him feel good. He asked me and [Mike] Kellie to record the album with him, but we were only available for a week.

Thunders' first product on Real, the single 'Dead Or Alive' / 'Downtown' was released on May 26, 1978. Featuring Paul Gray and Steve Nicol, the 45 was a triumphant revved-up rocker. Thunders flirts with his own fatalistic reputation on 'Dead Or Alive', while the flipside is an offcut from the later days of the Dolls. In co-producer Steve Lillywhite, who worked with Thunders on all his output for Real, the guitarist had finally found a sympathetic ear.

Back in London, waiting for the *So Alone* sessions to start, Billy Rath and Walter Lure recruited Steve Nicol and Henri-Paul to record a single, 'Seven Day Weekend' / 'Too Much Junkie Business', under the name The Heroes, with the intention of having it released on Speedball Records, a subsidiary of Island. Unfortunately, Speedball collapsed, and the tapes languished in no man's land for some years until they were released by Skydog in 1983.

In the mix and match warm-up to Thunders' solo debut, the unplugged Sid Vicious once again took his chance with the guitarist, approaching him with the idea of forming a band around a 'Living Dead' format as a regular thing, with his beloved Nancy at the managerial helm. However, as Sid told *Record Mirror*'s Jon Tobler:

VICIOUS Nancy's managing me at the moment, but I don't know if Johnny will have enough faith in her.

TOBLER So when will we see the results of Nancy's business acumen as The Living Dead get on the road?

VICIOUS I can't answer that. I'd like it to be today ... tomorrow ... but there's legal hassles ... and Thunders general unreliability.

Johnny shrugged the idea off as unsustainable: 'We got it together a few times, but it wouldn't have worked out.' Much like The Living Dead, who had now been fondly laid to rest, as Johnny confided to *ZigZag*: 'It was a good period. I like playing with different musicians. Actually, I got in a rut playing with The Heartbreakers for so long.'

Sid was once again left on the sidelines when the guitarist assembled Johnny Thunders' Rebels. Featuring Sex Pistols Steve Jones and Paul Cook with Henri-Paul, the Rebels began working on a new set that included a cover of The Chantays' echoing instrumental 'Pipeline', Nancy Sinatra's classic 'These Boots Are Made For Walking', and a collection of Thunders songs in a slower, more interior mood than ever before. He told *ZigZag* magazine: 'I always had a lotta slow songs, but they didn't wanna do 'em in The Heartbreakers. I always wanted to do 'em but we never did "It's Not Enough" onstage. Jerry didn't like playing slow songs ... I got my chance to do it now.'

The old love and drugs, and love *of* drugs, Thunders/Heartbreakers numbers now found themselves rubbing shoulders with more introspective material. From a past that most people didn't know existed, Thunders retrieved 'You Can't Put Your Arms Around A Memory' and reanimated 'I Am Confronted' (from his Actress period) as 'So Alone'. Other numbers followed, including 'She's So Untouchable', but just to show the poison sacs were still as full as ever, Thunders also introduced 'London Boys' from the tail end of the 'Breakers. What sweet irony to rebuke Rotten while playing with the rhythm section of his old band. Had the Rebels maintained their momentum, they may have proved unsurpassable, but Thunders' erratic drug induced behaviour took its toll on any new projects. Dave Hill:

> They had such empathy, Steve [Jones] and John together. It would've been a great band, it really would, but John just screwed it up and Steve and Paul couldn't take anymore and they left. So that was another chance down the drain. It was really great, even when they were only rehearsing, but they did play together a few times down at the Speakeasy.

Nick Kent offered his opinion in the *NME*'s April 29 issue:

> Immediate plans call for the band to record 'Pipeline' at the very least, and they will probably work as a unit for the whole of Thunders' upcoming album. As far as Thunders is concerned, though, it is his last shot. If he blows this one, it really is all over. Brooklyn sass meets Shepherds Bush rock action—an intoxicating mixture, no doubt about it.

Although the Rebels parted company, Thunders carried most of the material from their set on to the album which, like the 'Dead Or Alive' sessions, were recorded at Island Studios in Hammersmith. Featuring a dream team of musicians, participants included Paul Cook and Steve Jones, Pretender Chrissie Hynde, Phil Lynott, Patti Palladin, John Irish Earle, Walter Lure, Billy Rath, Steve Marriot, Only Ones Mike Kellie, John Perry, and Peter Perrett, plus Henri-Paul, as well as Xena Perrett's sister, Koulla Kakoulli, and Paul Gray and Steve Nicol. Representing the best of the class of '78, *So Alone* provided an opportunity for Thunders to refine his pure rocker credentials, under the steadying influence of Steve Lillywhite.

As with The Living Dead, not all of the musicians were present all of the time, depending on touring commitments, and the ambience was often casual, as Paul Gray recalled:

It was very loose, a few tracks turned into a few more, then a few more. I don't ever remember getting paid for it. I did a lot of tracks with Mike Kellie and Peter Perrett. Mike was a fabulous drummer to play with. There were all sorts of motley characters hanging out in the studio, it was nuts really, Christ knows how we actually got any recording done. Steve Lillywhite was the one holding it all together.

We'd get to the studio early evening and wait for J.T. to roll up and depending on what state he was in we'd figure how long we had to get stuff recorded. Often he'd play us a new song, we'd run through it a couple of times and he'd pass out so we'd carry on laying down the backing track, only for him to listen back to it the next day and play something completely different, so we'd have to start from scratch again. He was in his own world much of the time and you'd have to kind of figure out what he wanted. But it was impossible to get pissed off with him; he was such a lovely fella. It was an absolute pleasure playing with him.

Although Johnny wasn't in particularly good shape, his haphazard charisma and the ability to surface from the abyss and deliver usually pulled him through, with a little help from his friends. One of the key musicians throughout the somewhat chaotic proceedings, depending on availability, was Peter Perrett, whose vocals are clearly audible on what for many is the album's finest track, 'You Can't Put Your Arms Around A Memory'. Johnny may have been a man of few words, but he poured his essence into the number, encapsulating the soul of dejection in one of the most emotive ballads ever written.

Unfortunately, the same cohesion was lacking when it came to recording the title track, as Peter explained. 'In the middle of the lead break, he fell over. He just fell backward into Kellie's drums. The lead guitar stops and there's a great big crash. I thought they should have put it on the record because it summed up how things could get with Johnny.' Neither 'So Alone' nor a joyous version of Marc Bolan's 'The Wizard', featuring a guest turn from B.P. Fallon, made it on to the album, although both would be revived for a CD released after Thunders' death.

In August '78, Real Records began promoting the album with a glowing press release that proclaimed:

> A peerless collection of musicians held together by the dominant personality of Johnny Thunders. In fact, *So Alone* is the first solo album in many a moon to really reflect the personality of its creator. A complete album, it has plenty of balls, quirky humour and, perhaps most impressively, plenty of tender moments on emotive ballads such as 'Memory' and 'Untouchable'. *So Alone* is a rare treat of an album.

But Johnny's luck was running true to form, and after finishing the album there came yet another Home Office order to leave the country, as Thunders informed *ZigZag*:

> They escorted me on the plane and made me go back. I had a manager who never took care of all my business—my passport extensions and stuff. It got worse and worse and they threw me out. New York's really a drag. It's nothing like it used to be. All the kids I used to hang out with are either dead or in jail.

On Johnny's return, The Heartbreakers made it up long enough to play a run of shows at Max's. The *NME*'s Tony Parsons accosted fellow 'Breakers Rath and Lure at CBGB's:

LURE We're just playing together until Johnny goes back to England for that one-off date at the Lyceum next month to promote his album, *So Alone.*

PARSONS So it's just money for sweets, eh? Who you using for a drummer now?

RATH Anyone we can, man . . .

PARSONS But John's coming back to NY after that show ain't he?

RATH Yeah. He wants The Heartbreakers to reform when he gets back . . . but we don't wanna.

LURE He's too unreliable.

The Heartbreakers with their usual penchant for paradox set off on a mini tour that took them as far afield as Los Angeles and San Francisco. Fresh from the coast, Thunders then joined rhythm & blues combo The Senders, who had been stood up by their guitarist midway through a tour. While Thunders cited The Senders as 'the only good band in New York', they never broke beyond their home turf.

As a native of the city, Thunders was a star in New York's rock'n'roll demi-monde, but it was a tough scene, as English exile Sid Vicious was discovering. The former Pistol had been expecting a hero's welcome when Nancy Spungen arranged a four-night stand for him at Max's with a band comprising of Jerry Nolan, Arthur Kane, Steve Dior, and Barry Jones, aka The Idols. While the musicians acquitted themselves with aplomb, Sid was sloppy and the shows received mixed reviews. The 'authentic' NY life that Nancy had promised Vicious prior to their relocation quickly began to take its toll on the couple. After they were beaten up buying drugs, Jerry Nolan introduced them to his methadone programme and tried to look out for the couple as best as he could.

In the build-up to the release of *So Alone*, Real Records issued 'Memory' / 'Hurtin'' (B-side co-written with Henri-Paul) in both a standard seven-inch and a limited-edition coloured vinyl twelve-inch disc. Unfortunately, demand outstripped supply, and Thunders missed the opportunity for a potential hit single, despite regular radio play. The autumn of 1978 was a pivotal juncture in the guitarist's life, with *So Alone* as his calling card for a solo relaunch. Unfortunately, by the time he stepped on to Air India flight 116 to London Heathrow, he probably already knew that the album wasn't going to get an American release via Sire Records, which would have been a crushing blow. The doors to the American mainstream were to remain closed to Johnny Thunders for the rest of his life.

On Monday, October 9, the guitarist arrived back in the UK to prepare for the much-touted 'Allstars' show at the Lyceum ballroom. Rehearsals were booked at the Roxy theatre in Harlesden and included the nucleus of Paul Gray, Mike Kellie, Peter Perrett, saxophonist John Irish Earle, and The Pretenders' guitarist, James Honeyman-Scott. However, Thunders' involvement was erratic, his low mood underscored by the sudden departure of Steve Jones and Paul Cook from the ensemble, prompting him to tell the press:

> Malcolm wouldn't let them do it, said I might be a bad influence on 'em. Nuthin' was said, but Malcolm didn't want them involved. Paul, I get on with alright; Steve . . . he's an egomaniac, I think, nothin' specific just his general behaviour. He thinks he's a guitar hero. A pity he learned all his riffs from me, which is quite evident on the Pistol's album. I'm not losin' any sleep over them not playing.

Meanwhile, a minder was employed to stop J.T. going on drug hunts before the big gig, but the guitarist managed to elude him by slipping out of a hotel window. In spite of the turmoil, early reviews of *So Alone* were extremely promising, as Giovanni Dadomo's critique for the October 14 edition of *Sounds* attests:

> The first surprising thing to a lot of people will, I'm sure, be the overall excellence of this here recording. Mr Thunders is of course, one of rock'n'roll's more erratic luminaries—one night's Jet Boy, the next night's snailman. It's a part of his magic to be sure—like the Stones, his mistakes make him more loveably human, that much more believably real than those flawless characters who make up the Bruce Forsyth contingent which dominate rock as it does all other entertainment forms.

ZigZag magazine was equally charmed: '*So Alone* is a true album and so enjoyable it almost hurts.' The November '78 edition of the magazine carried a typically wry interview:

THUNDERS I'm pretty happy with the album, well, 99 percent of it anyway.
ZIGZAG What's the one per cent?
THUNDERS I don't wanna get into that. Might offend some people.
ZIGZAG How long did the album take to do?
THUNDERS About three weeks. Much easier than before. I was in complete control and had nobody to argue with.

The Lyceum gig, however, brought new challenges. 'Say, Mama, will ya come out tonite?' October 12, the anniversary of the death of black leather's first champion, the great Gene Vincent; also the night of the Allstars concert.

Johnny sways out first, a bleached figure in bandanna and gypsy velvets, and kicks off the set with 'Pipeline'—which instantly blows out his amp. Thunders looks through glazed eyes, mutters 'aw … fuck', and shakes his head. The rest of the gig is beset by various electrical problems; angry punters get tired of sonic whistles doing damage to their eardrums and start to heckle. Some of the crowd are angry at Cook and Jones's absence, others at the quality of the sound and the absence of Heartbreakers' material. Johnny teases out the introduction to 'London Boys' with, 'It's great to be back in London … I shoulda stayed in Queens.'

Next up is 'Great Big Kiss', Patti Palladin trading verses with Thunders, the teenage ghosts of Mary, Marge, Betty, and Mary Ann Shangri-La aching to join in. The show's oddest moment comes courtesy of a theosophical heckler demanding to know Johnny's religion, which met with the following riposte from the guitarist: 'Naw … I ain't fuckin' Jewish. Do I look Jewish … it must be the nose.'

'These Boots Are Made For Walking' runs into The Senders' 'Living End', followed by 'Born To Lose' and 'Japanese Socks'. The encore, 'Be

Bop A Lula', was for the spirit of Vincent, not the audience, and Thunders walked offstage without a backward glance. Still, the show made for some great photo opportunities that belied the true nature of Thunders' now precarious life.

It wasn't going so good for some of his friends and associates, either. The Speakeasy, one of the clubs most pivotal to J.T.'s story in the UK, became subject to a series of raids that would eventually result in its closure, while Sid Vicious was front-page news.

On Friday, October 13, Thunders rounded off the *So Alone* press campaign giving interviews and eating grapes for his sore throat while contemplating the fate of Vicious, who had been arrested in New York for the murder of Nancy Spungen. Andy Courtney spoke to him for *Sounds*:

THUNDERS Sid? Uh ... it's horrible. Well, he beat out Keith Richards for the story of the year. [*Richards had been busted in Canada for a sizeable amount of narcotics.*] That's heavy. Poor Sid. Wow. The poor guy, man. I feel worse for him than her. It's the worst thing that could ever happen to him anyway.

SOUNDS What will you be doing when you get back to the States?

THUNDERS My dream come true. I've got someone to finance me to go to New Orleans and I'm gonna try and find a bunch of old black musicians and start a band with them ... rhythm and blues, rock'n'roll, New Orleans is full of the greatest music you ever heard in your life.

SOUNDS What if the proposed band concept falls through?

THUNDERS I'll find somebody else; a sax player ... three chick singers.

SOUNDS How is life for you at the moment ... how do you feel about things?

THUNDERS It's progressing.

SOUNDS It's looking up?

THUNDERS Huhhh ... couldn't get no worse.

NINA Why, out of all the people you could have signed up, did you choose Johnny Thunders?

DAVE Why did I pick on Johnny? Because he was basically a hero, in a sense. I saw The Heartbreakers play in very early '77 at Dingwalls, and they were just one of the most exciting things I've ever seen. When the opportunity came that John wanted to do some of the other side of his stuff, less rock'n'roll, more of his personal songs... I'd heard some of the demos of those songs and I was really impressed with them, I thought it was a viable project. I mean, you had the rock'n'roll side *and* these really great songs. I thought we could make a great record and show people that John had a lot more to offer than just this image of a loser, a rock'n'roll loser. I still think he has a lot more than that, but that's why I wanted to get involved in it, really. I liked the guy, I thought it was incredibly exciting, plus I thought it would make a good record, which would have a very wide appeal.

NINA What was he like to work with?

DAVE Disastrous, really, that's the one word I can say, it was just totally untogether. It could have been so much better, if John had been in a better state, but he wasn't. Any money we had, he would just go and spend on drugs. It was all done very slip-shod, we'd waste a lot of money in the studio, we'd waste a lot of time in the studio. Considering how it was done, I'm amazed how well it turned out, but like I said before, I think it could have been a perfect record but unfortunately it isn't.

NINA Oh, I still think it was a great record.

DAVE Yeah, it's a really good record but I don't think it's perfect and I think John would agree, but also I think John was the reason why it wasn't a perfect record.

NINA Why didn't 'The Wizard' or 'So Alone' appear on the album?

DAVE 'The Wizard' never got finished, that was the thing; they just did that and sort of fooled around and it was never finished enough to put on the B-side. The title track of the album, 'So Alone', was never finished, and it was supposed to be. It was a great song and it was to have been a real focal part of the album, and it was never finished because John was too untogether to finish it . . . it was one of those days. Some of the days he'd go into the studio and everything would be just great and they'd get stuff done really quickly, and the next time it would just take hours for him to tune up a guitar.

NINA How well did it sell? It seemed to do pretty well in the alternative charts.

DAVE It did really well. The single was almost a hit but for various sort of record company reasons it wasn't, they didn't press enough twelve-inches. I think it could've been a hit. It caught them by surprise, it sold very well and I was really pleased with it. I think people consider it John's best work, I certainly do, I wish it could've been how we really wanted it to be. There's a lot of different producers involved in that, different people trying to produce it, one minute Steve Jones, the next minute it would be Peter Perrett, the next it would be Johnny, the next would be B.P Fallon, so it was all chaotic.

NINA How long did B.P. Fallon manage Johnny? It seemed to be about a month, not very lengthy partnership at all.

DAVE No, I don't think he could handle it. John would let anybody work with him, he was a very soft guy in the sense of, if somebody came along and thought they were trying to help him John would encourage them, so at the end there'd be all these people involved in it, just to add to the chaos. We had a week's rehearsals booked for the Allstars gig, and I think John probably rehearsed one day over that week . . . I made sure he got there the week before; but he just didn't do any work, didn't turn up for rehearsals, or turned up stoned.

NINA Apparently some people were disappointed at the Allstars gig because not everyone who worked on the album showed up.

DAVE The only people that were supposed to turn up who didn't were Steve Jones and Paul Cook. They were advertised to play and they were going to play but Steve Jones was in America and couldn't get back and Paul didn't want to do it without Steve, so that's why it didn't happen which was a shame. But I mean that concert was untogether in the sense that it hadn't been rehearsed properly, we'd planned for it all to be rehearsed and to be a really good concert, but it wasn't as good as it could have been, yet again.

NINA Did Chrissie Hynde enjoy working with Johnny?

DAVE Oh yes, she had a laugh. At one stage The Pretenders were talking about recording one of John's songs ... 'Memory' or 'Untouchable', something like that. A lot of people really thought they were good songs and John has a lot of other good songs as well. I just wish he could get it together to do those songs properly. Maybe it will happen but I doubt it somehow, but she really respects his work a lot, really does.

NINA Where were Johnny and his family living at the time of *So Alone*?

DAVE He was living in Soho with his wife Julie and his two kids, about two blocks away from my office. He was living above a brothel or underneath a brothel [in D'Arblay Street, over a 'sauna'] and there'd always be problems going on. I'd come to work about ten o'clock in the morning and invariably John would be sitting outside my office, on the floor, waiting for me to get in, demanding money, or there'd be some problem or other to sort out.

CHAPTER SIX

TOO FAST TO LIVE

In February's first, cold week in New York, Sid Vicious died of an 'accidental overdose' while on bail for the fatal stabbing of Nancy Spungen. One of the first people to have seen Vicious after his release from prison on Riker's Island, where he had undergone heroin detoxification, was Jerry Nolan:

Me and Sid were very close. The day he got out of jail, he was looking great, very clean, he had brand new clothes on. Malcolm [McLaren] happened to have bought him new jeans, new boots and a new sweater, and I gave him my black and white motorcycle jacket. We got to talking, the conversation started getting a little serious . . . he brought up Nancy . . . he said, 'I'm kind of feeling low,' though he wasn't into no suicidal talking—he said, 'You know, Jerry, I'm going to fight this thing.'

When Sid got arrested, the police made some not very clear comments about something that gave them some information, by what he said, that led them to believe that he did stab her. I knew Sid, he was pretty egotistical, but he wasn't the sort of guy who'd put himself on edge, just for the attention. He looked me dead in the eye, 'cos he knew that Nancy had been in love with me at one time. I never had a relationship with her, we were friends. I respected her and liked her because she was one of the few people that understood where The Heartbreakers were coming from musically. Sid knew this and he said, 'Jerry, I didn't touch her, I didn't stab Nancy.' I believe that.

It was left to Thunders, at a later date, to record an effective goodbye in 'Sad Vacation'. Often introduced live as being to 'My man, Sid . . .', the lyrics say it all:

> *I'm sorry I didn't have more to say*
> *Maybe I could have changed your fate . . .*

Even that's doubtful, but it was a well-meant premise. Talking of destiny, Johnny still hadn't made it to New Orleans. With his career seemingly running in a circle and his heroin problem now out of hand, the music papers, never his most loyal supporters after the Dolls, began branding him a loser and printing snide asides about his longevity—or lack of it. The Heartbreakers reformed for a series of 'farewell' gigs, Jerry Nolan occasionally making it back to the drum seat. As journalist Richard Gabriel put it, 'They still choose to play the parts of decadent bad boy rockers living dangerously close to the edge. It's really a sad and shallow image, but after all this time they wouldn't know what to do without it. It remains an article of faith that the entire band could be found slumped over dead in some closet at any time.'

If only the band had been play-acting, it might have made it a little easier. They weren't oblivious to the situation, but they were trapped by addiction, as Jerry Nolan noted:

> We were very selfish. We wouldn't go onstage until somebody delivered our drugs, and the kids were waiting two hours for us. The gigs come first. The gigs come before drugs, and that's where we made our mistakes. We put our drugs before the kids that came to see us play. That's why we got hurt, why we got punished, because we fucked them over many times. Sure, face-to-face, we

signed autographs, listened to their stories; it'd be in one ear and out the other.

We just couldn't wait to get into the bathroom and shoot up again. That's why we suffered, and we got our punishment. The kids had saved their money to see what was the greatest band in the world, to them, and they didn't want to be teased. You know, me and Johnny, in a way we would say it was just like going to a drug dealer's house. All drug dealers got something in common—they're on a power trip. They know you're strung out and sick, they'll open the dope real slowly and take their time while you're sweating. They're teasing you because they know you need them. They're being a musician, being onstage, getting all the glory, and we're suffering. We got the money, we got everything—give us the fucking drugs—but if you say that to them, it's, *Listen man, you don't like my drugs, go somewhere else.* What the fuck are we going to do? You can't play a gig sick, all the time, although we did it.

But you know something funny? No matter how sick we were, when we counted off one-two-three-four and started playing, you couldn't tell we were sick. Our music was so powerful; we were just as good as if we had shot ten bags of dope. The power of the music covered our sickness. Between songs, Johnny would walk up to me:

'Oh God, Jerry, how many songs did we do?'

'Johnny, we only did three.'

'Oh my God, it sounded like eight.'

'Look John, play and you'll get through it, play ten songs, don't get sick.'

Somehow we'd do it.

On July 6, Beggars Banquet released *Live At Max's Kansas City* and a single, 'Get Off The Phone' / 'Wanna Be Loved'. The set, which was recorded in late '78, is a fine example of live Heartbreakers, the only downside being Nolan's absence from the ranks. The band, with Ty Styx on drums, come across as much a part of NY (musical) mythology as the Alamo is to Texas (violent) legend. Max's manager Peter Crowley, who co-produced the album, noted of The Heartbreakers, 'These guys are assholes. Nobody will put up with them but me. They're the greatest band in the world—but what a bunch of assholes.'

The album is a testament to the band's ill-tempered camaraderie, as Lure and Thunders constantly try and talk each other down at the microphone, taking turns to insult the audience or demand that all the club's tables are overturned before they continue. The stigma of having once been thought of as London's own elite is sliced to ribbons—these guys are as American as a gunned-down president or eggs over easy. *Live At Max's* isn't intended to convert or convince, it's simply The Heartbreakers on home ground, airing their limited vocabulary, as Walter Lure concurred: 'It captures us as we really are, a great live band that's eating, living and breathing Rock'n'roll.'

Sounds' Pete Makowski gave the live album a four-star review, enthusing:

As people these guys are odious creeps (too real for their own good) but plugged in they are MAGIC. This features all the greatest 'hits'—'Milk Me', 'Chinese Rocks', 'Get Off The Phone', or (Getoffadafuckinphone)—the projected single, 'London'—dedicated to Joe Bummer . . . 'All By Myself' (à la cocked-up intro) . . . and Berry Gordy's 'Do You Love Me' as encore . . . 'Beg for it,' snarls Thunders.

Nick Kent had his own opinion, writing for the *NME*, 'The whole enterprise stinks and there is absolutely no reason for even the most rabid Heartbreakers fan to purchase this piece of shit.'

On one of their odd sojourns out of NYC, The Heartbreakers played Detroit, where they were joined onstage at Bookie's club by The MC5's former guitarist, Wayne Kramer, who was one Johnny's musical heroes:

I had always wanted to meet Wayne Kramer. He's one of my teenage idols. He jammed with us on 'Do You Love Me', and we got to be friends after that.

Johnny, who had seen The MC5 play in NYC as a teenager, jumped at the chance to forge an alliance with Kramer. Although the high-voltage kings of the late 60s were to have a profound influence on the sound of American hard rock, The MC5 never got their just rewards during the course of their short career. After the demise of the band in the early 70s, Wayne filled the void with drugs and crime and dreamt of getting a new group together:

On paper, the plan was to finance the new band by dealing drugs. As an organised criminal, I was a complete and total failure. I'm not a killer. I'm a pretty benevolent cat! I'm sensitive, an artist, I care.

After a three-year incarceration in Lexington, Kentucky, where he played in a prison combo, Kramer returned home in 1978:

I put a band together and worked around Detroit and met Johnny. Johnny came to Detroit and wanted to break up The Heartbreakers yet again. He invited me to the gig, said he had some bookings and would I consider using my rhythm section and we could do something?

That 'something' was christened Gang War, with drummer John Morgan and bass player Ron Cooke (later replaced by Bobby Thomas). Now all Thunders had to do was play his part. Newly clean, Kramer offered the hand of sobriety to the guitarist, who relocated to Dexter, Michigan, with Julie and the kids. It was, according to Johnny's agent, a 'healthier' environment, but Thunders couldn't kick the habit, and, in the bitter midwinter, his wife took off with the children, Johnny Jr, Vito, and newborn baby Dino. Despite everything, Thunders loved his family, but a heroin user is always going to have priorities that erode domestic life; the heart at odds with desperate need. There is no guilt or innocence, only loss and destruction. Thunders pinned the blame on Detroit but, as a self-confessed 'Kramer groupie', he stuck it out anyway.

Ditching any love songs from his repertoire, Johnny pitched straight back into dirty rock'n'roll. Although Gang War's repertoire mainly consisted of Thunders numbers, Kramer contributed 'Hey Thanks' and 'I Still Hate' (co-written with Mick Farren), plus 'Ramblin' Rose' from his MC5 days. The majority, however, was J.T.'s own work. For someone who is not usually the fastest of songwriters, he turned in 'M.I.A.', 'Alone In A Crowd', 'King Of The Gypsies', the obnoxious 'Just Because I'm White', and 'There's A Little Bit Of Whore In Every Little Girl'. From the remnants of the Dolls, he also brought in the instrumental 'Courageous Cat', based on the theme tune of a kids' cartoon show, and 'Endless Party'. Various covers were also given the Gang War treatment as well, including the Stones' 'I'd Much Rather Be With The Boys', Jimmy Cliff's brilliant 'The Harder They Come', Fats Domino's 'I'm Gonna Be A Wheel Someday', and Chuck Berry's 'Around And Around'.

With Thunders keeping only occasional company with his old band as Gang War shaped up and started playing live, The Heartbreakers began solo ventures. Nolan, of course, still had The Idols, with Barry Jones and Steve Dior. Walter Lure was seen with NY boys The Blessed. Billy Rath gigged with Iggy Pop on the *Soldier* tour from late '79 to early '80 and did some studio work with Ronnie Spector until the reformation of The Heroes with Walter, his kid brother Ritchie, and Billy Rodgers (Nolan's some time replacement in The Heartbreakers). The Heroes were short-lived, arch exponents of choice rock'n'roll but, after Rath fell sick and was forced to leave, Lure seemingly lost heart in the project and eventually, much to Thunders' amusement, got a job on Wall Street, leaving any musical activities till after dark. The *NME* reported that:

After five years, two albums, and a lot of screwing around abetted by Thunders decline into pathetic drug passivity, Lure and Rath formed The Heroes around 1980. An ace pop'n'rock band somewhere between The Byrds and the Dolls, The Heroes (in their time one of the best bands New York had) met with almost no critical or public response, and petered out by the end of '81, having recorded one 45 ('Crazy Kids') with producer Jimmy Miller that remains unreleased.

Heralded as a charismatic vehicle for both Thunders and Kramer, Gang War headed for New York, where they hoped to make an album. The offer came as something of a balm for Johnny, who was still smarting over Sire Records' decision not to release *So Alone* in the States. Sylvain Sylvain was approached to produce, as he told the *New York Rocker*: 'I'd like to know what kinda budget he has, first, I mean, I can work pretty cheap, but I don't know if I can work on his budget…'

Events turned out as they so often had before, and the task of releasing any of the band's material wound up with the bootleggers. After a year, Thunders' teenage loyalties started to dim along with his enthusiasm for Gang War. They played the 'Boys Night Out' at the New York Ritz on the same bill as The Lenny Kaye Band and The Senders, and a gig at Heat that was covered by Andy Schwartz for the February edition of *New York Rocker*:

While critics carped, the crowd gave Gang War one of those obligatory 'It's 3am and we paid $6' ovations. The band returned for an encore of (get this) 'My Sharona' / 'Ayatollah' (Johnny ranting unintelligibly about Iran, hostages, and Marines), followed by Chuck Berry's 'Around and Around'. Suddenly, Iggy Pop leaned out of the audience to sing and dance along, and the place went wild in a way that Gang War alone could never have inspired.

Gang War travelled on through Canada, Boston, and New England, stopping off long enough to talk Billy Rath into joining them briefly, before returning to the concrete heartland of New York. Back on Johnny's home turf, things got messy, as he explained to *ZigZag*:

> We did two shows over two nights and Wayne Kramer didn't wanna play 'cos I wasn't paying him enough money. So it ended up with me and Peter Perrett . . . and he only knew a limited number of songs that we both could do: so David and Sylvain came up and help't me . . . the real friends . . . THE REAL boys came through.

Wayne Kramer had a different take on Gang War's last rumble:

> The reason why we stopped playing together was, Tommy Dean from Max's had booked Gang War. The way that Johnny and I worked the band was as partners. As Johnny's habit got more and more out of control, he phoned me and said, 'Look, Tommy Dean doesn't want it to be Gang War, he wants it be Johnny Thunders, but if you come and play, I'll give you $100.' Of course I said, 'I'm not going to come over there and play for $100; I'd stay at home and watch television for $100.' Every time we'd try to set something up, he'd fuck it up.

IN COLD BLOOD

PART TWO

BORN TOO LOOSE

CHAPTER SEVEN

SOMETHING'S GOT TO GIVE

J ohnny's tattoo says it all: 'Too Fast To Live—Too Young To Die'. An overdramatic, self-perpetuating mythology that fits neatly on his arm alongside a death's head and a large unlucky thirteen. Johnny Thunders is hostage to an ill-omened iconography with the whole city as blind audience. He has no apartment, no manager, no record deal, and no motivation, until the renowned photographer Marcia Resnick chooses the guitarist as her subject for a proposed movie on nightlife and personalities.

In part-payment for his involvement, Thunders has moved into Marcia's place. It should be a simple arrangement but it isn't long before the film's producer, Christopher Giercke, receives a phone call from Resnick insisting that he help her: 'Get this guy out of my flat ...'

Few evictions result in second chances, but the subsequent meeting between the German filmmaker and Johnny Thunders has proven far-reaching. The guitarist appeared wasted and worn at that first encounter, but Giercke nonetheless refused to capitulate to perceived wisdom:

You know, I may perhaps consider it, but I don't give too much importance on somebody's reputation. I make up my own mind. See what I see, you know? When a person is called a 'junkie' it is a projection: you are supposed to react in certain ways. Say junkies are supposed to steal, so don't leave your purse out. If you tell a person that; okay, you're a junky but I still expect you to be responsible in other areas, very often that approach will work. When I decided to work with Johnny, to manage him, I rented him an apartment below mine. I gave him keys to my apartment and to the safe too. I told him, 'Look, if you need money, there is money; but be reasonable and tell me if you need to take some when I'm out.' Trust. Try and build up the details of the day on that basis.

I hope, over the past two years, it has been of some help to Johnny. If only to make him see that you don't have to steal, to take anything. He's never really been what I think of as the stereotype junkie. The people who have branded him in that mould, the press, they don't have the human experience to distinguish between different characters of people, they fail to look for the strength or the problem. They do their job to make their weekly wages, their payment for the story. They have short cuts to fill up their stories, and they don't concern themselves about what they write may do to the subject of their articles.

Every inch the mysterious stranger, Giercke has a background in film, having worked alongside actor Jack Palance, author Nelson Algren, and Andy Warhol. He is a creator rather than a manager of another's expression.

I look for a certain intensity in anything. For example, I don't have one particular form or style of music that I enjoy above others. I try to feel something that is behind the music, something inside the people who play the instruments; this may be classical or rock and roll. Johnny was trying to start a new life and I thought I could help him, at least part of the way. I can try and help him be what he wants to be, but he must have his own self-definition. Nobody can give him that.

Christopher Giercke has the ability to weigh a situation and its effect with the eye of an artist fused with a darkly abstract, almost secretive mind worthy of an assassin—an important combination when dealing with Thunders.

Heroin is the physical extension of an Escher print: the pattern repeats and repeats until its final fade into an irrelevant darkness. Imbibers always find a reason to use. The Chinese called it 'the time of delight', although a 'season in hell' equally applies. Heroin the absolute. It is the ultimate partner and ultimate price. If its use ends in death—as is so often the case, either by overdose or related illness—then it seems a necessary sacrifice, one more terrible expense in the life of addiction.

Johnny Thunders comes onstage with his eyes closed and starts the opening run into 'Pipeline'. His guitar isn't plugged in and he hasn't noticed. The audience is ecstatic. He starts to sing one of The Heartbreakers' songs: his voice sounds like a half-insane alto sax trying to get a point across in a crowded bar. He stops and goes into a story about faggots. He's almost incoherent, and whatever Johnny is trying to say gets lost in the three-watt wasteland between his brain, mouth, and microphone. It doesn't matter: the audience is delighted. Heroin the anti-hero.

Johnny's skin is a sickly, transparent blue under the fluorescent strip lights above the amps. His hair is tangled around his face like day-old spaghetti, and he's obviously having trouble remembering why he's at the club at all. Thunders is the danger line (most) of his audience wouldn't cross for a mention in Howard Hughes's will, but he stands as the fantasy symbol for a whole army of Walter Mittys who have grown up on William Burroughs instead of Edgar Rice. They flock to cheer every time he seems significantly unsteady on his feet: each slurred word and missed chord. Fuck the music. Look at the condition of this guy.

'Hey, I'm not a professional drug-taker. I just wanna make 'em dance.'

J.T., the sordid backstreet adventurer in the grimy white shirt and Spanish hat; a stylish loser with a perverse winning streak who somehow beats the odds and gives a one finger salute to everyone who bets on his staying down. Thunders acts in way that certain portions of his audience admire; hangs out in mean areas to pick up heroin and answers to no one, save for his maker. Stories circulate at every concert about how he might not show tonight because the Mafia want him, he's overdosed on the Lower East Side, he killed someone on the way to the date, the cops are looking for him. He is lowlife pulp lore.

The music press on both sides of the Atlantic need to add to their sales and Johnny Thunders makes good copy. He also provides a way in which journalists with little or no experience can attack the drug problem in such a way that avoids the need to go into print against more popular public figures who might just take legal action.

With Thunders, however, it's a long open season. Roy Traikin, writing for *New York Rocker* in January 1981, delivers one of the more sensitive articles ever written about the guitarist:

He has at once profited, and been made victim to, the rock dream as nightmare. He teeters on a tight-rope between life and death, living out our vicarious dreams of self-destruction and rocking Thanatos. Isn't it about time we all grew up and accepted the responsibilities of our actions before it's too late? There's no reason Johnny Thunders has to prove he's an artist by dropping dead for our amusement: all he really ever had to do was give us the guitar break in 'Vietnamese Baby' or the aching refrain from 'You Can't Put Your Arms Around A Memory', the kamikaze attack of 'Bad Girl' or the poignant, often self-mocking rant of 'Born To Lose'. Hey, Johnny, You ain't no loser to me. At least not yet.

* * *

Though exorcism is not one of the Christopher Giercke's specialities, he has managed at least to harness some of Thunders' demons, enabling him to commence gigging again. However, their bargain only seems to work when Christopher is present, as a chaotic tour of Sweden is to prove.

When people go to see Johnny Thunders play, they expect the atmosphere around him to be volatile. His image and his lifestyle are such that he comes on as a catalyst for obsessive extremes. In England and

TOP Lead singer and lead guitarist: David Johansen and Johnny Thunders. *Photo by Leee Black Childers.* **ABOVE** Forget the limos: the Dolls on their way to Escape Studios. Sylvain, not pictured, was held up at customs. **RIGHT** The New York Dolls in Johnny's closet at the Noodle Factory. *Photo by Leee Black Childers.*

ABOVE 'Catch them while they're still alive': a Heartbreakers PR campaign devised by manager Leee Black Childers. The 'blood' is melted chocolate. *Photo by Roberta Bayley.* LEFT Johnny at Max's Kansas City, 1976. *Photo by Phyllis Stein.* BELOW Steve Jones of the Sex Pistols, Henri-Paul, and Johnny at the Speakeasy. *Photo by Youri Lenquette.*

ABOVE An outtake from the *L.A.M.F.* shoot, showing The Heartbreakers' street sensibility. *Photo by Roberta Bayley.* **LEFT** Johnny onstage in London. *Photo by Michael Beal.* **BELOW** The Heartbreakers at another fancy location in New York. *Photo by Leee Black Childers.*

RIGHT The Heartbreakers'
enforced return to New York
saw them play well-attended
gigs at the Village Gate. They
are pictured here backstage
at the venue. *Photo by Phyllis
Stein.* **BELOW** The Heartbreakers
in London, with cityscape
backdrop behind them. The
'Guitar Hero' amplifier was
also used by the Sex Pistols.
Photo by Ray Stevenson.

Johnny Thunders

LEFT The perfect image to launch Johnny's first solo outing. *Photo by Peter Gravelle.* *BELOW* Pirate Love. Left to right: Jerry Nolan, Mr T., Tony James, Steve New. *Photo by Michael Beal.*

LEFT Jerry Nolan, a fighter to the end. His drums were the perfect accompaniment to Thunders' guitar. They never played better than when they were together. *Photo by Marcia Resnick.*
BELOW Johnny onstage in pensive mood. *Photo by Mick Mercer.*
BOTTOM Attempted *L.A.M.F.* remix session at Greenhouse studios. Left to right: Tony James, Christopher Giercke, Johnny. *Photo by Marcia Resnick.*

RIGHT Johnny's eyes really were the colour of night. *Photo by Marcia Resnick.*
BELOW What a racket: an attempt by Christopher to represent Johnny in a healthier light. *Photo by Laurence Sudré.*

TOP Johnny and Susanne: true love.
Photo courtesy SMS Records. **ABOVE**
Jerry Nolan and Christopher Gierke,
Manchester. *Photo by Nina Antonia.*
LEFT A sharply turned-out enigma.
Photo by Marcia Resnick.

ABOVE Johnny in fine form, playing to
the dedicated at the Gibus in Paris,
where he briefly reigned supreme.
Photo by Wayne O'Farrell.

LEFT A Jungle Records publicity shot for *Crawfish*, featuring Thunders and Patti Palladin. *Photo by Alan Horne.*
BELOW Johnny and the Black Cats: Henri-Paul, Keith Yon, Tony St Helene. *Photo courtesy of SMS Records.*

TOP Johnny and Mike Monroe share a quiet moment during the *Que Sera, Sera* sessions. ABOVE Just like the Shangri-La-la-las: John Perry, Stiv Bators, Dave Tregunna, Patti Palladin, Mike Monroe. RIGHT Shady guys: Johnny and Stiv, the very fabric of rock'n'roll. *All photos by Jane Simon.*

ABOVE Johnny with his James Trussart
guitar in Paris. *Photo by Angie/
Mama Productions.*

TOP The irreplaceable Marc Zermati,
founder of Skydog Records, with
Johnny and Jimmy K. **ABOVE** Johnny
and Patti Palladin under the
auspices of *Copy Cats*. *Photo by
Leee Black Childers.* **RIGHT** J.T. as
'Johnny Valentine' with his onscreen
amour in *Mona et moi*.

ABOVE Swash and buckle: Thunders in action at the Paradiso, Amsterdam, 1985. *Photo by George C Bekker.*
RIGHT Strike a pose: Johnny in Japan, January 1988. *Photo by Kasahiro Kobayashi.*

St.
Peter House
1005 St. Peter • New Orleans, LA 70116 • 524-9232
Toll Free # 1-800-535-7815

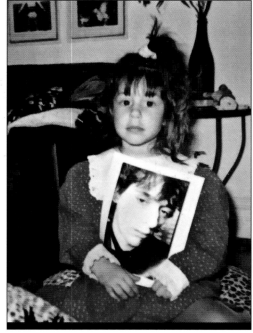

TOP Sweet dreams: Johnny and Nina pictured in a basement so cold you could see your breath. *Photo by Jon 'Boogie' Tiberi, colourisation by Gregg Skelley.* *ABOVE* Business card from St Peter House, New Orleans. *RIGHT* Little Jamie Genzale, who had only the briefest time in which to know her father. *Photo by Marcia Resnick.*

America, his reputation is known, accepted, even applauded in certain quarters by those who see him as their private martyr, but he *is* known. In Sweden, however, he provokes responses that range from the hysterical to the homicidal.

The band, comprised of Jerry Nolan, Luigi Scorcia, and Thunders, are initially delayed twenty-four hours by an extended recording session with The Rolling Stones' former producer, Jimmy Miller. Matters aren't helped in the studio by Thunders' tendency to go AWOL, as Miller would later explain:

Any excuse and he'd disappear. I mean if the headphones went and we'd have to change them, I'd ask Johnny to give us a minute and he'd be gone. It was very difficult. I feel like I never really caught him at his best time.

Booked to play Sweden's *Måndagsbörsen*, a prime-time TV music programme that went out live, the band's late arrival at the studio has upset the camera crew. Before Thunders & co even get to the point of a soundcheck, Nolan, who has been ill on the plane, has to have a doctor called out, who confirms he needs 'a good rest'. The technicians are again angry when the drummer doesn't show up with the rest of the band for a pre-recording run-though, although this could easily be facilitated in Nolan's absence. An agreement is eventually reached: Thunders will perform his four-number set, and it will be transmitted in the next edition of the programme.

Three hours late, Johnny staggers onstage looking the worst for wear and then some. The set starts with 'Green Onions'. By 'Just Another Girl', he is holding his guitar at arm's length and kicking it. Despite the carnage, Nolan, with eyes raised to the heavens, never misses a beat. Meanwhile, Thunders literally slides off the stage into the restaurant area, where he bums a cigarette from a mesmerised girl.

Despite having harangued his guest nation, Thunders invites the kids to come and have a drink with him, but it's too late, at least for a battalion of journalists, and by the next morning Johnny Thunders is front-page news:

'Burnt Out, Wasted: Mandagsborsen Main Attraction Stopped' (*Exspressen*)
'A Drugged Human Wreck: This Is Johnny Thunders, The Rock Singer That Mandagsborsen Didn't Dare Show' (*Afton Bladet*)

The producers end up shelving all the tapes of the performance, but the damage has been done. Overnight, Thunders has become the strung-out apotheosis of parental fears in a usually peaceable nation; more provocative than the Pistols confronting Bill Grundy and wilder than Jim Morrison at Dade County. In short, he is riveting. However, while it is impossible to defend him, there are mitigating circumstances; putting him on live television was always going to be a risk, but that's how it rolls with Johnny Thunders. Nonetheless, featuring the guitarist as a front-page shock story with photographic accompaniment in a city with a drug problem the size of Stockholm's is as hypocritical as it is over-sensational. Subsequently, his every move finds its way into Sweden's tabloids; his crying after the TV show, or his shivering in tour manager's Sukhedo Doobay's hotel room, as reported in another *Expressen* story:

I DON'T HAVE THE STRENGTH TO PLAY TONIGHT.
He looks wasted after a sleepless night. He looks terribly wasted as he walks over to his guitar. He sat shivering in a black dressing gown. No photos are allowed. When we are about to leave, he mentions tonight's show in Sundersvall; 'I can't do it. I can't do it,' says Johnny. 'Oh yes, you'll be fine soon enough,' says Doobay.

What follows is even more incredible. Aside from the much-circulated story that the Swedish Salvation Army want to kidnap Johnny in order to 'save his soul', circumstances turn the situation into one where it becomes a question of saving his jeopardised sanity for the duration of the dates. The next gig, with the macabre planning of a Joe Orton play, is in Sundsvall—for an anti-heroin event. Despite the police's efforts in stopping and searching the band, Johnny collapses onstage and pitches headlong into the audience. Again he makes front-page headlines, but the best is yet to come.

Having arrived at Bromma Airport en route to a gig, the band make life easy for any in-transit terrorists when they are surrounded by airport security, the local police, and a dog, after air-hostess Monika Emblard charges Thunders and Scorcia with raiding the plane's medical box for Valium. This too becomes front-page news.

As the newly appointed scourge of Sweden, Johnny finds himself revered by an audience of kids in search of a rebel icon and loathed by their parents in equal measure. Sweden's liberal front hold back for Johnny's return journey to their country, but by then the guitarist has come up with an explanation for all the furore, as he tells one enthusiastic crowd: 'You kids are okay . . . it's hard to believe your parents are so retarded. Is it the water they drink or somethin?'

By now, reports on Thunders' Swedish capers have begun to reach England, coinciding with the news that he is due to arrive in London any day. At a time when visiting rock'n'roll 'stars' have reached a limited impasse concerning credibility and stance, the return of the original bad boy generates, at least among his followers, a level of excitement and anticipation worthy of Jesse James.

A prevalent question, unasked and unspoken, in connection with Johnny Thunders, is: *Do you listen to him or do you live him?*

With a lifestyle like a warning television documentary, his fans have always tended to revel in every slip, every public outburst of narcissistic indulgence. Each time Thunders rolls his tongue, gathers saliva, and spits full into the face of the established order, his standing grows among the make-believe outlaws, the suburban outcasts, and the after-school desperadoes. But it isn't just the postulants who gather for Thunders; in his wake come the real shadows, the genuine dregs and seedy creeps who were always there, just on the perimeter—the night players, always waiting.

Despite the risks that Johnny Thunders takes in every city he plays, his dangerous journey is remarkably free of legal entanglements. Aside from one or two minor busts, he always remains under the radar.

With Jerry Nolan and Luigi Scorcia in tow, Thunders returns to England for a proposed two-month tour, its emphasis on the capital, with the occasional out-of-town gig. After a handful of dates the jaunty Scorcia is replaced by Steve New (Rich Kids, Vicious White Kids) and the line-up finalised by former Generation X bassist Tony James. As for their frontman, Thunders is holding himself together against the rumours and the reputation. Onstage he scowls and smiles, whines and curses, and above all demonstrates why he's one of the best and most original guitarists alive. He sways around the footlights, legs like gelatine scissors shrouded in leather, eyes glowing with poison while he swears like an expert in colloquial abuse at audience and musicians alike.

THUNDERS (*to soundman*) Hey . . . yo! Yo . . . can you give me some more reverberation on my damaged voice? Yeah . . . yeah . . . that sounds more like me.

AUDIENCE MEMBER Just play some fucking music!

THUNDERS Hey, scumbag, shove it up your mother's left nut.

—Hope & Anchor, April 20

THUNDERS (*unhappy with the sound*) Hey. What is this shit?

AUDIENCE MEMBER Oh . . . fuck off, Johnny.

THUNDERS (*reflectively*) Naw . . . as a matter of fact, I don't fuck at all.

—Kensington, April 30

THUNDERS (*scornfully*) You kids have some sense of humour, huh? What you kids do? Watch English TV? You laugh when the microphone's fallin' . . . awright . . . listen; a funny thing happened to me on the way to the show tonight. I took a taxicab—harharhar. Funny, huh?

AUDIENCE MEMBER Get on with it.

THUNDERS Hey. You don't like it? You paid your money—go home.

AUDIENCE MEMBER We paid our money...

THUNDERS Big deal. Go peek at your mother's pussy. Fuck you.

—*Rock Garden, May 1*

Even Jerry Nolan is treated to a brief sample of the guitarist's wit during the band introductions:

THUNDERS He's been with me just about as long as my mother...
naww...Jerry's my father, actually.

* * *

April 22. Clad in uncharacteristic denim, Thunders lurches through the still-drawn Venue curtains and tears into a set of Heartbreakers numbers cut with the mandatory Dolls infusion and including some of his more recent writings.

An incautious young woman stirs up her own trouble when she makes a pathetic grab for Johnny's zipper. She's rewarded by being dragged onstage and expected to perform an impromptu strip, bump-and-grind routine. A sudden burst of public modesty, probably brought on by the barrage of crude comments screamed from the audience, causes the girl to hide in an attack on the smirking guitarist. Johnny nimbly avoids her fist and pushes her toward a couple of bouncers, who drag her backstage by the hair.

Sylvain Sylvain, also on tour with his band The Roman Sandals, climbs onstage to Thunders' obvious pleasure, and together they go into 'Chinese Rocks', which Sylvain changes to '*he's living on Chinese rocks*'.

Sylvain would later tell the *NME* that there is 'a certain charisma about a guy that everybody thinks is about to drop dead. It's like when Daffy Duck blows up onstage and then you see him in heaven as an angel saying, Yeah, folks, it's a great show: but you can only do it once.'

Thunders and band play their last UK date on June 3 before flying to

Sweden minus Steve New, who is fired on the eve of their departure. It is hoped—God and Johnny willing—to be the beginning of a major tour, opening at the Facade in Gothenburg.

The tone is set for the evening when Thunders promptly collapses, seconds into the set. Thankfully, he manages to pull himself off the floor with the aid of a microphone stand that proves steadier than he is. Brushing his fingers across the guitar strings, Johnny starts the show again with customary charm:

> Hey. Turn th' fuckin' monitors up. Hey … hey! Is there a bartender down there? Huh? Listen, bring me a bottle of fuckin' brandy if you wanna hear more than three fuckin' songs … yeah, an' a pitcher of ginger ale …

The audience is getting more than restless. Jerry Nolan starts up the beat and Tony James pushes a vicious bass line into the middle of it, both hoping that Johnny will decide to start playing the guitar and/or sing. Instead, he walks slowly to the front of the stage and orders the house lights up. He notices the girls clustered around the toes of his boots and goes into a hardly audible insult tirade against them:

> Have ya ever seen such a motley crew? They don't know if it's the sixth month of their period … maybe … maybe … their boyfriend's left 'em an' they stuck somethin' frozen up their pussies 'cos they were so horny … an' it got stuck, huh? Awwright, darlings?

The concert collapses in a near riot, and Nolan and James drag Thunders back to the hotel, which they now have no money to pay for. Tony James:

> Three of us went, me, Jerry, Thunders. We just managed to make the plane, but that was in typical Thunders style. We're both on the plane waiting, and he ain't there. In the distance we can see

Thunders zigzagging toward us, totally not rushed at all ... couldn't give a shit. On the way over we fell out, 'cos I didn't bring my other guitar. Johnny didn't have a guitar—he'd flogged it—and I didn't realise he'd wanted me to bring it, so Thunders and me weren't talking.

When we got to the gig, I don't know, someone gave him something, and he wasn't very lucid; in fact, he was totally out of his brain. It was such a big deal, because the first gig was the one they were saying, 'If you get through this, we'll let you play the rest of the country.' All the Swedish papers were there to see if he'd fuck up again. He just walked onstage and fell straight off. Then he started insulting the Swedish girls. Someone managed to hold a guitar round his neck, and he started playing—I don't know what he was playing—he started this number, then he ran off. Me and Nolan started a twenty-minute version of 'Waiting For My Man', but the man never came, so we abandoned it. The audience were rioting and wanting their money back.

We didn't have any money to pay the hotel, and they threw us out, but Johnny would not get out of bed. Then, the next day, he wouldn't get in the van. I mean; he refused because we were both 'scumbags'. For some reason, it was *our* fault. We were, like, driving to the airport, and he's walking behind the van because he wouldn't sit in it. Eventually, we had to get the boat back. We were gonna do some more stuff, but then he got busted at the airport, and all that shit, and he flew back to New York.

Johnny finds it surprising that the tour has whipped such a semi-hysterical reaction in Sweden, telling journalist Kris Needs in April 1983:

I was there for ten days and they put me on the front page of the daily paper eight days in a row. I did nothing. I actually did nothing. I never warranted the attention they gave me. It was ridiculous.

I mean, what started it off was I played a television show and I played live—and I was too fucked-up so they wouldn't show it. That started the ball rolling with the press, and then they started following me to gigs . . .

* * *

Jerry Nolan has decided to remain in Sweden for a time, forming his own band, The Teneriffa Cowboys. They will release a single, 'Take A Chance' / 'Pretty Baby', on the Tandan record label in 1983, tour for most of the year, and then record another one, 'Havana Moon' / 'Countdown Love'.

Johnny probably wishes he'd followed Nolan's example in terms of location. Twin stories exist as to what prompts the guitarist's stay in prison in London, both erratic and both with typical discrepancies. All that seems certain is that Thunders was stopped at Heathrow and detained at Pentonville prison before being taken to court and fined fifty pounds for possession. Rescheduling his flight home, the guitarist went into Croydon's Wickham Studios and laid down some backing tracks, including 'Ten Commandments Of Love', 'Sad Vacation', and 'Give Me More', with Mike Hellier on drums and Malcolm Hart on bass.

Once home in New York, Thunders spends some time trying to secure a deal for the Jimmy Miller-produced tracks. In early July, he teams up with Walter Lure for a gig at the Peppermint Lounge; later that month, he celebrates his birthday by playing the Irving Plaza under the auspices of Christopher Giercke.

From this point onward, Christopher becomes a more apparent force in the guitarist's life. While the film project that initially brought Johnny and Christopher together fails to flourish, Lech Kowalski, who scored an underground hit with the documentary *D.O.A.*—a grubby expose of the Sex Pistols' last days—has begun making overtures to Thunders to star in his latest movie, *Gringo*.

The pitch is simple: an epic portrayal of Manhattan's junk kingdom, with Johnny as the guide to the underworld. The guitarist describes it thus:

It's a film about copping drugs on the Lower East Side of Manhattan and all the evil parts about it. It's just what the lifestyle's like: dangerous and dirty.

From the offset, *Gringo* is an uneasy alliance, plagued by disputes. Sequences involving Thunders in an assortment of scenarios—including onstage at the Mudd club and serenading a gathering of transsexuals with a delightful version of 'I'd Much Rather Be With The Boys'—are cut from the film. Meanwhile, Kowalski casts a new lead, the notorious Spacely, as Gringo, while annexing the footage of Thunders for another movie entitled *Stations Of The Cross*. (Although Roir Records will end up releasing a soundtrack in conjunction with Kowalski, the film footage itself won't see the light of day until Thunders' demise, when the director grafts the sequences onto yet another documentary about the guitarist, *Born To Lose*.)

Neither Johnny nor Giercke raises any objections when Kowalski removes the guitarist from *Gringo*, since it was Thunders' addiction that led him to the project in the first place. If Spacely has nothing to lose, Thunders has everything to lose—including the last vestiges of hope.

Lech Kowalski isn't the only man wielding a camera, however, and a more humane portrayal of Thunders is filmed in New York for a Swedish current-affairs programme called *Studio S*. The resulting footage is world-weary yet compelling. Thunders chain-smokes throughout, issuing stock answers to obvious questions. Clearly, he does not want to go below the surface, submitting to the interview as one might a police inquiry.

THUNDERS I hope this isn't going to be another boring interview about drugs.

INTERVIEWER Don't you like talking about them?

THUNDERS I'm not a professional drug taker—I don't think.

INTERVIEWER Do you remember when you started with drugs?

THUNDERS Yeah.

INTERVIEWER Tell me about it. How did you start?

THUNDERS I started smoking pot, the way the other kids do . . . got into heavier things, and I guess it's a hard thing to get out of once you've started.

INTERVIEWER Do you remember when you started shooting?

THUNDERS No.

INTERVIEWER Do you remember why you started?

THUNDERS Just to have a good time. There was no . . . nothing to escape from or nothing like that: no problems . . . like, a lot of kids start because they're bored or lonely, you know. It makes them feel like they're alive, I guess. I would *never* turn anyone on to drugs. It's a hard thing to handle, and once you get into it, it's *really* hard to get out of . . .

Drawing the interview to a poignant close, Johnny reminds the public that 'I have a heart, you know. I'm still a human being.'

Johnny's partner in crime, Jerry Nolan, is interviewed for the same programme and is both communicative and evasive, showing diplomacy even when pressed by the most banal questioning, and leading off with a conflicting account of their early heroin days:

NOLAN That whole drug era in the late 60s, for some reason, even though most kids my age were getting into drugs then, I never got into it, really. Not even smoking pot, not drinking . . . but then, when it was all over, even after the Dolls were over, I started experimenting with drugs and, unfortunately, with the wrong kind of drugs: hard— real hardcore, addicting drugs like heroin . . . and . . . well . . . me and Johnny sort of got into that at first for a while.

INTERVIEWER At the same time, or had he [Johnny] been on it a longer time?

NOLAN No. Not really . . . it's like I say, very late in life: but heroin is *such* an addictive drug it was a little too late before we found out enough information about it, before we realised what we were getting into. It was much too late.

NINA Did you know Johnny prior to the 1982 tour?

TONY Maybe around The Heartbreakers period. I know I met Walter and Jerry, so I'd probably spoken to him. Thunders was always one of my heroes so it was great meeting him and brilliant to actually play with him: I mean, I could play 'Jet Boy' legit with the man that wrote it.

NINA I believe you put Johnny up during the tour?

TONY He only stayed here for two weeks but it felt like three years. Things kind of fall apart all around Johnny, it's like having E.T. in your house. I'd be lying in bed and I'd hear him running around disconnecting everything. He always had this big fear of leaving things plugged in. I might be pissed off and I'd come home in the morning to find he'd unplugged everything in sight—pulled all the wires out of everywhere, records all over the place ... God. It was like the chaos in that scene from *E.T.*, when he's pissed. It's just Extra-terrestrial Thunders.

NINA I heard that you were going to maybe produce Johnny.

TONY (*laughing*) Johnny? Produce him? Fuckin' hell. I wouldn't walk him across the road, let alone produce him. He'd probably want to stay here again. Never, never again. Johnny's got quite a clear idea of his own ... and I don't think I could add anything because I have a very similar approach.

NINA What's he like to work with?

TONY A nightmare ... but it's good fun. I found it more fun playing with him than I did playing with Generation X because he plays the sort of music that I *really* like. It has this great unpredictability about it—a great attitude—just going out and playing. Never rehearsed once. They taught me the numbers in about half an hour before we did the Venue. Just taught me them here on an acoustic guitar, then he handed me a list of about thirty songs that I was supposed to have learnt, and we went and played the Venue. He was carried unconscious into the soundcheck, but he went out and played. Absolutely no bullshit involved. I think he has a heart full of soul—I mean, there are *no* groups that have got that soul . . . that real rock'n'rollness in them. They play from the head, from what they read in books. I think Thunders is a living legend. The only thing I don't like is, obviously, him being so fucked-up on heroin. I don't think it's cool to be a junkie, it's fuckin' stupid to be a junkie. That was the only problem I had—being the only non-junkie in the band. I mean, people think that I do junk but I don't. I'm totally against all that shit. It's such a waste of talent and a waste of human life.

CHAPTER EIGHT

THE ART OF COSA NOSTRA

With the familiar confusion that always surrounds Johnny Thunders, 1982 grinds to a vinyl finale that spills over into the New Year. With the participation of Parisian label New Rose and, to a lesser extent, Jungle Records in London, Thunders aficionados suddenly find themselves with a flood of imports to choose from, along with a surge of bootlegs of Swedish origin.

New Rose started the disc-spinning by releasing an unauthorised patchwork of live and studio cuts under the title *In Cold Blood*, which includes the tracks produced by Jimmy Miller. But as the guitarist informs *17* magazine, he is none too happy about it.

It was a double album; but it was only meant to be an EP. It was only demos that were put out, they weren't finished works and I'm not really pleased with it.

In Cold Blood is later withdrawn and subsequently put back on the market minus the live album, in a new sleeve. PVC Records then releases a remixed version of the same tracks with the inclusion of 'Endless Party', under the title *Diary Of A Lover*. Meanwhile, Jungle Records begin their involvement by issuing a live single, captured in 1977, of 'Chinese Rocks' / 'All By Myself', followed up with *D. T.K.—Live At The Speakeasy*. The release of the single and album create new problems from old ties both contractual and personal in nature.

Before he and his manager reach an understanding with Jungle, Johnny is adamant about the album's position: '*D. T.K.* is illegal. I'm involved in a lawsuit with them.'

The second week in April sees Thunders and Christopher Giercke in London to negotiate with Jungle, who have now released a three-track EP entitled *Vintage '77*. Returning to Soho, Johnny, Christopher, and Tony James take their time in the Ship pub on Wardour Street before going to see the inimitable Dr John play a set at the nearby Marquee . . .

* * *

Johnny is looking quite healthy, considering the deluge of stories that he'd died four or five times that week. He smirks and rests his glass on the overcrowded table:

> In Paris, I died three times. It was in the papers. Jerry Nolan phoned up from Sweden and friends phoned up from London. Your guess is as good as mine who starts the rumours. Probably someone at New Rose or Jungle or someone records, I guess.

Life is no less complicated when Johnny attempts to get into the Marquee club for free. 'I'm Johnny Thunders,' he tells the girl at the front desk, but she doesn't believe him and goes off to find someone who can verify his claims.

Alan Hauser, the man at Jungle Records who instigated the company's decision to reissue as much of the Johnny Thunders / Heartbreakers catalogue as possible, sits in his office, surrounded by pyramids of Thunders promo badges and related material. Alan knows exactly who Johnny Thunders is and why his music matters.

> Leee Black Childers mentioned that he had these tapes, and he didn't think anyone would be interested in them except maybe in France. He went off, didn't get a deal, came back, and I said that

we'd be interested. At that time, Johnny hadn't been heard of for a couple of years since he'd vanished from the scene. He wasn't a name on everyone's lips. I'd had his singles from the early days of punk, loved them, and was sure lots of other people did, so . . .

We knew we had a live album, and we got the *L.A.M.F.* tapes back from where Leee had left them in France. Just as we were ready to release them, I saw in the papers that Johnny was playing Sweden, and that was the first that had been heard of him for ages. He'd got all this press there, so, consequently, *D.T.K.* sold four or five thousand copies on export to Sweden, and it got into the national charts at number 33, I think.

But what did Thunders think about old tapes being pressed into albums and sold when, at the time, he and his manager knew nothing about it?

Well, Leee hadn't been in touch with Johnny, and Johnny hadn't been in touch with ANYBODY—no one knew where he was when we did the original deal. Leee was in the right: he was the management company and when Track Records liquidated, the rights to all the tapes reverted back to him. Johnny didn't realise this . . . and also, Leee had lost a lot of money in his management of The Heartbreakers, and I think he was justified in getting some of it back.

Eventually, both parties came to me to try and sort it out. Leee spent three months in London just looking through papers. At this time, Christopher was in Katmandu or wherever. We sorted it out.

* * *

Johnny sits curled in a corner of Tony James's sofa, eyes narrowed against the smoke that curls from his cigarette as he mumbles his set of stock answers to the person attempting an interview from Flexi-Pop. *Performance* is playing on video, and Thunders finds it a lot more interesting than answering the same questions over and over. At last, the man from the paper realises he's lost to Fox and Jagger, hands down, and leaves.

Performance over, Johnny puts on a fresh video, *Cannibal Holocaust*, while Christopher makes a never-ending series of phone calls, alternating between arranging European dates and finalising the details of their move to Paris. Thunders can't stand the bright sunlight illuminating the room and starts dragging most of Tony's furniture over to the window to build an unsteady barricade against the day.

Flashing a crazy Gomez Addams-style smile, Christopher puts his palm over the telephone mouthpiece and nods toward the video screen, where a cannibal is dining on human flesh. 'Finger lickin' good,' he quips, before returning to a serious conversation across the wires.

Johnny ejects the cannibals and starts watching *Christiane F.*

Slowly, Friday turns into evening, and the room is suddenly very quiet. Johnny is gently playing a match along some tin foil, smiling while Christiane gets her first taste of heroin and throws up.

* * *

For a generation or two of cinematic hoodlums, the term 'Cosa Nostra' has evoked images of Al Pacino or George Raft. Well aware of the mythology associated with the name and his Italian American heritage, Thunders has christened his latest outfit Cosa Nostra. With Billy Rath on bass, Jerry Nolan on drums, and Henri-Paul on guitar, the band played a three-night stint at the Gibus Club in Paris. Any further activity was put on hold when Johnny succumbed to a severe bout of pneumonia, which gave rise to a particularly unpleasant series of rumours, including death, overdose, and paralysis.

This time, Thunders isn't available to comment, but in his absence ROIR Records in New York has released an album-length tape, *Too Much Junkie Business*, which, despite his later disowning of it, Thunders has agreed on, to the extent of providing a narration between songs. Christopher, for no obvious reason, would describe the cassette as being 'a positive point against drugs'.

Even in Sweden, where Thunders is seen as the very incarnation of penny-dreadful villainy, his commercial potential has begun to outweigh other considerations. The decent-quality bootleg *Cosa Nostra Never Sleeps* reveals Thunders breaking the Swedish hex in Sodertalje Park before a massive audience of adoring kids. After one of the shows, Johnny meets an attractive hairdresser named Susanne who is to join him in France and become an almost constant companion.

Following a well-received and much bootlegged tour around Europe, Thunders returns to Paris, where he begins working on a movie with the award-winning director Patrick Grandperret. The film, originally called *Go Back To Go* (and for a short while *Personality Crisis*), is to feature the guitarist playing a character with a past not a million miles away from his own. Thunders, in the precision-made shoes of Johnny Valentine, describes the plot as being about 'a guy on heroin who knows he's got to get his life back together. He's walkin' out onstage and collapsing. I guess it's about different relationships I have with different people, like my manager, who plays the lawyer in the movie.'

Ultimately, Grandperret will settle on the title *Mona et moi*, and, although filming has commenced, plot changes and the eternal quest for funding slow the project. However, when Jungle Records put out their first major video release, *Johnny Thunders And The Heartbreakers: Dead Or Alive*, it includes early outtakes from the film as a teaser.

* * *

In London, the ground is already an icy mirror and the sky a dull grey, but Giercke's manoeuvres have taken the band away from the dismal surrounds of their last visit. Billed as Johnny Thunders' Cosa Nostra, their one and only concert at the Lyceum is a sell-out, surprising everyone except Thunders. His newfound confidence is largely due to his trust in Christopher, in whom he has found not only a manager but also a friend and guide—one on whom he relies perhaps a little too much. Thunders' increasing popularity in Europe, especially France and Sweden, coupled with his self-proclaimed efforts to cut down on his chemical intake, appear to have given him a drive that the years have slowly chipped away.

I ask Johnny if he regrets the past. He grins, pausing slowly as he lights the latest in a seemingly endless line of cigarettes. 'Well, I'm glad it's over. See, now is a new start. I finally ended my career as a drug addict . . .' He smiles again, contemplating keeping his last line reserved for future press interviews.

It's a freezing cold afternoon when Cosa Nostra arrive for the soundcheck. Burly roadies strain under electrical equipment while poker-faced bouncers check that the locks are still secured on the outer doors of the venue's baroque entrance. The Lyceum's crew belong to the ranks of the terminally pissed-off. Under these circumstances, it's hard to imagine that the once fine venue was managed by Bram Stoker and used to possess a florid dignity.

After a brief inspection of the dressing rooms, the band returns to the dimly lit ballroom. Johnny positions himself next to Susanne on a roll of carpet and insists that the bar staff ignore licensing hours by serving him a drink. Jerry Nolan, meanwhile, turns jetlag into an art form. Having just moved from Sweden back to New York, he's barely had time to catch up with himself before flying to London. Part of his drum kit has been lost in transit; after telling the road crew to 'wake me up when you find it,' he pulls the brim of his hat down over his eyes and goes to sleep. Billy Rath fluctuates between his normal surly impatience, pacing around and checking his reflection from various angles, while carrying on an affable conversation about some recent production work he's been doing in New England.

Two hours later, Nolan's cymbals have been found, and the band— including Michael Thimren, who has taken over from Henri-Paul— soundcheck for the evening's show. Johnny leads into the *Pink Panther* theme, which turns into 'Jet Boy' into 'Subway Train'. While Thunders is explaining to the soundman, as always, that he needs reverb—'turn up th' fuckin' reverb'—Jayne County (tonight's support act) slips quietly into the hall carrying an armful of shopping bags, hat pulled down as low as Harry Lime on a wet night, collar turned up to add to either the incognito effect or the eccentric normality. By the evening, Jayne has metamorphosed and turns in an effective performance to a hungry crowd. Wearing a silver lurex ensemble, she sits on her knees under the spotlight, washing in the metaphorical blood of rock'n'roll.

Upstairs, the dressing room is full of smoke and tight nerves. A large table has been filled with fruit and drinks but no one really bothers with it. Jerry Nolan is sprawled out on a sofa, making it clear he is not in a mood for conversation by letting his silence build an effective wall around him. Johnny is putting the final touches to his appearance before a full-length mirror. He catches the reflection of Patti Palladin as she slips into the room, late. Johnny half turns toward her to ask where she's been. Patti shrugs. 'My clutch went.' Thunders returns to his minute inspection with a faint grin around his lips: 'Yeah? Sounds like one of them female things.'

One of Peter Perrett's children is running around with a banana. Finally satisfied, Johnny surrenders the mirror to Patti and strolls across to talk with Perrett senior. Billy Rath sprays his hair and pats it into place. Anita Pallenberg, clad in traditional spy uniform of trench coat and black glasses, goes over and greets him warmly.

Downstairs in the ballroom, the capacity crowd start stamping their feet when the house lights abruptly dim. Thunders picks up his guitar and leads Cosa Nostra along the backstage walkway, which is now filled with well-wishers, Tony James, Stiv Bators, Siouxsie Sioux, and Dave and Laurie Vanian among them.

A syringe lands at Billy Rath's feet as he walks onstage. He checks the needle has been removed and throws it back. Flowers would have been nicer. (Half an hour before, a couple of dealers, one dressed in black PVC with face powder thicker than a Japanese hooker, argued with Christopher about his policy of keeping them away from the band. When attempts at a cold politeness fail, he gestured at the nearby bouncers, who roughly escorted the dealers from the area.)

The set lasts over two hours, and Thunders paces himself like an expert. Obviously happy with the night's strength, he sings, jokes, and curses with a calm assurance that works better than his normal indifference. The absence of a guitarist of the calibre of Walter Lure is noticed when Johnny goes offstage at one point to talk with Susanne and Christopher in the wings. Michael Thimren, the second guitarist recruited from Jerry's Swedish band, cannot hope to cover for him.

Moments later, Thunders returns for a solo acoustic interlude that includes 'Memory'. Even he looks mildly surprised as the audience starts singing with him. Not one for sentimentality, Johnny lets the guitar hang around his neck while he tries to buy a joint: 'Hey. Nobody got a joint tonight? I don't need batteries for my fuckin' brain, somebody gotta have a joint: I got a quid if you got a joint.' Thunders ends negotiations by burping loudly into the microphone: 'Awright ... awright. I'd like to bring up my friend Peter Perrett ...'

The rest of the introduction to the former leader of The Only Ones is lost in a burst of applause. 'I'd like to bring up little Patti Muppet from *Snatch* ... you know that old whore ... I'd also like to bring back Jerry Nolan and Billy Rath.' The audience pounds its collective feet loud enough to be heard above the trademark roar of Thunders' guitar. Johnny interrupts the final chords of 'Pipeline' with a nonchalant wave. He's very obviously aware that if he ever lost London, he's just won it back.

* * *

Returning to France, Thunders sets out on a short tour that mainly concentrates on the south. When the dates are done, he starts working on *Hurt Me*, an acoustic album scheduled for a November release on New Rose.

The Lyceum concert brought him some of the most favourable reviews he'd received in England for a long while, marking a slight thaw in journalistic attitude. Like anything given grudgingly, it is now to be taken back. Even the *NME*, who seem to have an editorial policy against anything Thunders does, have let their man on the spot, David Quantick, muse over why: 'It's a paradox the way Thunders goes from suicidal gloom to defiant euphoria in the space of two songs...'

Sounds' Robin Gibson wheels out the soapbox to report:

> He didn't fall over and he wasn't so noticeably arrogant. Thunders thankfully concentrated simply on playing with his—slightly shaky—panache, and with a surprising coherence. The legend, the lifestyle and the cringe-inducing tribute to Sid Vicious, all of those stink: the rock'n'roll though—highly predictable, yet immensely pleasing—does not stink. That understood, all that can be expected is that Thunders will keep on playing it, and to this evidence he's still very capable of doing so.

* * *

Toward the end of November there is a small, low-key announcement that Thunders is going to re-form The Heartbreakers and play a short tour. Then these plans are shelved for financial reasons. Instead, to coincide with the release of *Hurt Me*, Thunders returns to England for two small dates, at the Brighton Escape on December 5th and Dingwalls on the 6th. By all reports, the Brighton gig is a winner, but on returning to London Thunders gets antsy to score. As a consequence, he is two hours late for the Dingwalls show, and the manager, facing a full house, starts to panic. The staff at the club search for Johnny's hotel phone number to confirm whether he has left for the gig. He has. The venue is so packed one can barely see the small figure wandering into the venue and eventually on to the raised platform that serves as a stage at Dingwalls.

Just Thunders and guitar. The club is unbearably hot, the audience so densely crowded that only the occasional glimpse of Johnny's black hat is visible. Even the spaces around the video screens that are transmitting the show are filled. Like a voice in the wilderness, Johnny plugs a gig later that evening before withdrawing to the dressing room. He's been paid and, from his unfocused eyes and slurred speech, so has his medicine man. His companions, Peter Perrett and his wife, and are not exempt from the chemical alterations.

At the Pipeline, deep in the heart of Soho, Thunders passes a test pressing of *Hurt Me* to the DJ to play while he gets himself ready. By word of mouth alone, the tiny club is packed beyond capacity, and a percentage of the audience eventually leaves, thinking the album was the man. Nonetheless, by the time Thunders walks slowly onstage in the early hours of the morning, the place is still rammed. In a reflective mood, Thunders busks his way through a collection of his own songs, reinforced here and there with Rolling Stones and Bob Dylan covers. Toward the end of the set he is joined by Peter Perrett—for whom it was to prove a memorable night, for all the wrong reasons:

> He made me play acoustically with him. I must have realised it was going to be bad, 'cos I turned up late. I was meant to be playing with him at Dingwalls. The only reason he was doing it acoustically was to have more money to spend on drugs—he didn't have to hire equipment or pay musicians. Later that same evening, he was supposed to play a set at Gossips and, as I was there, I had to go on with him. I agreed to do it, even though everything told me not to, but he had this way of acting so hurt. I was given an acoustic guitar; it didn't even have a strap on it. There was one mic between us, and the audience were two feet away. I don't mind the audience being close while I'm confident and enjoying it, but when you're feeling like that, *What am I doing here?* ... it was the only time I've been embarrassed onstage.

Thunders is a hard man to resist, as Peter would admit: 'He would just look at you with those big sad eyes and how could you say no?'

Retiring to spend Christmas in Sweden with Susanne, Johnny watches as *Hurt Me* reaches number 22 in the charts. The album's liner notes have been written by the guitarist, and next to 'Cosa Nostra', in his inimitable scrawl, it says 'Kiss me in Italian', a reference to the fatal endearment used by hit men familiar with their target. Although missing the essence of what Thunders can present live, *Hurt Me* is still more than just an experimental acoustic record by someone for whom electricity was invented. With a gentle clarity on his production, it offers a new spin on familiar territory, years before *Unplugged* became mandatory for any artiste wishing to be taken seriously.

Returning to London in February, Johnny again puts a new slant on some established material, this time aided by Tony James. The pair are ensconced in Greenhouse Studios, hunched alternatively across the mixing desk or around the gas heater, trying to restore *L.A.M.F.* to what it should have always sounded like. Thunders sits immobile by the tapes, ignoring the early dawn chill that has everybody else present huddled into coats and blankets. Susanne is somehow attempting to catch a brief nap on the sofa underneath one of the huge speakers. The latest in a seemingly endless line of untipped cigarettes hanging from his lips, Thunders pounds his fists on his knees, miming the drum intro to 'Born To Lose'.

'Do it harder, harder. The first crash has gotta be harder—really bangy.'

Christopher arrives, pleased at the productivity around him. The present situation, for perhaps the first time in almost a decade, allows for a (very) careful optimism. During 1983, Thunders played forty-five sell out concerts, established himself with production work, and now, less than a month hence, a Heartbreakers reunion concert is planned with a live album and video.

Patti Palladin makes a grand entrance. Tonight is her birthday. Christopher opens a bottle of champagne and raises a plastic beaker in toast to the Brooklyn singer: 'May all those things you dream of come true.' Thunders wishes her a 'Happy Birthday, scumbag' before jumping up and chasing her around the mixing desk.

Johnny takes a deep drag on a joint before offering it to Tony, who waves it away in favour of another bite of cold pizza. Thunders holds up a hand and then intones slowly, 'I don't need society to open up my pride for me,' before pressing a button that releases the remixed 'All By Myself' into the room.

Tony James decides that 'a miracle has been performed'.

Johnny just nods. 'Yeah, the tape sounds better.'

Christopher lights another cigar and does a headstand worthy of Gomez Addams. 'I can drink on my head, too.'

Johnny looks at him in some amazement. 'Four in the mornin', too.'

The Heartbreakers pull off an unexpected coup on the ears of England when, on March 24, Radio One's Richard Skinner puts the censored and remixed 'Get Off The Phone' on the deck as a preface to interviewing Thunders on his early evening nationwide show. Johnny, despite sounding like Dustin Hoffman doing his 'Ratso' voice, is very much on the ball. Even his one-liners are well thought out and sarcastically witty. The DJ leads him through a string of obvious questions about the Dolls until he generates the guitarist's interest by asking him if it was in 1975 that he first met Malcolm McLaren:

THUNDERS Yeah—and that was a large part why everything went the way it did.

SKINNER Why?

THUNDERS Why?!

SKINNER What was the influence of Malcolm McLaren on The New York Dolls, in the end?

THUNDERS Malcolm had this thing that he thought we only hadda dress good, and he didn't really care about the music much. I mean we played good, we just ... we never hit it off together. He was English and we were American. A sea apart.

SKINNER Was he practising, in a way, for what he did later?

THUNDERS Well, if you're asking me—there's your own answer.

SKINNER You're not going to say any more than that?

THUNDERS Do I have to?

The interview continues with Richard Skinner's surprise that Walter Lure, one of New York's most respected and better-known guitarists, is now working on Wall Street as a commodity broker.

THUNDERS Believe it or not, yeah.

SKINNER That's great. He's having a quick vacation with The Heartbreakers?

THUNDERS He goes back to work on Wednesday.

SKINNER If people want to see you in London tomorrow, where will they see you?

THUNDERS The Lyceum.

SKINNER All right. Have a good gig.

THUNDERS Okay. See ya. BE THERE OR BE SQUARE.

'Chinese Rocks' marks the end of Thunders' stay at Radio One. Richard Skinner comes back on the air laughing.

That's a terrific record . . . 'Chinese Rocks' from Johnny Thunders & The Heartbreakers. I saw them live 'round about 1977, '78— terrific night. The sight of Johnny Thunders dodging glasses will stay with me for a while to come.

* * *

A red minibus containing the band pulls around the back entrance. Billy shakes his head.

'Do you see that crowd? We've sold fuckin' out.'

Jerry, ever dour, with a manic, humorous edge, fixes the bass player with a poker face and half a smile. 'What did you expect—only our moms would check us out?'

The addition of a film and recording crew has typically unnerved Johnny, and in response he downs eight double vodkas in record time. It will be a passable performance, but not the greatest he's ever given. The gig is heralded by the blasting instrumental of 'The Man With The Golden Arm'. Following a split-second lull, The Heartbreakers take their places onstage, Johnny stumbling theatrically before they launch into 'Pipeline'. The unspoken aggravation between Lure and Thunders' guitars produces a mesmerising tension. Both take turns on lead with equal ease and urgency.

At one point during the set, Johnny tries to attract Billy's attention by walking over and kicking out at the bass players legs. Rath's stony glare is enough to instantly send Thunders pirouetting back to the stage front like a demented prima donna. Jerry Nolan, as always, ignores the antics of his colleagues and continues to pummel the drums into submission. There is something hilariously sinister about watching this rabid pack of debauchees singing 'Seven Day Weekend', twisting the innocent lyrics into something much darker.

Thunders cuts short his acoustic spot.

'Awrite . . . that's enough of this shit . . . I'll get th' boys back on . . .'

The Heartbreakers are back, gunning from the lower levels. Time has made them harder.

Thunders is drunk . . .

Rath looks annoyed . . .

Lure looks nonchalantly bored . . .

Nolan looks unmoved . . .

During a guitar pause in 'So Alone', Johnny decides to add a touch of blasphemy to his public sins: After a storytelling tangent that sees him tarry rather too long on the subject of a kid on the Lower East Side who loses his virginity to a 'big black guy in leathers', he piously makes the sign of the cross before intoning slowly, 'Our Father who art in heaven, hallowed be thy name . . . fuck you.'

* * *

In early April, Johnny is once again featured in the Swedish press, only this time the tone is a great deal calmer. Under the simple headline 'I Will Be Back', a reporter notes:

Last night Johnny Thunders left Sweden and took the ferry to Abo,
from Stockholm. When the boat left Swedish waters he picked up
his guitar and played a free gig in the restaurant. It was, said Johnny,
'A private protest against the Swedish bureaucrats'.

Thunders has been in Sweden for a week, unable to play his advertised
concerts due to claims made by one Gunner Oldenir (63) that the guitarist
would be taking employment from Swedish musicians. Oldenir's obscure
and stupid reasoning has won Thunders a certain level of sympathy from
within the Swedish music business. Johnny tells the press that Oldenir's
statement is 'dead silly, to stop me for that reason. Besides, I'm free from
my drug problems; I've been on methadone for the past two years, and
I've quit that too. It happens that I drink quite a lot, but which rock star
doesn't?'

Describing how his only controversial gig during the last Swedish tour
was an 'accident', he explains to a party of journalists that he was so drunk
he couldn't keep on his feet. The guitarist's attitude combined with a rare
display of public diplomacy wins over the press, who start describing him
as looking 'healthier' and 'alert' every time they mention him.

A 'healthy' and 'alert' Johnny presses his media victory by telling them,
'In a week I'll try and get a new work permit. I won't judge Sweden by one
bureaucrat. I like being here. My girlfriend, Susanne, is from Stockholm,
and the audience has always been one of the best.'

Leaving Thunders to sweet-talk the papers, various music and
promotion companies go to the Minister of Culture to complain about
Gunner Oldenir's obstructive behaviour and to try to effect a change in
the law concerning foreign performers who cannot get work permits.
Thunders' Swedish promoter, Lasse Lindros, insists, 'We have to stop this
nonsense. Every musician is unique. You can't replace Johnny Thunders
with someone else. The Home Office's motivation is stupid.'

In Finland, where the tour has started up again, Johnny requests
written reports of his four gigs there from both the local police and the

Home Office, in an effort to make the Swedish authorities retract their decision. 'I'm not gonna give up until I can play to my Swedish fans again.'

By June, the Swedish government has backed down. Thunders returns with what he calls the Revenge 84 Tour, consisting of Jerry Nolan, Billy Rath, and Sylvain Sylvain. As well as covering some of Sylvain's material—including 'Teenage News', which dates back to the Dolls—Thunders sings a couple of new songs, namely 'Size Ten Shoes' and 'Have Faith', which feature on a range of T-shirts. Unfortunately, the concept of faith is wearing a little thin in the once reverential English press, where the release of *Live At The Lyceum* is met with less than favourable reviews.

CHAPTER NINE

ASK ME NO QUESTIONS

J ohnny Thunders likes publicity but hates giving interviews. He has an armoury of stock answers to most questions that are slurred into every tape recorder placed before him; either that or chanted in a *Midnight Cowboy* monotone that makes it clear he'd rather have stayed in bed. Frequently, his manner during interviews is enough to give all but the extra-thick-skinned a confidence crisis. His fingers play with whatever's around at the time: a book of matches, a lighter, a television set—anything to distract him from the boring question and answer routine. Certain aspects of his private life are taboo, which is, of course, Johnny's right. The most frustrating thing about him is his left-field sense of humour and bleak, almost Runyon-esque one-liners that usually surface once the interview is over.

From the off, Thunders has made it clear to me that all doors would be opened to enable the book's progress, but pinning the man down for an interview? We talked plenty, but that was off the record. However, as *In Cold Blood* develops, along with a sense of familiarity, Johnny opens up as far as possible.

Could you speak up a little, Johnny?

JOHNNY I hated school. I always did terrible anyway, couldn't wait to leave. I quit when I was about fourteen. See, school in America is very social, I guess. And I never really joined a gang, I used to have more fun just hangin' out in the neighbourhood parks. Kids get involved with the street gang scene for lots of reasons ... for protection ... 'cos their friends are in one, you know. Background has lot to do with it too. Certain areas, stuff like that. I was brought up in Queens, which is sort of a middle-class area of Manhattan. I used to play baseball all the time, ever since I can remember. I grew up with just my mother and my sister. We lived in a one and half room apartment till I was about twelve or thirteen. Then we moved into a big house with my grandmother—her husband died, so we moved into the house with her. I guess I stayed there right up until I was fifteen. My mother got married, so I moved out and found my own apartment.

I still see them or talk to them on the phone or whatever. It was good living with a sister who was older than me. I got to listen to all of Mariann's records, lots of the 60s girl bands like The Shangri-Las, The Ronettes, The Crystals, The Angels. I liked music ever since I was a little kid, Eddie Cochran and Gene Vincent. Yeah, music's always been important.

NINA You must have been very young when you came to London the first time?

JOHNNY Yeah. I was really young then. It was '69, something like that. A friend of mine in New York was workin' for a magazine, so I got to borrow their press pass, and when me and a girlfriend came to England, we just kinda went around checkin' out all these bands for free, you know. I saw, must have been fifty or sixty bands. I saw Tyrannosaurus Rex. It wasn't long after I went home that I got into music myself.

NINA So, The New York Dolls would have been your first band?

JOHNNY Yeah, more or less. We were called Actress for a time.

NINA Does it bore you, answering questions about the Dolls period in your life?

JOHNNY Sort of ... not bore me ... but, you know, you kinda run out of ways of answering the same questions after a million times or so. And nobody was that interested at the time the Dolls existed, but I guess that's often the way, huh? I mean, I still play with Jerry sometimes, and I had Sylvain in my band a couple of times. I've run into David; I never see Arthur, but nobody sees Arthur. I did hear he got married and lives somewhere in Brooklyn. Who knows? To have been a part of it was great. In the beginning we had a lot of fun. The Dolls played some great gigs—we played the Waldorf Astoria, one of the biggest hotels in New York, on Halloween. We had all these crazy people coming to see us in all kinds of weird make up and stuff. The Dolls set a lot of styles. We got ripped off then and we got ripped off now. I thought the band had gone as far as it could.

Toward the end we had Malcolm McLaren managing us, and he wanted us dressing in red leather and stuff. Me and Jerry thought it was more important to get a new set together. We had five or six new songs, and we wanted to get back to New York—we were in Florida—and work on them, but David thought we should stay with Malcolm ... and he liked calling the shots, so me and Jerry just split back to the city and started up The Heartbreakers. I don't gotta name names to tell you how much the Dolls influence is still around.

The Dolls had a couple of managers, Leber and Krebs, who didn't give a fuck about us at all. They just wanted to make lots of money for themselves. I've always had problems with managers, though.

NINA Tell me a little about The Heartbreakers.

JOHNNY What's to tell? Me an' Jerry, we got back to New York and we got hold of Richard Hell, who'd just left his own band, Television. We thought it'd make a great combination, and it did for a while. Then we found Walter Lure, and we stole Waldo away from The Demons, his band. Richard had this thing—kinda an ego thing, I guess—he wanted to sing all the songs himself. It wound up with me getting one song a night to sing, and Walter getting one song a night, and Richard doing all the rest. I'd had it with that number. I'd backed up a frontman long enough.

Anyway, I was gonna quit, but Richard saved me the trouble. See, he got Jerry and Walter together and tried to suggest they get rid of me, but he didn't know Jerry. So we just kinda threw Richard out and got Billy Rath in on bass. It was a lot better with Billy. So that was The Heartbreakers. We got Leee Black Childers in as manager. We played Max's, CBGB's—we musta played every fuckin' club for miles, and we had this really big hardcore following. Every place we played was sold out.

NINA But you had some trouble with record companies, didn't you? Some trouble getting an actual recording deal?

JOHNNY SOME trouble? We invented the word. See, the companies was after kinda safe products, and The Heartbreakers had the worst reputation. Lots of people put the finger on me and Jerry for splitting the Dolls, and the press liked to write stories 'bout, all The Heartbreakers wanted was drugs and sex and stuff . . . and I guess the big companies thought we only wanted a deal so we could get an advance and go blow it on drugs and die . . . naww . . . we wanted to make records as well. The bottom line was, they were afraid of us. They wanted a band they could control, and we obviously didn't fit that description. Then Malcolm invited us to England to do the Anarchy tour, so, of course, we went and played it. We enjoyed it a lot. It was fresh or something.

NINA And you got an album deal, too?

JOHNNY Yeah . . . we did *L.A.M.F.* for Track Records. They treated us okay at first, but they had lot of underhand things going on, that we didn't find out about for a while. Tax business or some shit. Typical fucking music businessmen.

NINA Was that one of the reasons behind The Heartbreakers splitting up?

JOHNNY. I guess it had something to do with it, but there were other reasons apart from Track pretendin' to go bust. See, none of us was happy with the album mix. It sounded okay when we played the songs in the studio but when we got the tapes back it was fucked up. We mixed the album, right and I went back to New York. Then Walter, who was still in England then, came in and mixed it again and fucked around with it. And then Jerry, who didn't get along too well with Walter, came in and remixed it again. I mean, fuck, nobody knew who did what in the end. Anyway, between them it came out, and it hadda wait years before I got the chance to get back into a studio and fix it up the way it always should of sounded so Jungle Records could reissue it. Anyway, like I was saying, then Jerry quit the band. Walter an' Billy did a couple of singles together, I think, and I stayed on in England to do a solo album with Real Records.

NINA That was the *So Alone* album . . .

JOHNNY Right. I got the chance to do a couple of slower songs on that for the first time, things I'd written up but would've sounded kinda out of place on an LP by The Heartbreakers.

NINA What did you do after *So Alone*?

JOHNNY Vanished. Naww, I went back to America and tried the family life for a bit. I got three kids: Vito, Dino, and little Johnny. I did other things, too. Moved to Detroit and met up with Wayne Kramer and started Gang War. That coulda been a good band, but it just didn't work out. See, me and Wayne were different generations, right, and we didn't understand each other. It was a great idea, but that's not enough.

NINA Do you think your career, your life, would have run a bit smoother without heroin?

JOHNNY Of course. In certain ways. I mean, obviously it bothers me when I got busted for drugs or something. Nobody likes that shit. I mean, I would never advise anyone to start using heroin. All it does is fuck you up. But, at the same time, I ain't no fucking preacher either. I ain't gonna lecture people on how they live their lives. See, I was very young when I started using heroin. Young and innocent, and I thought I knew it all, right? But I didn't know it all, and I'd never have conformed to it even if I did . . . I had nobody to warn me off, to tell me it wasn't right. I guess I was about eighteen when I started using heroin. I tried it and I liked it, and in some ways I don't regret ever having used it.

I loved taking drugs, right? I thought I was having a real good time, taking drugs and playing rock'n'roll, but I wasn't. I only realised that when I started playing without drugs. See, for me, it's much the same at the end point anyway. I can play great without drugs, but I can play great with drugs, as well. It's real easy to start, right? It's when you come to stop you find out you got problems. Like, I've had to go on all sorts of methadone programmes and it's ... well, it's horrible. You find that you get to kind of depend on drugs in certain situations, and it's much harder having to deal with them straight. But really, drugs just cocoon you, cut you off from the real world, alienate you from the entire fuckin' world. But the problems are still around, you know? After the drugs, you always still got the same problems.

NINA Does it make you angry when people want to see the legend rather than the man?

JOHNNY I don't feel nothing about it. I get up onstage to make a little money, make the kids dance. I play for the kids who come to hear me play guitar. Maybe some of my audience come to see me because of something they heard or something they've read, but not too many. Writers write whatever they want, people think what they want to think. I don't live up to anything except myself. I don't usually read anything anybody writes about me ... it might distort my mind!

NINA Do you feel you've changed much over the years?

JOHNNY I still feel the same way about music. I still won't compromise it and I still ain't rich. I've maybe changed more in certain smaller ways, like, the way I write songs or something. I used to write a lot of songs about objects rather than people. Like, when I was young, I used to pick all my girlfriends by their shoes. If they had nice shoes, I'd be interested in them. Other things, too. My tattoos, for instance. I was crazy. That was something I always wanted when I was a kid, so I just did it. I wish I never did ... but ... I like staying home more now, watching videos or something.

NINA Are you content with the way your career is going now?

JOHNNY I don't think it's too smart to ever be content. So much can happen so quickly. Since *So Alone*, I've done so much ... I've played all over the world and made records. I've started to make a couple of movies. That's a good example, see: when I was in Paris, I started this movie about an American rock star getting off heroin and all that shit, right? I was also doing one which was, like, a gang movie, real violent—I get to kill about twenty-five people—and I was really looking forward to doing them, and what happens? One runs out of money and the other movie, the guy behind it gets busted for a kilo of cocaine, and he'll be in prison for ten years or something.

You never know in this business. I like living in Paris and London, but New York is always home. I'm dying to go back there and get those motherfuckers with my new band, you know, 'cos they're used to seeing me with Nolan. We gonna do all new songs. I'm gonna start the show with me in a tuxedo singing 'New York, New York'—that's gonna be the intro of the show. You always gotta move. That's why I produced the *Hurt Me* album, and I've produced other bands too. I've produced Justin Trouble, and I'm gonna produce this band in France called The Untouchables. I'm gonna do a single with Patti. We're gonna do a song called 'Crawfish'—it was on Elvis Presley's *King Creole* album.

Things look okay, but you never know. You can trust yourself ... some of the time anyway ... but it's everyone else you gotta watch for. I started the Dolls with managers who didn't give a fuck about us or our interests, they were just out for money. They showed me how cold and nasty people can be, and I just couldn't see what that had to do with rock and roll. It's really hard to trust anyone in this business, and we were all so young in the Dolls, we didn't know what we were doing. The way we were treated was really, really rotten. Then, when I started The Heartbreakers, it was the same shit . . . and I was just amazed to see how people just blatantly rip you off, you know? Then when I made *So Alone* with Dave Hill, and I thought he was a nice guy, but it was just another story of somebody else ripping me off in another way. It's just sad, the way they used us, all the different people. It's a real bad business if you don't understand it. It's a real bad business even if you do. It's . . . it's just a rotten business. It's worse than being a whore.

NINA And now?

JOHNNY Now I try to be more positive. I have Christopher managing me—it's really good. I look on him as a friend. I never really had anybody before, a manager that I was a friend with. If you play rock'n'roll, though, you always got problems. If I can have the same amps and the same PA every night on tour, then I'm happy. It's so defeating when you play with different equipment every night . . . and it's different every night.

CHAPTER TEN

CHRISTOPHER AND HIS KIND

T he small Chinese restaurant in Soho is hot and without ventilation. Christopher Giercke obviously has more on his mind than dehydration as he toys, with great dexterity, with chopsticks and sweet-and-sour spinach. Looking in from outside it might almost seem that, with every live concert and record release, Thunders public stature continues to grow. From Christopher Giercke's point of view, things are far from black and white, and it's his job to manage matters with a mixture of tact and (subtle) tyranny.

Christopher waves a black-draped arm in the general direction of the Marquee Club that is playing host to Thunders and two Heartbreakers for the entire week. Each night sold out as well.

Of course, it's good that things are going well but things can complicate each other so quickly. At the moment, I have enough business problems without having to also worry about the personal lives of the people whose careers should be my fundamental responsibility. I mean, right now I am restructuring deals for Johnny with Italy, Japan, and Spain. Also, an English tour with Hanoi Rocks is being set up.

Christopher Giercke is a strange mixture of manager, artist, and philosopher. While more than able to keep pace with the various sharks that infest his financial waters, he still has the nature of an individualist and looks on his charges with a gaze at once humane and abstract.

So, that is more than enough for one man. Johnny and The Heartbreakers still have to he considered a problem. Not one that cannot be surmounted, but . . . Johnny thinks everything is fine. He's a 'big star' . . . but they have a tendency when everything is good to get greedy. Today they didn't want to pay for batteries for a tuner, yet they get $150 a day. They sent the soundman out to buy strings for them.

Now, Johnny decides he doesn't want to play Dingwalls, thinks it will spoil his reputation. Okay. It's not a great place, but it'll pay a couple of bills, perhaps. They don't appreciate money. It may be their ruin. I try to present things to them in a diplomatic way to make them understand they have to be able and quick like everyone else living on this planet. Yesterday they are supposed to go to Foubert's *Valley Of The Dolls*. They are given taxi fares and people are waiting to see Johnny, a different Johnny—journalists, press agents, lots of fans waiting—and what happens? Johnny doesn't want to go.

Most problems for The Heartbreakers, it is generally assumed, result from their having more faith in narcotics than in themselves. Giercke nods.

Drugs are always such a danger. Three years of hard work to make sure everything goes smoothly. Then, one single shot, and OUT! Tours broken up, health broken up, thrown out of the country maybe for just £50 worth of smack: but that's it! ARE THEY OUT OF THEIR MINDS?!?

Johnny's real problem is lack of responsibility, that's why they never got anywhere. When there is no leadership, then that's where the problem is. I suppose that's what I'm trying to teach him: leadership, standards, and certain rules.

The Marquee is overflowing with punters. Out front, the 'House Full' sign is already up, but people are still pushing to get in. It's the hottest August on record for years, and the overpowering stench of sweat and beer in the club isn't helping. The dressing room offers no respite. Neon Leon and The Bondage Babies sprawl around, pondering the wisdom of playing saunas. By the end of their five-night stint as support, the entire band are stir crazy and spend much of their last set throwing cornflakes to the audience.

It's 20:45 and an otherwise tranquil Christopher Giercke is taking frequent glances at his wristwatch. The Heartbreakers, of course, are late when the door swings and Johnny, clad in an undertaker's frock coat, strolls in and politely requests that the dressing room liggers be cleared out. Jerry Nolan follows dressed like a priest who's decided, on a whim, to become a pimp. He sticks to his customary pre-show regime, finding a quiet corner and staying in it. A few minutes pass and then Billy Rath wanders in, seemingly unaware of his surroundings until someone hands him his bass and his eyes suddenly snap into focus.

Nobody talks very much. It's hard to say if the silence is brought on by nerves, drugs, surly dispositions—or all three. Walter Lure and Sylvain Sylvain were supposed to be playing tonight, but both are still in America, held back by Wall Street and a family illness, respectively. Jerry comes out of his corner to ask how the book is coming along. He also confides he's thinking of writing one himself but has a 'real terrible memory'—a distinct problem. 'Well, there are lots of people around I can ask, you know ... see if they remember what I was doing on such or such a date.'

With the band all present, Christopher visibly relaxes and circulates from band to road crew reminiscing about the days he spent in the Amazon. Hanoi Rocks are crowding the bar, waiting for their main inspiration to take the stage. They and the audience don't have long to endure as backstage things are at the critical phase when there's nothing left to do except plug in the guitars. Jerry is devastating an apple with real hatred while leafing through a French magazine called *Losers*, which has a large article about Johnny and The Heartbreakers in it. Thunders passes him a copy of *Red Patent Leather*, the New York Dolls live album that Sylvain mixed, which has a sleeve shot of the band in their ketchup-hued phase. It used to be a bootleg and now it's official. Like most 'under the counter' items, it had a certain charm but, as a legit release, it's unlikely to help the Dolls already legendary reputation. Thunders slings it into his empty guitar case.

The lights out front have dimmed to a dull red glow around the equipment and the baying has begun in earnest. Untroubled, Johnny goes through his pockets slowly and comes up with a cigarette which he ignites, straightens his shirt inside his black and purple spangled trousers, and, just like every night, pauses to give Susanne a kiss before preceding Billy and Jerry onstage.

Make 'em wait. Thunders stands with his back to the crowd for a long minute with crushing, unfamiliar notes shaking from the speakers. He turns, his frock coat curling around his ankles, and prowls quickly to the centre microphone.

'Well if you lookin' for trouble, you come to th' right place ... I'm tellin' you, baby, don't waste my time ...'

Johnny surges through 'Countdown Love', 'Hoodoo Voodoo', a couple of bars of 'Alone In A Crowd', and a wall-shaking 'Personality Crisis' before pausing long enough to tug loose his tie and toss his coat to the side of the stage.

'Man,' he gasps, 'it's SO fuckin' hot. Holy shit.'

Thick clouds of cigarette smoke filter sluggishly through the stage lights giving his skin a moist translucency. While Thunders grabs a few seconds to breathe, a guttural chant for 'Jet Boy' starts up. Johnny teases his guitar into the opening notes and then drops it.

'Uh ... this is about a guy I useta know ... 's called "Too Much Junkie Business".'

These words, together with the chords that accompany them, produce an acrobatic psychosis in the audience. Burly blokes spray sweat in every direction as they hurl themselves forward in a convivial attempt to drag underfoot as many as possible. One of the more athletic lemmings actually makes it to the stage, where he goes into a frenzied spin until a large roadie sends him somersaulting back into space. Thunders gives a wary backward glance to where Susanne is standing on the stage, to check on her safety, and, once satisfied, finishes the number.

* * *

The Italian restaurant, while still within the clichéd corners of Soho, is a lot more upmarket. At least the bill is. Christopher muses over it briefly, before returning to more pressing matters. He is still worried about drugs—temptation and effect. Thunders is almost, for the first time in many years, free of his addiction to heroin. His methadone intake is also decreasing. Christopher wants to keep it that way.

> Some equations are obvious and must be made. If you drink ice water you get a stomach ache, and if you shoot up with dirty needles you get an infection. Johnny is very talented, and that gift takes away the right to indulge in self-pity. Once you have a talent you also have an obligation to express it. You can't go out onstage and not know where you are. You can't. You can maybe get away with it for a short time but, in the long run, there may be a time to bring all that beauty together, and if you can't do it, then the gift might be taken away.

He pauses for a moment, his thoughts obviously on Billy and Jerry.

> Of course, it's also possible to make great music and, in reality, be a scumbag. Billy and Jerry are sick in medical terms. If you have to take 60ml of methadone then you are sick. But they are closet queens about junk—they want to be applauded and yet make problems in not being healthy.

Don't you think it's possible for them to clean up their acts?

> They've broken promises hundreds of times . . . but I don't write anyone off. We all have to make decisions. We all have to try and survive, don't we? They have to be clean from their dominating obsession with self-pity. I mean, they are not leprous outcasts with some fatal disease. They are very privileged and talented and fortunate. If only they could see those privileges and talents. There are so many junkies living without talent, without hope or attention.

Was Johnny very ill when you met him?

> Well, a while back I took Johnny to a corrida . . . a bullfight, you know . . . and it sickened him so much he almost passed out. Every thrust from the Matador's sword was more wounding, more terrible to the animal. It was in great pain, but would not fall. Does that answer your question?

What made you decide to take Johnny on in the first place? 'It was his birthday and I thought I could help him.'
Christopher smiles and lights a cigar.

> Johnny is much more critical now, and that is good. As an example, when we filmed the Lyceum show, March 25th, '84 . . . we had a twenty-four-track unit so they can see and hear what they do. On the Saturday everybody is using junk, right? On the Sunday, the night of the concert, the dealer does not show. So Johnny drinks eight large vodkas and goes on; when he watches a video of it now, he is embarrassed and critical. You have to learn to know your weakness and to project. The process of changing is slow. Inside, perhaps, the first step is to be aware and curious. With heroin, you can't do that, and I think Johnny knows that now.

Outside the restaurant, it's almost cool for the first time in days and the air smells of rain. Christopher decides we've spent too long over the meal and is forced to hurry the half block back to the Marquee, dodging traffic and tourists, only slowing down when he sees Johnny and Susanne sitting quietly on a car outside the club.

'Sad Vacation', as always, is dedicated to Sid Vicious. Dozens of Instamatics take advantage of the night's traditional gentle moment and Johnny is illuminated by flash cubes exploding in sequence. That bit of the repertoire over, he gives Patti Palladin another affectionately licentious introduction as she joins them onstage for three numbers.

Alone again, The Heartbreakers tear through various of their classics until, during 'I Wanna Be Loved', Johnny lets the bass carry the tune as he mops his face and starts to say goodbye:

Thanks a lot, kids, it's been wonderful but it's hot ... we had a really good time ... I'm hot, you're hot ... everybody is hot. We ... we need a little fire to cook up some 'Chinese Rocks' for you now and we ... we'll see ya.

Everybody has been screaming for this song from the minute they took the stage, and nobody is disappointed. If anything, it's even better than when they first released it. 'Can't Keep My Eyes On You' and 'Pipeline' serve as encores, and then it really is over.

* * *

The taxi driver sticks his head out of the window to hurl a stream of abuse at the lady in the grey Jaguar that had cut in front of us. He continues scratching at a heat lump growing from the middle of a blue ink tattoo until he draws blood. After what seems like forever spent driving around the clogged rush hour arteries of Kensington, he stops outside a block of apartments that could have been designed for a Chandler film. Susanne opens the door and Jerry sticks his head out of the bathroom in greeting before vanishing for the rest of the afternoon. Johnny is relaxing before another round of interviews. Just before coming over to play the 'Thunders Week' at the Marquee he had, once again, been filmed by Patrick Grandperrett as well as gigging in Sweden and Finland. On August 18 he played in Amsterdam and then headed off to Rotterdam for Pandora's Music Box, a mini festival that also featured John Cale and The Gun Club.

Susanne likes the apartment they're staying in for the duration of the Marquee stint. It's more like a flat than the normal faceless hotels they usually wind up in. She's carefully unpacked: neat lines of guitar cases surround the bed, and scarves and belts tilt over the room's single chair. On a table beneath the window sits the latest of Thunders' hats, this one boasting a stuffed cobra coiled around the brim.

Susanne Blomqvist first met Johnny when he played her native Sweden over a year ago and has been with him ever since. She remembers her parents' fears when she told them she was going away with the guitarist, and how those fears were slightly quieted once she brought Johnny home to meet Mom. Since then, she's been living his nomadic life and longing for a settled base in either New York or London—but not Manchester, where the next gig is. Even the horrific summer here is submitting to autumn in premature apathy. The pristine modern technology of an empty Hacienda lends the day an unreal element of sci-fi.

The atmosphere is tense and building to an argument nobody wants.

Johnny slowly breaks the tip off his cigarette and considers my question if he's been enjoying this stage of the tour. His response is somewhat muted. 'Not especially, no.' In Nottingham, someone had thrown a bleach missile which had left Jerry Nolan temporarily blinded for part of the set. Billy is standing by the table, testing a selection of relish laid out in a large tray in the small cafeteria at the side of the club. Jerry hasn't said a word all through the soundcheck and continues to sit apart from the others, managing to dominate by his silence. Christopher mentions that a Swedish record company have been wondering what condition the band are in. Conversation turns to their last tour of Finland, which had come to an abrupt conclusion after the band hightailed it out of the country five hours in advance of their scheduled flight, upsetting the Finnish promoters.

'Everyone' remarks Christopher, 'lost 1,000 marks [about £125]. Sylvain felt great about it.'

Johnny matches the irony. 'That's too bad for Sylvain.'

Jerry looks up abruptly. 'I live my life for Sylvain.'

The manager turns more fully toward Billy and Jerry before continuing.

GIERCKE Look, I'm going further in the red and I see that drugs are bought. I can't pull a gun on you—it's your own life, your own choice . . . but you deprive yourself. I can't go to a record company and say, 'They're in great shape'. I have to admit I'm helpless. It's not good.

RATH C'mon . . . you've been saying that for a year now.

GIERCKE I'm worried you could get busted . . . anything could go wrong.

Jerry suddenly stands up—'Just pay my salary and air fares and I'll do my job to the best of my abilities'—and walks out of the room.

* * *

Evening. Going into the club, everyone pauses to look over the audience. Johnny smiles faintly at the dozens of black hats, swaying around the dance floor, that mimic his own. By day, the Hacienda's dressing rooms double as a hairdressers, and as we enter it, Susanne sniffs knowingly: 'Hairdye.' The small fridge in the corner has been filled to their specifications with champagne, orange juice, Perrier, and beer. Christopher opens a bottle and falls into conversation with Johnny and Susanne. Jerry is asleep. Billy is explaining how, by positioning yourself in just the right spot in the middle of an open road, you can avoid being swept up by a tornado.

They clatter up the designer interior fire escape and under the house lights. The audience is clustered tight in front of the stage and the band is as good as ever, but something is missing, Johnny obviously isn't having as much fun as he does in London. He is doing the encore when he finds himself alone onstage. Billy and Jerry have already made it halfway back to the dressing room when they hear him singing and pivot back up the stairway to finish the short set. Everyone seems pretty emotionless on the drive back to the hotel.

* * *

With only days to go before the co-headlining Thunders / Hanoi Rocks concerts begin, Billy Rath and Jerry Nolan have left and are back in Sweden. Their replacements are adequate but no more, and the entire weight of the upcoming shows will be on Johnny's shoulders alone. With a bad cold, Johnny and his band join up with Hanoi Rocks and play a series of dates, including an unadvertised twenty-minute guest spot at the Lyceum.

By any standards, North London's Savoy Ballroom is the absolute pits. Just like in the song, the plaster's falling off the walls. Outside the toilet someone has artistically placed the two bottles of champagne, a heap of plastic cups, and a crate of beer. If the toilet light is used, a roadie for the ballroom warns, it will fuse the hallway and the entrance to the stage. The show is okay but has nowhere near the edge of the Marquee gigs. The best moments come in the encore, when Thunders parodies Thunders and Mike Monroe does a David Doll. The audience, perhaps caught up in the spirit of their surroundings, remain lacklustre throughout.

The bar is no less depressing. Trying to inject a little glamour into the evening, Mike lies dramatically across the length of the bar like he's posing for a calendar photograph, but his performance barely raises an eyebrow.

Johnny is remembering the recent date he played in war-torn Belfast: 'Those kids are starved for music . . . I really felt something for them.' He recalls the tanks in the streets, going back and playing 'Chinese Rocks' over and over for them. Johnny socialises for a while and then decides the party that never was is over. Jungle Records' Alan Hauser offers a lift back to the hotel. When the car pulls up in the Maida Vale courtyard, not a light is left on. A tired Johnny waves goodnight as the elevator door closes.

CHAPTER ELEVEN

PRIVATE WORLD

In 1984, Johnny Thunders played ninety-five concerts spanning continents in an almost endless series of soundchecks, hotels, and suitcases: Russia, Italy, Sweden, England, Spain, Holland, Germany, and Japan. The dates spill over into 1985, the backing bands changing from city to city. For the last few months, however, Thunders has acquired a more stable outfit. Out of the group that toured the UK with Hanoi Rocks, only bass guitarist Keith Yon remains. Experienced in the sudden call to arms, Henri-Paul has once again been drafted, but how long he will remain is uncertain. His position, according to Christopher, is 'more then than now'. Only the new drummer, 'T' (Tony St Helene) is an unknown quantity to Thunders' English audience. Having previously played with Keith Yon in the reggae/jazz outfit The Tribesmen, T had come to Thunders as a replacement for Terry Chimes, who, in turn, joined Hanoi Rocks after their drummer, Razzle, was killed in an automobile accident in December '84.

Mid-February. Thunders and Giercke are back in London for casual negotiations with the Beggars Banquet record company. A futile meeting takes up most of the first day. As evening falls, they decide to go out for dinner with friends. In a small Italian restaurant just off Regent Street, Thunders is practising his celluloid alter ego, Johnny Valentine, a mixture in equal doses of De Niro and Pacino's hood from Havana.

Thunders as himself is an almost intangible presence, polite and insulting, charismatic and insular. Johnny ignores social norms like flies on the wall. He sits at centre table, black hat tilted to the nape of his neck. A white dressing gown hangs around his shoulders while he breaks bread with members of Hanoi Rocks and Lords Of The New Church in an absurd reflection of the last supper. The spectacle of J.T. holding court is an experience for others in the restaurant, shyly peering around menu cards to catch a better look at the Lewis Carroll table behind them. Mike Monroe is presented with a small box wrapped in a print of Mount Fuji that Johnny has brought with him back from Japan. Waiters hurry backward and forward to keep pace with the conflicting orders.

Johnny has returned from Japan with a good impression of both people and place. Each concert sold out well in advance of his arrival. Even the journalists liked him and treated him with a respect rare in that profession. A miracle not unnoticed by Christopher Giercke: 'They didn't ask stupid questions about drugs. Johnny was just perfect ... he fits in there.'

Thunders rises from the table, takes Susanne's arm, and wishes everybody a casual goodnight. Stiv Bators departs soon after with Mike Monroe and Terry Chimes following. Christopher lights another cigar, wipes the smoke from his eye, and orders coffee. A question about the immediate future for Johnny brings a tired smile:

> Well, you know, we have to keep our fingers crossed for the unseen ... but if all goes well, we play some dates in Norway before a return to Spain to finish off a television special and then, on April the first ... a date which is unfortunate ... we start three nights at New York's Irving Plaza.

Christopher pauses while the coffee arrives, pulling on his cigar and warming to his theme:

> New York should be quite something. Lots of Johnny's friends will be turning up to maybe do a guest spot with him—Walter Lure, Jerry Nolan, Sylvain Sylvain. It should be good. Johnny Thunders

comes riding home. I think if he is clean when we get to New York, free of all medication, then he would be a real hero. There is nothing in his way then to stop him. He could be another Lou Reed or John Cale ...

While still remaining very careful, Christopher is hoping that Thunders can at last shake off the 'junk-sick rock star' tag: 'Three years ago, out of twenty-four hours, he would sleep twenty-two. All that has changed now. His level of methadone is down to 15ml, so it's all up to Johnny.' The Marquee week was a turning point for Thunders, which marked a return to peak form. Night after night he had stalked onto the overheated stage, flanked by Rath and Nolan, and delivered a set of raw perfection. One of rock'n'roll's last surviving icons, a man without dreams or peers, the best.

A common idea is that Thunders needs The Heartbreakers before he attempts another leap at the stars. The band's grainy romanticism is a tempting one. Even the journalists that came to hate their innards never denied their power or style. In retrospect, The Heartbreakers have left a mythology that's almost impossible to follow or imitate and the band themselves know it.

Walter Lure says, with just a trace of bitterness, that nowadays he would 'just shut up and play for the money. It isn't really as exciting as being part of a group—so I guess I don't do it for the pleasure of it now.' Billy Rath has exiled himself to Sweden: 'I love to produce bands. That's what I'm actually working myself into now. In lots of ways, I think I prefer it to playing.'

And Jerry Nolan? His relationship with Thunders spans some thirteen years; it's a friendship that has often touched on blood and a subversive loyalty to one another. Nolan is someone on whom Thunders was once dependent; Giercke described them as 'animals who went hunting together.' Yet despite the recent separation, they are kindred.

Thunders' warped humour and his onstage lectures and tirades that might've made Lenny Bruce blush come as no surprise to his regular audience. Much to Thunders' amusement, his new band comprised of two self-assured black musicians creates some consternation among the more knuckleheaded of his fans. Too bad. It's the music that counts. Tony St Helene:

> I know Johnny gets his kicks from playing with us. We have a lot of fun seeing people go, 'What?! Black men playing with Johnny Thunders?' But the same way we have to adjust our perspectives is good for them too.

Christopher is amused by the radical swing in the Thunders image and sums up with perplexing abruptness, 'They say, *We are Rastaman*. Okay, it would be as easy to say as *I am superman*—it all turns to cultural fascism.'

Jungle Records have entered the video sales business with a forty-five-minute film of the Heartbreakers show at the Lyceum Ballroom. America and Japan are placing import orders and Jungle, headed by Thunders expert Alan Hauser, have attempted to make the product as alluring as possible within the realms of their limited resources. They incorporate clips from *Personality Crisis*, which includes, along with a brief sequence featuring an attractive actress in gratuitous nude cameo, Thunders singing 'Hurt Me' in a seemingly deserted recording studio.

Jungle also stepped in to rescue the collaboration between Patti Palladin and Thunders—a cover of 'Crawfish' paired with their self-penned 'Tie Me Upon' the flip-side. Originally it was to have been on the Swampland label, but arguments over the cost of the final mix caused friction and delays. Jungle's intervention let the record be released in seven- and twelve-inch formats, together with a limited-edition picture disc.

David Johansen, on one of his periodic visits to England, is playing two nights at Dingwalls to promote his latest album, optimistically entitled *Sweet Revenge*. The core of his show rests on the past. At least a quarter of the set is taken up with a New York Dolls novelty pastiche—a depressing medley featuring Johansen dressed in a Florida bowling shirt set off by an outsize pith helmet. He waves an umbrella with a toy ostrich hanging from it, trying desperately to convince the audience he doesn't care about fame and fortune, only having a good time. When the gig is over and the dregs of the show have been drained like the night's dirty glasses, Johansen and band set about getting drunk over a chicken dinner around a large table at the back of the club. The singer has changed from his jungle garb into a flying helmet with goggles swinging from the long ear flaps. It's something past three in the morning and David is now tired and drunk. He manages to keep the smile on his face and, when he hears Thunders' name mentioned, passes Johnny off as, 'Ahhh ... a guy I used to know who plays guitar an' used to play baseball.'

Ex-baseball starlet Johnny Thunders reaches across Susanne and shakes a cigarette out of the pack from the bedside table. Keith Yon and Tony St Helene are crowded into the hotel room to watch some television. On the small screen, like some pompous psychedelic Buddah in shades, Todd Rundgren is talking about his astral artistic abilities. Thunders nods at the flickering image with calm distance.

'He produced one of my albums once ... what an asshole.'

T and Keith leave, and Johnny starts looking through various photographs for possible use in this book. 'Naaah ... I don't really like these, you know. It's really important to have some good pictures too. I mean, my idea of a good rock book is, like, eighty percent photos and twenty percent text. That's what I like, anyway. I tell ya, I got some good photographs back in New York. I'll bring you some.'

I ask Johnny if he's pleased with the video.

'Jesus. Ain't it borin'?'

Susanne protests that it isn't and points out that the guitarist's fans will like being able to buy an official, good-quality videotape and not have to pay exorbitant prices for a barely watchable print bootlegged from the States or Europe. Thunders, who had to redub some of his guitar and vocals for the video, is adamant. 'Nawwww. It's borin'.' He sprawls out on the bed and asks Susanne, 'Hey, we going to go round an' see Jerry tonight?'

Jerry Nolan is due to fly into London to headline a concert at the Fulham Greyhound the following week with The London Cowboys. The one-off concert has been advertised in the capital as a 'B.A.M.F. (Bad Assed Mother Fuckers) Clean Bill Of Health Gig'. But the drummer's luck is almost the equal of Thunders—mostly B.A.D.—and on the night of the concert it's left to one of the Cowboys to announce that Jerry has been arrested. Nolan had returned to Sweden on a brief visit and been stopped by the police at the airport. With his passport held over, the drummer has been unable to return to the UK in time for the concert.

Johnny finishes off a second packet of crisps and groans loudly.

'God. I'm so fuckin' hungry. You girls wanna go out an' get some Chinese food? I'm starvin' to death. Get me some shrimps in hot sauce ... and some sweets, huh?'

On our return, Thunders gets into bed with his shrimp dinner and starts talking about his favourite audiences:

The best audiences are in Sweden. I go down real big in Sweden, these days ... Japan was great, I really enjoyed it. The first gig was on this little Island called Kochi, off the mainland. I had such jetlag, I went right to bed. I woke up and the clock says it's twelve, you know, so I phone room service to order breakfast and they say, 'What?! It's midnight.' Great place, the kids really liked it. Even the press were okay. I can't wait to play there again.

Susanne remembers how they had returned home with about thirty kimonos as gifts for family and friends at Christmas. Johnny is watching a news programme on television, intensely. The reporter is talking about a Brazilian agency that sells babies to foreigners wealthy enough to afford them. He flicks the set off— 'fuckin' disgusting'—and falls almost instantly into a deep sleep.

Susanne shrugs. 'I doubt we'll make it over to Jerry's tonight.'

Later that evening, as I'm about to leave, Johnny wakes up and walks me to the door, offering some final advice on the book. 'Listen, make the end the beginning, something new. Whatever that is. I don't know.'

CHAPTER TWELVE

HURT ME MORE

I n Paris, the sun still slants between the spires of the old church atop the Rue Lepic but there is trouble in the city of poets. Despite an astute appreciation of art and artistes, the tourist-motivated Parisians have declared war on junkies. Henri-Paul goes out to buy cigarettes and is detained for looking the part of the enemy; Johnny is picked up by the police in Montmartre and beaten up. Understandably, the incident leaves him shaken and paranoid. The city that he's had some faith in suddenly becomes hostile.

The brutal police action also jeopardises plans for the guitarist to gradually detox, Christopher having located a young doctor to whom Johnny has responded well. It's not going to be an easy task: Thunders is sick and prone to terrible mood swings, but if he continues to use the outcome is bleak.

Johnny Nine-Lives on the eighth.

Several weeks later, Christopher, still disgusted by the needless setback, is hoping that perhaps the situation can be restored:

Without the intervention . . . it might have worked out but what has happened has happened. Even though the detoxification failed for now, at least Johnny attempted it. Maybe he will have learnt something else about himself again. Bit by bit he's gaining some inside information about himself and that might just turn out to be the most important factor of all. I hope so.

Christopher is much more of a friend to Thunders than a manager. They don't even have a contract. Trust is to be learned and earned. If Thunders understands that, the battle's half over. If he doesn't, then that Sword of Damocles may well be on a very thin thread, getting weaker by the moment.

* * *

March is fading with magnum grey skies over London. Thunders and band are in Tin Pan Alley Studios to work on a demo tape. I ask the engineer how it's going. His only answer is a good-natured grin and a roll of his eyes as if hoping for help from that great technocrat in the sky. The studio is a sixteen-track operation, now mostly used by pre-contract bands.

After a quick checking out of his new surroundings, Johnny positions the band in their places and the soundman, Hessu, behind the mixing desk. He begins the warm-up by picking out some morbid blues that echo Howlin' Wolf's 'Spoonful'.

Tony is just picking up on the beat when Johnny slaps a hand to his head and makes with a string of curses. Keith Yon looks up from his bass to ask, 'What's up, man?'

A suddenly animated Thunders spits out his cigarette and opts for sarcasm. 'Wrong? Oh, nothin' much. I just forgot the fuckin songbooks with the lyrics in. Shit . . .'

Johnny pushes some money in my hand. 'That should cover the cab.' Five minutes later, I'm heading back to the hotel to collect his lyric books from a forewarned Susanne. The object of the journey is a small, unlined notepad with a Japanese print cover. 'New Songs' is scrawled in large letters on the first page. Thunders' odd jottings turn up throughout, often with large blank spaces between them; a few one-liners on a single leaf, a title here and there. Sometimes the odd familiar phrase, like 'King Of The Gypsies', all carved in his strange, almost occult writing, with its phonetic spelling that is reminiscent of Marc Bolan's unique script.

Back at the studio, Johnny and Mike Monroe are on their knees searching for a block of dope they've dropped. Monroe at last locates it, and Johnny produces a pack of rolling papers. 'I'm gonna dedicate this joint to you.'

The engineer's voice comes over the studio intercom: 'Are we ready to roll yet?' The band attempt Jerry Nolan's 'Countdown Love', but the song doesn't quite come off with the power it should, and Thunders decides to take a break.

After a stale cheeseburger lunch, I take the opportunity for a few words with the bassman and drummer while Johnny tunes his guitar and goes over some lyrics.

I ask Keith Yon how he felt about working with Johnny.

It's a whole different world of music, like nothing I've ever been involved with. The audiences are different, obviously. I've been in quite a few bands but none that have ever done very big gigs or anything, apart from one band called The Tribesmen. That's where I met T. We've been playing together for about three years now. Since The Tribesmen, we've been playing in jazz bands and doing different sorts of things . . . some poetry stuff, totally different to what we're doing with Johnny. We get to travel a lot with him, that's an advantage. You couldn't say Johnny was ... easy ... to work with. You just have to accept his moods.

On the subject of travel, I ask Tony how he felt about playing Johnny's hometown.

New York? This is the first time I'll be working in the States. I've been as a tourist once, but this is something else. It's daunting because most of the musical standards are really high. It's sort of like bringing coals to Newcastle. But it should be okay, people come to see Johnny Thunders, you know. When we played France, I was really surprised just how big he is. They love the guy. He's very much the centre of what's happening. He has this aura that draws

people to him. Maybe it's his fatalistic attitude or something. Most
of the time it's great. Mind you, when we played in . . . I think it was
Berlin, someone threw a full can of beer which hit me. Perfect aim,
'cos I was right at the back of the stage. I wouldn't mind so much,
but when we were coming into Germany, the cops dragged me off
the train and strip-searched me.

Overall, I'm really happy working with Johnny. For me, it's
a brand-new perspective. Everybody's got different parts to their
characters that you don't always get a chance to use, you know?
People are more comfortable being what they are—what they think
they are—without endangering their environments. So sometimes
I think it's good to step into another world.

* * *

Johnny's health has shown little sign of improvement, and by the third day
in the studio a bad cold has also caught up with him. His eyes are hooded
and his skin the colour of a 1931 Hollywood vampire. The afternoon's
recording stops and starts around his coughing fits.

Over the months and years, Thunders has come to put a lot of faith
in Christopher Giercke's ability to sort out any business or personal
problems that follow the guitarist like a shadow, and when word gets to
the studio that his manager may not be joining them for their New York
homecoming, Thunders becomes morose and worried. It was Giercke
who pulled Johnny from the mire of the 'lost legend' gutter and has since
tried every way to make him understand that the first step of the artist
is to respect himself. Once that is done all that is left is the honing of
the gift and its presentation to a public that has, more so in London and
New York, almost always been prepared to recognise that a guitarist like
Thunders can only be counted out when someone ties a tag to his big toe.

Johnny is sitting in a chair in the middle of the floor, head bowed and
sombre in black; his boots are resting on his guitar case with the 'Cosa
Nostra' sticker across it.

Stiv Bators, small face almost hidden by an outsized pair of sunglasses, is waiting in the doorway to see what's going to happen next.

Mike Monroe stands just behind him, looking like a blank and beautiful Roger Vadim creation.

At last Thunders, the fragile devil in the flesh, gets to his feet and orders Monroe and Stiv to take their places behind the mic stands.

'One more time, guys, okay? Try for "Trash",' he requests, 'like th' old Dolls song.'

Johnny raises his arm like a demented choirmaster as they obediently reproduce the harmony backing. He lights another cigarette and winks.

'Boy. You guys really sound like th' alley cats, huh?'

Sometime later, with Johnny out of the studio on a periodical hunt for junk food, Henri-Paul, in a very dazed state, is wandering in circles, trying to get his guitar part right. Tony and Keith try and offer the young Frenchman advice, as does the soundman, but then Johnny wanders in, rubbing his hands together and asking, 'What's been happenin'? Anythin' exciting?'

Someone plays him the tape. Thunders starts to light a cigarette and stops, the match halfway to the end. He sounds out his words slowly to make the meaning threateningly clear:

'Henri. What th' fuck is that? Do you wanna rewrite it or somethin'?'

'No, Johnny.'

'Okay. Then maybe this time you'll go and play it the way I showed you yesterday?'

Henri-Paul staggers back into the sound booth.

Stiv Bators raises his sunglasses and seems surprised that the light has almost faded. The former frontman of The Dead Boys, currently in The Lords Of The New Church, Stiv has long regarded Johnny as an inspiration.

I met Johnny back in 1973 or something. The New York Dolls were playing in Cleveland, with KISS as their support, and I got to meet him after the gig. What I really liked about Johnny was his attitude, you know? He had this spark in his eyes . . . I'd never met anybody so smartass before. Everybody back then was so tame and here was this crazy, real cocky little guy picking fights with these gigantic bartenders. I wasn't really in a band then . . . it was like, you know when you get into a rut and nothing inspires you? That type of scene. And then the Dolls came along, and their record really fired me, made me wanna do something, you know? I was a real big fan of Johnny's, just through the papers, and he didn't let me down when I met him, the way a lot of people do when you get to meet them.

The Dolls had broken up before I'd managed to get a band together, and I guess the next time I met up with Johnny was maybe about 1975, he came back to Cleveland with The Heartbreakers: just Johnny and Jerry and Richard Hell. It was great because all the audience had turned up dressed as Dolls fans, and then Johnny walks out with a DA haircut!

We've known each other a while now. I even have his pink jacket that he wore on the sleeve of the second Dolls album. I traded him for a pair of snakeskin shoes. Johnny Thunders is very important. People should respect that. I mean, I never told him this 'cos he's big-headed enough, but a lot of the time, when you just seem to be spending your whole life slogging around bars and cheap dives, you need an inspiration, you need a dream or an image, and Johnny gave it. It was just his general attitude . . . nobody else was like him. I remember one time when Cindy Lang, Alice Cooper's girlfriend, had followed the band to Cleveland, and we were walking down the street, going from one bar to another, and she's running after him with her shoes coming off all the time . . . she had these stupid high heels . . . and she's shouting, 'Johnny. Johnny. Hey, Johnny, wait for me,' and he doesn't even turn around to look, you know; just says, like, 'Shut up, bitch.'

We don't see each other all the time, just sort of run into each other every so often. Before this, me helping out on these demos, I guess the last time I saw Johnny was in a bar in New York. He was attacking the drummer out of Tom Petty's Heartbreakers because they'd stole his name.

Johnny Thunders is a rare breed. A very rare breed.

* * *

The subject of the conversation sticks his head out of the recording studio and commands everyone to come in and listen to a playback of the embryo 'Crawfish.' Thunders is half satisfied and straps on his guitar for a brief moment of improvisation while chanting lyrics dealing with Mafia and murder. Mike Monroe attempts an accompaniment on harmonica while Stiv positions himself behind the drums. Keith Yon has almost decided on a suitable bass riff when Johnny stops and tells the impromptu band he wants to try a version of Marc Bolan's song 'The Wizard'.

Monroe raises his eyebrows and looks toward Keith Yon, who shakes his head, just as perplexed at Johnny's sometimes obscure musical tastes. Yon leaves the room, slightly nonplussed.

'Shit. I don't know what Johnny's playing half the time!'

The situation is resolved by the sudden arrival of Christopher, sweeping into the studio with a heavy black overcoat draped across his back and shoulders like a cape. He is briefed on events and proceedings and then ushers Thunders to one side for an impromptu business conference.

The last thin strands of daylight have long since vanished when Christopher Giercke sits down in the office. With the band finished and the technicians left for home, the studio takes on an antiseptic silence. Christopher looks out of the window at the changing neon jigsaw below, the only time of the day when London looks picturesque. He slowly unwraps a cigar, turns speculative eyes to the tape recorder, and sighs, more in thought of the scope of responsibilities than the prospect of recorded speech.

'You know,' he begins, 'the great task of any teacher is to eliminate himself from the situation. He must do it in such a way that he is always there from a spiritual point of view, in case he is needed, but something is lost if he is depended on too much.'

Do you think that perhaps the danger exists that you may be looking at the situation too sympathetically?

He raises a hand slightly and rotates it in that timeless gesture of equivocation:

I hope not. I don't think so. You see, over the past three or four years, my absences have been very deliberate. I want to build Johnny's self-confidence; make him realise he can take care of situations on his own without any help from me or anyone. Johnny wants me to fly out to New York with him, but I am going to join him at the end of the week instead, to see if he can do it alone. I am very seldom happy, but I feel almost happy now. After he plays New York, he'll rest up for a while, then the important thing is going after a record contract. We are going to have twenty-four copies of these demos made on Monday to send around. Everything must be done in stages.

He flicks ash from one black sleeve before continuing:

You cannot ignore Johnny's problems. Detoxification, or trying for it, has terrible emotional effects on him. It's time to stop. You cannot go on smashing in all the windows, threatening to throw guitars out of windows, getting beaten up by the police. It is more dangerous than ever now, with him living in Paris, as the police are on a campaign to clean Montmartre of junkies.

Everyone who uses these kind of drugs reacts to criticism in different ways. In The Heartbreakers, for instance, Jerry Nolan was the only one who could be honest about it. Jerry would say,

'I will do my job, and a good one, but I will still take heroin.' You have to respect that. He is honest about it, while Billy and Walter just lie, perhaps to themselves as much as anyone else. To deliver what is expected is not enough. Johnny has the responsibility not to present a fucked-up image to the world, it is very selfish.

There is a big difference in heroin addiction and having a good time. In fact, they have nothing in common at all. Liquor is the same kind of weird perversion, to drink until you fall over. I mean, Richard Burton and Peter O'Toole are great actors, but it's a similar kind of perversion in that everybody around them is made extremely unhappy to see it. They had a sense of accomplishment, as Lenny Bruce had, but it would be nice to keep it lighter. Much lighter. If there is a responsibility to be donated from them, it is to learn from their tragic downfall.

Christopher rises to leave the studio, then pauses.

'You know, it's not really a management's task at all. It's a friend's task to develop his responsibilities to those around him.'

* * *

New York is waiting, and Thunders and party are caught in that frustrating vortex of pre-travel chaos that always seems to descend at the last moment. It's just before eight in the morning and the floor is a maze of luggage and musical instruments. Johnny Thunders is dressed in a neat, black gangster suit with a narrow stripe running along the slender line of his frame. The hometown dates mean a lot to his personal prestige, and he wants to go back in style.

Downstairs the keys are returned to the desk and Johnny and Susanne join the others in the lobby. Christopher arrives and glances at his watch. The taxis ordered to take them to Heathrow are, of course, late. A phone call to the firm provides no satisfaction, and Giercke slams the receiver down with an aggressive curse. Everybody piles outside to try and wave down passing cabs. The Maida Vale air is shot through with thin shards of rain and no taxis are in sight. Thunders shivers forlornly and lights a cigarette. Everyone stands in a motionless group with their eyes fixed on the road. The whole scene is like a slowed-down sequence in a Peckinpah movie, before the violence and the soundtrack return.

Heathrow Airport is reached with only a few minutes to boarding time. The band line up at the departure gate with passports ready. At the counter, a blonde hostess gives Henri-Paul a crocodilian smile and tells him that his work permit has run out that morning.

Henri-Paul looks up at her with the wide-eyed disbelief of the perpetual unfortunate: 'What? It can't be . . . it's in order.' The hostess flashes a row of absurd dental work and continues, in her official monotone, 'I'm afraid you must have made a mistake.'

Christopher pushes Henri-Paul to one side and calmly plucks his documents from the woman's hand and glances at them quickly before tossing them back on the desk before her: 'You are the one who's made the mistake,' he snaps, 'check the dates.'

She is still forming a frustrated apology as Giercke guides Thunders and company through the gates and toward the plane.

PATTI PALLADIN INTERVIEW

NINA You and Johnny have similar backgrounds. What was it like growing up in New York?

PATTI To survive in that sort of environment, it's essential to develop your 'attitude' at a very early age. Although I grew up in Brooklyn and Johnny grew up in Queens, the similarity of our backgrounds is strong—the basic neighbourhood mentality. The neighbourhood was sliced into 'gang-governed territories'; my neighbourhood was more or less shared by the Phantom Lords and the Hell Burners. Jerry was a Young Lord. The letters D.L.A.M.F. ('Down Like A Mother Fucker') and D.T.K. ('Down To Kill') were as common as one-way signs. Yet STYLE, not violence, was the main motive; your main concern was really your profile. Mind you, there was a fair amount of bloodshed over who had more style—violence was merely the result of too much style and too much attitude. I can't erase all that, and I'm sure Johnny and Jerry can't either, but I also can't erase the fact that I've lived in London for the past ten years.

NINA You've known Johnny from way back; what do you make of his self-destructive edge and the kind of folklore that surrounds him?

PATTI There are moments when Johnny is absolutely definitive and every damaged cell is legend in its own right, but sometimes he is just sooo jive. He respects so little, he's a cunt, really—well he always tries it on. You gotta love him—you gotta hate him. He's got a lot to live up to, you know he always will. The Dolls were so fucking brilliant, it must create a constant pressure—plus, the obsession with his death plays such a major role in his career now, it seems his success is gauged by it. I suppose the value of his catalogue would soar. This could explain why so many major names appear to be brain dead! Johnny is the ultimate self-destruct hero, the sheer essence of what rock'n'roll is said to be. He always seems to be within arm's distance of an axe, even if he had to crawl to it, regardless of what state he's in, you can throw him a guitar and yell 'Jet Boy' and he'll play it ... well, he'll certainly have a go. If it's totally unrecognisable, he'll probably tell you: 'Something's wrong with your hearin'—I played fuckin' great tonight!'

He's had so many line-ups. Some have been flawless, some have been absolute shit. Yet to some degree the band is irrelevant, 'cos Johnny usually gives his audience what they came to get. For them, that's great, but for him, well, I don't know—it does get pretty brutal sometimes.

NINA I heard another bad rumour, that Johnny has pneumonia and is in hospital.

PATTI Yeah, someone told me something really awful. I didn't say anything to you because I don't like hearsay on Johnny at all. I get really annoyed when people come up to me and ask, 'Is Johnny really dead?' In fact, someone told me quite recently that he was in hospital in Paris and that he was paralysed on one side or something, but, as I said, it's grapevine bullshit. I never really listen to it—I usually wind up calling his sister to find out if anything really bad has happened to him.

NINA Johnny is in a strange position, really. I mean, he's made brilliant records that should have kept him at the top, but he's still in an unstable position.

PATTI He's made some superb records. If he was receiving royalties for inspiration—for the influence he's had on so many other musicians— he'd probably have to seriously dodge the taxman. The Dolls' albums, even with all the bad production shit, are brilliant. *L.A.M.F.* was great, too—once again, the content was so strong, bad production couldn't totally destroy it. *So Alone* was a real gem; 'You Can't Put Your Arms Around A Memory' is classic. It's a real shame—lack of know-how and commitment really anchored that record. Basically, bad deals, business or otherwise, blew it! His reputation, that's his main problem—his bad reputation. It keeps him in demand, it keeps him at the bottom—ridiculous, eh? It's really just all the social taboo about junk: it lingers, the big boys don't want to know, and it's much too intense. It's so illogical and irresponsible, they can't control it, and they just don't need the aggro. I can understand that. Basically, it's just too risky to command serious financial commitment. Johnny's reputation is so lousy, he'd probably have to stay spotlessly clean for a decade before anyone in charge of the purse-strings would believe him. It's unjust, really. He has calmed down considerably. I think, with a bit of serious interest, he'd probably deliver. I'd love to see him get the recognition he deserves.

NINA What do you think about Christopher Giercke and his relationship with Johnny?

PATTI Ah yes, 'darling Christopher'—a most peculiar creature. It's a bit incongruous, really. He's articulate, well read, well dressed, etc, so why manage Johnny? Curious fascination? For art's sake? Maybe a deep-rooted Marty Thau fixation … why manage anyone? Perhaps it's a need to control—I don't know. Christopher is quite an intricate character; he's got a great sense of drama. He loves a good crisis; he really is quite amusing. It may seem strange, but I do think that respect is a very important issue to Johnny, he has little regard for most things beyond his own existence. Yet if he respects something, he protects it, it's typically Italian really. Christopher is German—fire and ice. I think they both enjoy the game, they both enjoy the power, the struggle.

NINA You've collaborated on a lot of stuff. What's he like to work with?

PATTI Working with Johnny seems such a natural thing to do … besides, it's the only real chance I ever to play 'the cocky dumb bitch from Brooklyn'. I suppose it's obvious, really. I couldn't think of playing that role for anyone else: Johnny genuinely does in many ways see women as dumb bitches. He's playing that Stanley Kowalski role, and he needs someone to play it against. I can't think of anyone else in London who could do it better, can you?

CHAPTER THIRTEEN

QUE SERA, SERA

The well-publicised Thunders luck doesn't desert him. Arriving back in New York just far enough in advance of the dates to contract a voice-annihilating throat infection, the guitarist is still well received throughout a four-night stand at the Irving Plaza. During the course of the concerts, he welcomes onstage guests Walter Lure, Sylvain Sylvain, David Johansen, with even the reclusive Arthur Kane climbing up alongside Johnny long enough to show New York that he is still breathing after all. A little while later, Thunders mentions that some of the difficulties he encountered aren't entirely related to his throat condition: 'I dunno . . . I went to New York to conquer it . . . I fucked up. I really fucked it up. Next time, eh . . .'

The disappointment of NY fades to an almost insignificant memory by comparison with his next move. Having promised to attempt another detox, Susanne and Johnny take a flight to Stockholm. Brooding on the various setbacks that have afflicted his return to Gotham—a cancelled opening spot with Dr John, his voice going, the financial losses of the concerts—Thunders finds solace in a bottle of Valium tens during the long journey. While the tiny blue tranquillisers once prescribed to harassed housewives may appear innocuous, when taken in excess the consequences are far from sedate. Through an anaesthetised veil—nerves frayed to a hair trigger; speech slurred but not enough to disguise the insults—Johnny is rude to his girlfriend's family, who have agreed to pick them up at the airport. After spending the night at Susanne's mother's place, he is moved to a hotel. Reacting to Thunders' drug-induced attitude, Susanne terminates the relationship.

Christopher Giercke, still in his Paris base, is informed of the guitarist's movements but decides to stay in the shadows for a while, to see if Thunders can manage to 'plan things—to see if he can fall on his own two feet. To keep giving Johnny support is perhaps the worst thing I could do for him right now . . . for that reason, I think he should try and make out alone for a time.'

Confused and in a bad state of chemical depression, Thunders doesn't take the time to analyse Christopher's actions, which he regards as a form of betrayal, and resorts to the tested analgesic of releasing his hurt in accusations. With an almost paternal detachment, Giercke remains immune to any barbs, and Thunders finds himself really so alone.

* * *

Early May. Johnny drifts back to London, briefly residing at Stiv Bator's empty apartment before moving on to Patti Palladin's sumptuous hideaway. Hidden amid the dishevelled grandeur of Patti's mock baroque living room, he waves away her dog, which has been sprawled across his legs, to search for some cigarette papers.

'I dunno how she finds anything in all this stuff . . .'

Some minutes later, he pulls them out from under the mound of blankets he's been sleeping on. Judging by his unusually dishevelled appearance, it is obvious that Thunders is unhappy, and the effort he is making is forced by pride rather than self-belief. Taking a small plastic bag from one of the two suitcases that are pushed into the corner, he spills the contents onto the mattress. Fanning the various scraps of paper and phone numbers around like a card-sharp, he locates an age-yellowed photograph of a very attractive young Latin kid with heavy black hair holding a large, carefully posed book before him. Johnny remembered my request and has brought it back from his mother's home in New York.

I ask him how old he was then, and he tells me eleven or twelve.

Brushing the ash from a joint across the front of his light blue shirt, he slowly falls asleep.

Leaving a trail of smashed-up apartments, broken glass, and burned spoons in his wake, Thunders swings between London and France, leaving Christopher to concede that he 'isn't ready yet to start working too closely with anyone'. For a short while he stays in an apartment block near Hyde Park, but without a telephone in his room or change for the payphone he can't call up Chief, the man he will eventually elect as road manager/personal assistant.

A burly six-foot veteran of the London rock'n'roll circuit, Chief has quickly discovered that 'taking care of business' also involves the guitarist moving into his cramped flat for a spell—a less than easy domestic situation in which to set up a series of dates.

Their relationship began in a period of confused adjustment to one another and, even though eventually the situation appears to even out, it will never mature beyond a short-lived and tenuous association. Chief makes the arrangements; Thunders plays his own games. No one can compensate for Christopher Giercke.

Despite an initial run of gigs being blighted by cancellations and postponements, mainly due to work-permits not being sorted out in time, Johnny has seemingly gained strength from the previous month's slide, and a fragile stability is maintained. By the time Cosa Nostra reach Manchester on July 4, the concerts had fallen into a more regular pattern. Although Johnny promises something special to celebrate American Independence Day at the Hacienda, by the evening he's forgotten the date.

The following morning, the band drive back to London, Thunders deciding en route that they should stop off in Hammersmith to check out the venue of that night's gig, the Clarendon Ballroom. Casting a weary eye over the empty hall, the guitarist leaves the talking to Chief, who tells a member of the Clarendon's road crew that they'll do their soundcheck after the two support bands, Bone Orchard and Chelsea, have finished theirs.

Thunders returns to the venue in the early evening, wearing a billowing mosaic-print blouse, Chinese slippers, and a faint scowl. In the main dressing room, he learns that Cosa Nostra's equipment has been buried under Chelsea's, making it difficult to dig out in time for the soundcheck. Although he has little interest in the dull quandary, Johnny is instantly surrounded by the Clarendon's roadies, bitching about the necessity of doing the check. Gene October, Chelsea's frontman, adds his comments and receives for his trouble a steely glance from Thunders on his way out and a poisonously adamant refusal to share the dressing room with them.

By night-time, the venue's tiny spare equipment room is heavy with a thick, grey net of herbal smoke. There are no lighting facilities, and, as none of the paint-stained ancient windows will open, T is just about to ram a fist through one for some fresh air when Johnny arrives and motions the band to follow him.

Cosa Nostra wind they way through the tightly packed audience and climb up onstage. The theme from *The Man With The Golden Arm* comes screaming out from the speakers to signify the start of the gig. Bouncers crouch on their heels stage-side, muscular ball boys ready to fling any unwelcome trespassers back in the field, but this evening's trouble comes from more technical sources when, halfway through the set, the power cuts out. T maintains a steady beat until it's clear that the problem is going to hold out longer than Thunders' limited enthusiasm with the hecklers. He leads the band back once electricity is restored and they finish the set. Not a classic performance, but under the circumstances . . .

Costa Nostra go on to play the Marquee on Johnny's birthday before briefly parting company. After making an appearance at Dingwalls' 'alternative' Live Aid show, Thunders travels to Canada for what should have been a solo acoustic tour: instead, he teams up with two guitarists from the Canadian band Teenage Head and uses Chief on drums. And then it's back to London's West 3 Studios, to commence working on an album with a suitably serendipitous title: *Que Sera, Sera.*

* * *

Sitting around a small black-and-white television while picking at the remnants of lunch from the local fast-food takeaway, Johnny, Tony, and Keith have called another halt to the recording session's progress. The pace is as best leisurely, and afternoon TV provides Thunders with a welcome distraction.

'Hey! *The Streets Of San Francisco*. Ahh... I seen this one before. I been to North Beach, you know. The place is full of whores an' guys in purple an' yellow striped suits.'

Thunders is at West 3 to record his first studio electric album since *So Alone*, seven years earlier. Rather than position the band in their individual partitions in the studio and work systematically through the songs, Johnny periodically picks up his concentration from where he last threw it, straps on a guitar, and commits his music to tape in short bursts. Later, they listen to a replay of the backing track for 'Endless Party', and everyone is mildly pleased. Thunders slowly puts a match to a cigarette:

It's supposed to speed up a bit toward the end... okay... leave it for a bit. Let's try 'Short Lives'.

'Short Lives' (a song paradoxically close to most people's expectations of the composer himself) takes up the majority of the afternoon. By teatime, Cosa Nostra are back in front of the television but watching Johnny instead as he tries to roll a joint, the contents of which keep spilling onto the floor.

'Rizla Orange, man,' he gripes. 'Fuckin' disgusting. Like goddamned school paper or somethin'.'

Johnny looks up and sees the tape recorder, then nods toward T.

'He wants to say it's the best thing in the world to play with a white musician, it's the best thing in the world...'

Peering over the peeling papers in Johnny's lap, T laughs.

'You should have a chapter called *Johnny The Spliff Vampire*, you know...'

Johnny leans right into the tape recorder:

THUNDERS Keith and T are both scumbags.

T We're learning from the greatest scumbag of all.

YON We're serving our apprenticeship in scumbaggery.

THUNDERS You got to be a scumbag for six months to play in my band. Then I accept you. T's time is nearly up, but Chief's gotta long way to go. Lotta dues to pay . . . you'll thank me for this one day.

As the weeks pass, the album begins to pull together, with various friends dropping by the studio to lend a hand, including Patti Palladin, Wilko Johnson, Stiv Bators, and the legendary Only Ones guitarist John Perry. In effect, Thunders is attempting to return to the ensemble ethic of *So Alone*.

Despite *Que Sera, Sera* being the most controversial of Thunders' albums to date, his regular supporters either loving it or hating it, the album offers the most current view of his music on offer. But not the most realistic. The songs carry the familiar topics with the same sneering 'fuck you' intonations, but the guitar is either too low or even occasionally filled in by one of the guests.

* * *

With *Que Sera, Sera* completed and a major tour in the offing, Thunders flies out to Stockholm to see if he can repair his relationship with Susanne, who he is missing a great deal. Not long after his arrival, fate throws yet another punch at the star-crossed guitarist when someone is supposed to have slammed a car door on his left hand, fracturing it and leaving him unable to play for several weeks. The American tour is put back and a copy of the doctor's certificate sent out to the understandably suspicious promoters.

Talking to Thunders on the telephone in Sweden, he sounds healthy and in good spirits, despite the 'accident', and looking forward to taking off on a short European tour with Cosa Nostra, which will commence without any further incidents. They open in Holland before crossing over to Sweden and Finland, finishing in time for Christmas, when Thunders once again returns to Stockholm.

In February, the Johnny Thunders US Tour '86 goes ahead without any further delays. The extensive seven-week itinerary of club dates successfully fulfils the anticipation of both audience and press as Thunders meets head on the rumours and reputation that his very stance generated. Cosa Nostra are tight and J.T. is at a performing peak (unlike his previous stateside jaunt), but the customary chaos is also a part of the legacy.

Three dates into the tour, in Boston, Chief calls it quits, failing to complete his apprenticeship in scumbaggery. Half-mad from lack of sleep and the rigours of working with Thunders, he devises his own redundancy payment in lieu of what he perceives to be his rightful earnings and makes a shaky exit in the dead of night.

The curse of the dead presidents (US currency) tails the tour back to New York, where Keith and T accuse Johnny and Chief's successor, Stephen Hoda, of pilfering the band's funds. Incensed, they throw Thunders' clothes out of the window of the Chelsea Hotel. Fortunately, he isn't wearing them at the time.

With the echo of their parting threats still ringing in his ears, the guitarist leaves the maelstrom for the sanctity of Stockholm. After a couple of weeks' rest and recuperation, he resurfaces in London in early May, ostensibly to work alongside Jerry Nolan on an album by Japanese rockabilly guitarist Jimmy K. The project—coordinated by Thunders' old friend Marc Zermati, head honcho of Skydog Records, and Japan's premier rock journalist, Gaku Torii—has prompted a ceasefire between Nolan and Thunders. Despite all of the exacting interludes, rock'n'roll's answer to Bonnie and Clyde work best against the world rather than each other.

Young Jimmy K has high hopes that their credentials will rub off on him, but that isn't the kind of thing money can buy, even with substantial record company funding. With Johnny in the producer's seat and Jerry taking care of the drums, however, the opening stages of recording look promising.

Between takes of the album, *Trouble Traveller*, Jerry is happy enough to comment on his long and often volatile relationship with Johnny.

Listen, if I had it my way—and Johnny, too, I think had it way down deep in his heart—we would always have played together, but certain things happened where we had to separate for a while, which is too bad, because we sure do work well together. We bring the best out of each other. Even socially, friendship-wise, we bring a lot of good out of each other, as well. Sometimes we bring bad out of each other too, but musically, we're really good for each other. It's more than just playing, it's creating.

With Nolan's wife Charlotte acting as business administrator, Jerry and Johnny have planned a fifty-fifty partnership, recruiting a new band that consists of former Sex Pistol Glen Matlock on bass and Barry Jones from The London Cowboys on guitar. An inaugural gig at Dingwalls is pencilled in for May 13 with second guitarist Matt Kellett, while Jimmy K has been promised a cue at the encore.

A relative newcomer to the trauma team but nonetheless dedicated, Gaku Torii likes to hand out a business card that simply states 'Rock Is My Life'—a risky motto in the circumstances. Gaku:

I stayed with Johnny and Jerry in a flat in Baker Street. It was absolute fucking hell. At the beginning of the recording sessions, Johnny was okay, but he was getting stoned in between. The record company began to get nervous, and I ended up acting as middleman. In the end, Johnny produced the A-side of the album. One day, Johnny and Jerry had a big fight in the studio, Johnny started telling Jerry what to do with the drums. Suddenly, Jerry blew up: 'Motherfucker—you don't know anything about drums!' Another day, Jerry hit Johnny with a wine bottle. Johnny was crying like a child, telling Marc Zermati he wanted to go back to Sweden immediately, but there was a show to play at Dingwalls.

Aside from all the ongoing strife, Thunders is edgy about Keith and T, who have made it known that they would be at the venue. Holed up at the bar, it becomes clear that they don't really intend to harm the guitarist, just freak him out a little, and their tactics work. Johnny is so sloppy onstage he's nearly seasick, and he manages to forget about Jimmy K, who is waiting in the wings.

After the gig, Thunders asks me for my critical reaction, to which I respond, with some trepidation, 'Ohh ... it was horrible!'

While such a response might well have offended many artists, Johnny finds it highly amusing, and it breaks the tension of the night. But it is to be a short-lived respite, according to Gaku:

At the Dingwalls show I was waiting with Jimmy K, because he was supposed to join Johnny onstage for a couple of numbers, but Johnny was stoned and forgot about it. Later, Johnny vanished for the night, but the rest of us went back to Baker Street. When we got there, Matt started complaining about something. Jerry said, 'Fuck you, don't talk about Johnny like that,' and hit him with a big flowerpot. His head was bloody, and the neighbour wanted to call the police. The whole thing was a bad experience, but I understood that this was rock'n'roll.

Despite Jerry's earnest torment when it comes to his relationship with Johnny, he holds no truck with outside grievances from short-stay passengers, whatever the circumstances. The broken pottery and scattered soil from the ruined flowerpot will remain on the floor of the apartment, along with other accrued debris and damages, until the party check out, leaving the chambermaids to nod their heads in disbelief when they finally gain access to the hotel suite.

After briefly touching base in Sweden, Thunders and company fly to Tokyo, where they play to enthusiastic audiences of more than four and a half thousand people in just four gigs. In spite of all the terrible capers that punctuate Johnny's life (and the chemical instabilities), there is no one better on a good night, and in that electrifying moment the slate is wiped clean, the bad gigs forgotten.

Although Gaku was driven to distraction in London, he is more than pleased to hook up with Thunders on his home turf. While Johnny continually tests the limits of all around him, he possesses the ability to be uniquely endearing due to a genuine vulnerability. How one survives is up to the individual. Gaku:

> Johnny came back to Japan with Jerry and Barry Jones and Glen Matlock. He was very well, and the shows were great. He also played a big hall in front of three thousand people for television. The promoter of the event had been made an offer by some Japanese musicians who wanted to back Johnny, so he booked a studio, but Johnny didn't want to rehearse—he said the musicians knew his songs. The promoter, who was very straight, got really wound up about it.
>
> Johnny did have to do a soundcheck at the venue, but he didn't like the sound of the amp. The promoter had ordered a vintage Marshall that Johnny had already used at one of the gigs but before the television show, his mood changed, and we started running out of time. I told the promoter to take the amplifier away, then I went to see Johnny in the dressing room . . . 'Okay, we'll find a replacement amp.' We just brought the same one back.
>
> Then the promoter wanted to know which guitar Johnny was going to use. Johnny said the Les Paul Junior, which was like his arms and fingers. However, later that day, he was given five or six guitars by a guitar company, including a red Stratocaster. Just before the show, he changed into one of his pink suits and was looking at himself in the dressing room mirror when he gets the thought, *Pink suit, red Stratocaster, good for TV!* but he was on in ten minutes, and the red guitar was back at the hotel. He turned round and asked the promoter where it was. You should have seen the guy's face!

The band continue to tour through the autumn, though a two-week stint in Australia is marred when the bus rolls over. Once the dust has settled, Johnny is the first to scramble out, but Jerry has broken his collarbone and has to take an unusually gentle approach to his drumming for the duration of the dates.

In early November they head for Spain with a new tour manager in tow. Going from working with The London Cowboys to taking care of Johnny is an easy progression but not an easy task, as Mick Webster discovers:

Jerry introduced me to Johnny, and the first tour I did was in Spain, with Glen Matlock, Nolan, and Barry Jones. After that, on January 1, 1987, we went to the States. Johnny and Jerry had equal billing, and Arthur Kane and Barry Jones were in the line-up. That was a good tour, from one side of the country to the other, right down to Miami.

My job couldn't be classed as an ordinary tour manager—I was on twenty-four hours a day. When Johnny was awake, I was awake; when he needed to go somewhere, I had to be with him. Some of the places we went to, you wouldn't want to visit in your nightmares, they were so bad, but I had to get him back safely so he could do a show. He walked a very thin line. It wasn't my job to judge him. It was my job to look after him.

When I first started working with him, he told me I could never stop him doing what he did. Someone once tried, and he turned it around on them—they were doing what he did inside of five days.

Sometimes it was difficult to get him onstage. He'd be in the dressing room enjoying himself. He always made the audience wait until it was right to go on. The promoters would be creating havoc, but Johnny knew how to time it. The audience would be keyed up and ready for him; it seemed to be like a part of the show. The guys who had booked the gigs would inundate us with calls at the hotel, especially in America. They would worry, and things would get blown out of all proportion.

We had a lot of problems getting work—we were always being accused of cancelling dates, but the only dates that were ever cancelled were scrapped because either it was impossible geographically or somebody would book a gig and we hadn't been told about it. Some promoter would say that Johnny was playing and then collect the money on the tickets—that happened a lot. There was always this 'is he going to show up?' routine, but it was pure nonsense.

* * *

As tapes filtering back from the two-week US tour testify, the band are hotter than molten lava, Nolan clearing a steady path for Thunders' cascading chords, Kane and Jones creating a perfect balance. Although the majority of the gigs stick to fairly familiar material—'Pipeline', 'Blame It On Mom', 'Dead Or Alive', et al—and a midway acoustic break, the sheer force of performance is truly exhilarating, breathing new life into a bunch of oft-paraded numbers. Unfortunately, the truce between Johnny and Jerry has broken by the end of the dates, money matters and concerns over a possible album souring the pitch.

Thunders arrives back in London, minus Nolan, on February 15, primarily to work on a single version of 'Short Lives' at Matrix studios. Somehow, however, J.T. and the recording process just don't get on well. Being placed under pressure to deliver is an edgy business for the guitarist, and he often prefers to goof off rather than just get down to it, finding distraction after distraction, like a magician producing a million multicoloured handkerchiefs from a top hat.

On February 19, Thunders enters Remaximum studios with Patti Palladin, Glen Matlock, and J.C. Carroll (on mandolin) to cut a cover of 'Que Sera, Sera' as a late accompaniment to the album. Despite it being an afterthought, the results are fetching if a little off the wall, Thunders adding his own touches to the song that Doris Day made famous.

When I was just a little brat
I asked my teacher, what will I be
Will I be a mess?
Will I have success?
Here's what she said to me . . .

While the single is in production, the immediate future snaps into focus when Thunders and Palladin begin to consider the logistics of making an entire album of covers as a dual venture. Likewise, Jungle Records have worked out the logistics of paying for such a project. Alan Hauser: 'They negotiated with us to spend £20,000 on the album, which was a reasonable price. Out of that they took a personal advance of £12,000. Two thirds of that went to Johnny which only left £8,000 for the studio but they thought that was sufficient.'

A hit list is drawn up consisting of songs that were once the signature tunes of artistes as diverse as Judy Garland, Mitch Ryder, and Otis Redding, but this initial selection is eventually superseded by choice cuts from The Seeds, Roy Head, Natalie Wood, The Shangri-Las, and Dion, among others. However, the project is held in abeyance when Johnny returns to Paris to resume filming at the request of director Patrick Grandperret, who has finally managed to find new backers for his movie. Although Grandperret's film would took even longer to make than the entire Godfather trilogy, the director is tenacious and keen to get rolling after the considerable delay. Numerous plot and title alterations, from *Go Back To Go* to *Personality Crisis*, are eventually ditched in favour of *Simple Simon*—the story of a fan and his relationship with Johnny—but as the storyline develops, the film takes a different turn, metamorphosing into its final evolution, *Mona et moi*. Grandperret:

The film took up five years of my life but just four and a half weeks to shoot. *Simple Simon* was a little like *Sid & Nancy*, but as I got to know Johnny, I wanted a lighter dope angle with more humour. Johnny did not have a big part in *Mona et moi* but his role is very important. He was very easy to work with; he didn't like to compromise but there were no problems because we were in agreement with most of the ideas. I would direct from sequence to sequence, the actors would make up their dialogue; we would rehearse, then shoot. After *Mona*, Johnny wanted to make a film about the life of his manager, Christopher—that was his idea. He wanted to play Christopher and direct. We would have to find someone to play Johnny, but I'm sure he would have made a great director. He was visual and had very expressive taste.

After filming the additional sequences for Grandperret's movie alongside a young cast that includes rising star Denis Lavant, Johnny returns to London to warm up for the covers album. The finer details are still up in the air, save for the title *Copy Cats*—part playground refrain and a distant echo of a 1962 Gary US Bond tune. Later, Thunders would tell an American reporter from *Records* magazine, 'It's a project I always wanted to do ever since I heard the John Lennon album *Rock 'n' Roll.*' However, recreating the jukebox of Thunders and Palladin's childhood, the tunes that tumbled out of clubs that were still adult territory, the music that came from behind the door of a sister's bedroom, the whole formica-topped, milkshake flavoured, tear stained, hip-shaking, heartbreaking concept is a multifaceted project rather than a basic rock album.

Rehearsals begin with the core of players from the 'Que Sera, Sera' single session, but it swiftly becomes apparent that an album with such a vast sweep of styles requires an orchestrated approach. Eventually, an impressive roll call of twenty-eighty musicians would contribute to the album, but first they must be mobilised. Thunders sends out signals to Nolan, but the drummer has stayed in Sweden.

Meanwhile, nobody seems to know where to find guitar supremo John Perry. Eventually, Patti Palladin manages to track down a Spanish telephone number, and Alan Hauser calls the Catalan coast. Perry, a seasoned veteran of such calls, well used to 'urgent' Thunders demands, doesn't break his holiday but returns at the end of the month. By the time the former Only One makes his entrance, the sessions, already underway at Falconer studios in Camden, seem to be going nowhere:

> When I arrived, I found an unusually despondent Johnny sitting on the steps, well away from the studio, with his head in his hands, disjointed snippets of music drifting down the corridor. The sound of nothing happening. John leapt to his feet, flung out his arms, hugged me, and asked, 'Fuckyabinman?' Never seen him so animated. Once inside, it was pretty clear that the sessions had been drifting for weeks—though nothing prepared you for actually *hearing* the tapes! Began to see why John had been so pleased to see me.
>
> Remember, *Copy Cats* is an album of covers, and if you intend to cover a song, it helps to know the changes. Of course, John could blag his way through any song and come up with something kinda presentable—or at least, something that sounded like *him*—but the method was useless for a band. Two guitars, bass, keyboards all playing different chord progressions . . .
>
> So, the first thing was to jot down some charts, note the chords and mark where the accents fell. Far as I could tell they'd been working for a fortnight, but nobody was willing to play bandleader . . . least of all John, who just wanted to be Dion anyway. What did we do? I think we scrapped the lot and started again from scratch. New band, new tapes. Quicker to lay down new tracks than patch up old ones. Sessions were fun from there on though John was getting a bit scattered. Used to vanish, then we'd get urgent, whispered messages from callboxes saying the CIA were following him— mortal danger—Alan *had* to send over fifty quid in a cab *now*! Hard to see exactly how the latter would solve the former . . .

* * *

Despite the support of his fellow musicians, Thunders has entered an emotional vortex. Any stay in the same place for too long is always dangerous, and, in London, mounting cocaine psychosis overtakes him. Alone at night he unravels, the shadows assuming demonic proportions, while his worst fears manifest when he imagines that he had been arrested and has had to turn himself in for an early morning court appearance. Fortunately, he oversleeps and wakes up a free man.

While Patti Palladin continues to supervise *Copy Cats*, Johnny flies to Stockholm on June 8 to be with Susanne, who is some seven months pregnant. As the summer burns up, so does Thunders' throat. When he returns to put his vocals on the album, recording is briefly halted until the mystery affliction that has periodically affected his singing has cleared.

Reaching the dimensions of a Phil Spector production, the *Copy Cats* cast list has now expanded to include a horn section, castanet player Maribel La Manchega, and Chrissie Hynde, whose backing vocals grace Patti's tender rendition of The Shirelles' classic 'Baby It's You'.

Back in Sweden, Johnny is having to deal with his own version of the same theme as he looks into the eyes of his newborn daughter, Jamie, for the first time. Jungle, meanwhile, have been holding crisis talks over the album's rising budget.

For most of the autumn, Thunders stays close to home, aside from a sojourn to Paris for two shows at the Gibus. With Patti Palladin at the helm, *Copy Cats* enters the mixing stages, just as this biography goes off to the printers.

IN COLD BLOOD

PART THREE

BORN TO CRY

CHAPTER FOURTEEN

FATE AND FATALITY

On November 10, 1987, the first edition of *In Cold Blood* was launched in a converted church. The (London) Limelight had a full congregation as Johnny performed a twenty-minute acoustic set to mark the occasion. Afterwards he pulled me into a smoky corner of the former joss house to show me some snapshots of Susanne and Jamie. He was happy. Such a simple statement—I wish I could have used it to describe him more often. He glowed with a poppa's pride and, whatever the downside of the guitarist's history, in theory he possessed traditional morals and was already fretting about Jamie's first date. With some concern he detailed how he was going to shadow the courting couple from a distance, just to be sure that his daughter was safe.

I signed off with a cautious optimism and an awareness of the fragility of such sentiments when it came to Johnny Thunders. Wishing him all the luck in the world was the best that I could do.

* * *

In the final descent of Johnny Thunders' life, he tried to pull back from the tailspin, make some changes, but the ground was coming up too fast to meet him. Despite or perhaps because of the positive press interest in the forthcoming release of *Copy Cats*, Thunders played a truly disastrous gig at the Town & Country club on December 2, 1987. Accompanied by drummer Chris Musto, bassist Adam Pierson (ex-Red Lorry Yellow Lorry), and Michael Thimren, the gig was a watershed in terms of Thunders' ability to self-sabotage. Even Carol Clerk, who had always championed J.T., turned in a concerned review for *Melody Maker*, stating, 'I've seen Thunders clean, on form and brilliant, I've seen him stoned and absolutely bloody awful, but I've never seen him like this, so listless, so tedious, so depressing.'

Once again, Johnny Thunders had fallen prey to 'big gig syndrome'—a tendency to sabotage key events. However, in drummer Chris Musto, the guitarist would find stalwart support. Musto had been introduced to Thunders via Marc Zermati and Patti Palladin, and being of an amiable disposition he developed a protective streak toward the guitarist:

> The third show we played together was at the Town & Country club, and it was a disaster. Poor old Johnny, he got in a real pickle. It was my first experience of the 'London Syndrome'. The day before the gig, Johnny decided to start losing his voice—it was an obsessive thing. At that stage he had a blank about London, as he did about New York, Los Angeles, and Paris—most of the major cities. He knew he was going to be criticised because he was Johnny. His defence mechanism would go into overdrive, and he'd end up in a mess. The emotional mess would start a day or two before, then just speed up. Then there was the so-called 'fans', the kind of people who would offer him a line of coke, thinking that they were being cool, but with Johnny's chemical makeup it would turn into a psychosis. It was the worst thing for him. He would become a monster, especially under pressure.
>
> After two vitamin B12 injections, we got him on to the stage of the Town & Country club, and for the first couple of numbers I felt confident, but then it just became shambolic. It was awful. Johnny was out there and he was an absolute mess, although he still looked great. He always had attitude. After the show, he realised what he'd done; the people who ran the club were appalled, and he'd never be able to play there again. He'd effectively blown the major London venue circuit, and I nearly left.

The debacle at the T&C, Johnny stumbling sightlessly in a self-induced delirium, was something of a career nadir. Although he was unable to reverse the insecurities that clawed away at his personal life, he began to make changes, musically at least, which were eventually unveiled by the summer of 1988. Tired of the inconsistencies of pick-up bands and in-fighting with older amigos, Thunders recruited a group of relatively fresh-faced musicians. With only one troublemaker in the ranks—Johnny himself—he could be sure of a more stable environment.

Retaining Musto, Thunders next discovered nineteen-year-old guitarist Stevie Klasson playing at a biker party in Stockholm. Stevie:

> After the show, Johnny came over. He wanted to know how I'd ended up in the band, and then he tried to trade me for my leather jacket. I invited him to this club I was running called the Pipeline, and we ended up jamming until the early hours of the morning.
>
> Two weeks later, he came back and we played some more. He gave me his phone number and suggested that we get together. He hardly knew anyone in Sweden; he was mainly looking after Jamie while Susanne was working.
>
> About a week later he showed up at the club again, and asked me if I wanted to go on the road with him. Two days after that, he phoned me for my passport number.

As far as the new line-up went, the only problem was the geographical distance between the musicians. With the musicians based variously in London, Stockholm, and New York, group gatherings became a complex and costly manoeuvre, yet Johnny persevered. Back in '78, Thunders had talked about putting together a 'revue'-style band; now the moment had arrived. While Johnny in his post-*So Alone* reveries had wanted three 'chick' singers, Stephen Hoda's girlfriend Alison Gordy, a theatrical blonde bombshell in the Ursula Andress mode, more than made up for the shortfall in numbers. Alison:

My boyfriend introduced us. We were round at a friend's house, Patti Palladin was there as well, and she was playing tapes of the *Copy Cats* album. I picked up a guitar and started singing, then Johnny came over to see if we could do a duet and we sang a couple of things. One tune that stuck out was what turned into 'Birdsong'. I said, 'That's great, you should finish it.' He was like, 'I'm working with it but I'm not sure what I'm going to do with it.' Then he played an alternative version, which was a love song ['Some Hearts']. He came back to New York in the early summer that was the second time we met up. We were in a cab and he said, 'You want to put something together?' He had a gig coming up at the Limelight. He asked if I knew anybody else that could sing, and I told him that my friend Jill [Wisoff] could sing and play bass.

The NY contingent of Thunders' new band was rounded off by the addition of a convivial sax player named Jamey Heath, who joined Alison Gordy and Jill Wisoff onstage at the Limelight on July 24, 1988, alongside drummer Jeff West and bassist Tony Coiro, who frequently backed the guitarist in his home town.

In time, Heath, the clean-living antithesis of the stoned saxophonist of jazz lore, traded sides, falling under the deadly spell that occasionally consumed people in Johnny's orbit, but it was an independent process. From a distance, demoralisation may be seen as a (perverse) form of seduction, but Johnny Thunders was the most poignant anti-drugs statement that ever there was. Stevie Klasson, in particular, became aware of Thunders' later stance on drugs: 'Do as I say, not as I do':

He was always lecturing me about drugs because he knew that was why things hadn't always gone the way he wanted them to. One time, we were on tour and we got a little too drunk and wanted to get something to put up our noses to wake us up, so we went to this place but they didn't have the right thing, they only had heroin. I said, 'Let's get some of that.' He smacked me in the face as hard as he could, I hit the floor. For a month he lectured me every day about it.

Johnny was fond of saying he was an entertainer, which downplays his musicianship. However, the new band—christened The Oddballs after Thunders jokingly used the phrase to describe them to a journalist— afforded him the opportunity of a more mature approach. After all, the old way had been killing him in public. Neatly sidestepping the quandaries of grown-up rock'n'roll, Thunders remained an alluring and exciting performer. The occasional inclination to play around with his vocal range became more pronounced, as *Copy Cats* attests, while his songwriting grew increasingly contemplative.

Everyone looks for clues, the veiled prophecy in the doomed artiste's last repertoire, but Johnny's is more telling than most. Aside from personal concerns, be they the open letter to the music press that is 'Critics Choice' (aka 'I Tell The Truth Even When I'm Lying'), the hurt bravado behind 'Disappointed In You', or the betrayal that infuses 'It's Not What You Say', Johnny began to address subjects outside of his usual remit such as 'Children Are People Too', 'In God's Name' (co-written with Patti Palladin), and the superb 'Help The Homeless'. The humanity that he had tried to anaesthetize with drugs—that he so convincingly submerged as an all-seasons reprobate—surfaced gasping for breath, especially on 'Society Makes Me Sad', which brings the heart to its knees. But could he get a major deal on the strength of the material? Could John The Baptist have kept his head? Naaah, behind the glass towers of the record corporations where an outlaw is the ex-wife's mother, no one was about to reprieve the condemned man of rock'n'roll. Still, he lived in some hope, although that faded too. Even Thunders' sublime adaptation of Dion's 'Born To Cry', from *Copy Cats*, failed to make any impression on its release in November 1988. Johnny knew all too well that his career would fare better in death, and he noted it for posterity in 'Disappointed In You' when he wrote, 'The only way you get respect is when you die.'

From 1988 to his demise in April '91, Thunders did he what he had always done: took to the road.

Backed by The Oddballs, the gigs had revue flair, Johnny in his candy-wrapper-coloured suits bringing a little considered showmanship to the party. Describing the vibe of the band to *Records* magazine, Thunders stated, 'It's sort of a 60s-ish Motown feel with my kind of sound. The madness is more controlled. I definitely think it's a part of me growing up.'

If Johnny had addressed his creativity, he was unable to do the same emotionally, despite his intentions. Chris Musto:

> He was a pleasure to work with and stylistically, he left everybody to it. It was very varied onstage but basically it was improvised rock'n'roll. To do that properly, you've got to know what you're doing. The only thing that irritated me about Johnny was his lack of self-respect, which was brought on by what he used to do himself, that hedonistic approach was so frustrating. He gave the impression that he never analysed himself, but he did. He existed by his heart, he existed passionately. He did things first then thought about them later. His desires were very basic: he wanted to be loved, he wanted to have a nice place to live, he wanted to be comfortable.

The home life that Johnny Thunders craved was attainable, but he couldn't diffuse the ingrained capacity for self-sabotage, no matter how wretched the consequences. In January 1989, Thunders pulled the plug on a short Spanish tour in a desperate attempt to salvage his relationship with Susanne. Sadly, he failed. The introduction of a baby into their lives irrevocably altered the status quo: Jamie came first, and Johnny's lifestyle became more of a threat, as Christopher Giercke explained:

> Susanne had a great love and gentleness for Johnny but at the point that she had a baby, the protection of the child became the all over importance. It was difficult enough to live with Johnny,

than to live with Johnny and a baby. Susanne made the instinctive choice, and Johnny could not understand that, consciously. The last weeks before they split up, I was in the Himalayas filming and Grandperret was shooting another film, and I think he was left too alone. He eventually returned to New York, which didn't stabilise things, but he did fall back on his feet.

Although Christopher would remain detached from Johnny, the guitarist had learned from the association and tried to put some of those lessons into practice. Johnny Thunders returned to Gotham with a weary finesse, bolstered by some enthusiastic local press and a flurry of hometown gigs, including two nights at the Beacon Theatre, supporting The Replacements on March 30 and 31 with The Oddballs. Back to familiar transient ways, Johnny crashed at bassist Jill Wisoff's place, along with Stevie Klasson, for a couple of months. Before she cracked from having Thunders as a house guest, Wisoff set up and paid for some demos, but the results were disappointingly lacklustre.

A second shot at capturing some of the new material also failed in less than auspicious circumstances when Thunders, accompanied by Jamey Heath, Stevie Klasson, and filmmaker Rachel Amodeo, travelled to Rochester, where an outfit called The Chesterfield Kings had organised some gigs and free studio time. All went well, according to Amodeo, until they got to the studio:

The gigs were great but the recording didn't go so well. The Chesterfield Kings were big fans of Johnny's, and when we arrived, they were like, 'Oh my God, my hero's here!' By the time the weekend was over, they weren't so sure. Basically, Johnny wasn't musically compatible with them, he played from the heart and they got impatient.

However, according to a spokesman from The Chesterfield Kings, the sessions did go well, save for outside interference from the studio owner, which Rachel wasn't aware of. An attempt at 'Society' was scrapped due to some reticence on Johnny's behalf, but a version of 'Critics Choice' later surfaced after the guitarist's demise, on an EP alongside 'I'd Much Rather Be With The Boys' and a live cut of 'London Boys'.

In Paris, Patrick Grandperret was finalising the details of *Mona et moi*, which included the possibility of a soundtrack album in collaboration with Jungle. On his home turf, Thunders was once again blending into celluloid at the behest of Rachel Amodeo, who was making her directorial debut with *What About Me*, an account of the perilous existence of New York's street denizens, from the exiled to the outcast and homeless:

> I thought I would write a story about bad luck. I decided to base the situation in my neighbourhood park, Tompkins Square Park, where a large homeless community developed, until the park was closed. I had already met Johnny once before, when he was staying with a mutual friend called Patti Giordano, then one night I saw him doing an acoustic spot and realised that his music would be perfect for the film. I told Patti Giordano that I wanted to talk to Johnny about the soundtrack and he called right away and came over to see it. We became friends and I decided to write a part for him.
>
> The first role that came to mind was that of a priest or a gangster. I asked him if he had any ideas about it, and he said, 'I think I should play your brother.' Johnny was a natural actor, very professional and charismatic. When I asked Johnny what his character's name should be, he said, 'Vito, because that's my son's name.' He thought of Napolitano as our last name. His character was very sincere in the film, very true to his character in real life.

The last message to his lost sons was sent out like a flare in an unknown night. While Johnny knew that Susanne would never bar him from Jamie, the fate of Vito and Dino, who he had not seen in ten long years, haunted him. Indeed, he would always carry a small, time-weathered photograph of the boys taken at a party. When Emil Genzale passed away, during the period Thunders was still living in Sweden, the guitarist expressed regret that he had never gotten close to his father. For reasons outside of Johnny's control, it was now too late to break the second cycle of separation that had originally begun in Michigan when his wife, Julie, suddenly took off with Dino, still a babe in arms, and Vito. Johnny Jr was similarly whisked away. At first, Julie kept in touch with Johnny's family, as Mariann Bracken explained:

> She contacted us and told us that due to Johnny's drug habit, she couldn't put up with him anymore. At the time we agreed, not knowing that her habit was as bad as his. She kept in contact for a couple of months, making us promise not to tell Johnny that we knew where she was. We complied with it. We told him we knew but weren't telling him unless he straightened out his act. One day we called the number that she'd given us, but she'd left.
>
> Johnny tried looking for her. Jerry Nolan's mother had something to do with a tracing agency called Child Find. In one period of three years, Julie had eight different addresses.
>
> Johnny and I didn't see a lot of each other in later years, he was on the road, things like that but he'd call me at least once a week; if he didn't have the money, he'd call collect. He would tell me if he was depressed, he didn't think anybody cared about him. He would tell me he had nobody, no friends, he'd say, 'All I have is you and Mom.' The main thing that ate him up more than anything else was the fact he couldn't find Vito and Dino. He didn't want to be a father the way his had been.

Julie did not let the family know the whereabouts of Vito and Dino until after Johnny's death.

* * *

In early August, Thunders flew to London to pick up his regular methadone and Valium script from his private doctor and seal a deal with Jungle Records. Skipping on the idea of a soundtrack album for *Mona et moi*, Johnny and Alan Hauser came up with *Bootlegging The Bootleggers*, a retort to all those that had profited from his work with illegitimate product, effectively short-changing the guitarist.

When Johnny Thunders didn't play, he didn't get paid. *Bootlegging The Bootleggers* provided a short-term solution to his perpetual financial instability. Between a selection of live tracks culled from 1985–89, Thunders narrates *Bootlegging* like a bouncy hybrid of Bugs Bunny and Louis Armstrong. Ironically, his introduction to the opening number, 'M.I.A.', points directly to his final destination, New Orleans. If he hadn't yet bought his ticket, he knew the direction.

Through the endeavours of an old friend of Johnny's called Abbijane, the guitarist took part in a rock'n'roll charity pool tournament aimed at raising awareness of the destruction of the rain forests. Attitude triumphed over technique when Thunders made it into the semi-finals, where he encountered David Johansen. At the celebrity bash afterward, Johnny met a promoter who subsequently booked the band for two tours, the first of which kicked off in Winnipeg on August 28. However, this Midwest jaunt almost ground to a halt at the starting post when the tour bus was impounded by customs officers who held Johnny at a hospital until the legitimacy of his methadone script was established, via a fax from Marc Zermati in Paris. Further difficulties ensued at the border when it was discovered that the non-US members of the band lacked the correct working papers. Alison Gordy:

> The Midwest tour was kind of a fiasco. We couldn't bring Chris and Stevie across the border, so Jill and Jamey went off to Winnipeg with Johnny to salvage the gigs, which they had to do acoustically. Originally, we were supposed to get $5,000, but it ended up being $750, which they spent trying to get to Minneapolis. I was pissed

off with Johnny—he had put me a bad position because I was driving as we crossed the border, and my license and reputation was now involved.

Johnny wasn't in good shape either, just dragging himself around. He'd binged out and wasn't that together, although he did do a good show in Minneapolis. Jill and I weren't getting along either, so I told Johnny I was going back to New York. Johnny needed Jill more than me to finish the tour. He thought I was pissed off at him and that's why I'd left, but it wasn't. When they all got back into town, we went out for something to eat, and Johnny told me he'd been to Jill's apartment to collect some things and he had it out with her. Then we got a tour in California, and Chris's friend Stuart [Kennedy] came over to play bass. We rehearsed once with Stuart, then off we went.

The twelve-day West Coast tour began with a flourish on October 13 amid high hopes that Thunders would be able to get a deal for the new material. Chris Musto acts as tour guide:

We played LA, which was great, packed out an old church, a well-known venue called the Second Coming. San Francisco went well, but the funniest show was in San Juan Capistrano. Johnny completely forgot that the band were there. He kept stopping the numbers halfway through to play acoustically. We walked off. By the time Johnny finished the set, there was about three people left in the club. He was standing on one of the tables with his acoustic guitar going 'name a song' to what was left of the audience, and they would call out 'Pirate Love' and he'd go, 'Yeah, I ripped that off Bad Company. Name another one.' It became this really funny routine of 'name a song, any song, and I'll tell you who I ripped it off from'. Then he sang the same song, twice.

I started apologising to the manager of the club, but the guy said, 'It's fantastic, bordering on genius,' and yes it was, but I was astonished he felt the same way, too. I can't say that the band weren't pissed off, though. We were sitting down to breakfast, and at that time of the morning, Johnny was probably last person I wanted to see. He said, 'What was it like last night?' I said, 'Where were you? It was like watching a one-man club act.' 'Was I funny?'

Midway through the tour, Thunders, like a poltergeist, began kicking up dust clouds of chaos in his wake. The promoter, who'd come along for the ride, retired early from the fray while the windows of the band's hire van mysteriously shattered from the inside. Johnny's wide-eyed hypothesis on random acts of street malice failed to convince the aggrieved parties. Then a massive earthquake rocked California. Caught between Long Beach and San Jose, Chris Musto wondered if it was a psychokinetic side-effect of the tour but, once the tremors subsided, the dates continued, sparking A&R interest from five different record companies.

After going back to New York with the band, Thunders returned to LA for a benefit gig, which he later mentioned in the course of an impromptu, unpublished interview with journalist Brian Paisley:

> At Thanksgiving, I did this benefit in Los Angeles with Clem Burke, Frank Infante, and Will Sexton. We gathered a $1,000 and gave the money to a mission so they could buy turkeys. I went to the mission myself and played three songs in front of a podium, with all these old people playing with their toes and stuff. It was the scariest thing I ever did in my life. I've never been scared onstage. Ever. It's the most secure place. When I put this song out ['Homeless'] I want to dedicate all the money to soup kitchens, because what goes on is such an injustice, especially in America, you know, it's one of the richest countries . . .

In spite of the positive reactions, Thunders' drug need unfortunately became too apparent, and, after spending a little too long in California, he blew his hard-won amnesty with the majors.

On January 24, 1990, Johnny returned to London to see his doctor, before meeting with the languid Luca Mainardi, an Italian prodigy and former student of classical ballet. The native success of Mainardi's first album, *Rock And Roll Clown* (1985), enabled him to lead an orchestra. Inspired by *Hurt Me*, Luca tracked down Thunders through Jungle Records, and so began what was possibly the strangest of all of the guitarist's musical encounters. Luca:

> My music concentrates on different languages and cultures, I never ask anybody who plays with me to perform their usual stuff. A session was set up for Johnny at CTS Studios in Wembley. We spent the first night at a hotel where the French Institute used to book free rooms for me, and the staff always addressed me as 'Maestro'. That evening Johnny destroyed everything; he fell over and broke the sink in my bathroom, his own room was terrible. We had to creep out in the morning. I've never been back since.
>
> My next mistake was renting a flat in Maida Vale for us and a couple of my Italian friends, for two weeks. It became unbearable; my nerves were shot. The problem was that you never got any sleep. I always had the feeling that disaster was imminent. We had many arguments but the biggest came after I nearly stepped on a syringe that had been left on the floor. He apologised and said he wanted to talk to me alone; he was very sad because his mother wasn't well, and of course not being able to see his children always played on his mind.
>
> Things got better once Stevie Klasson arrived. Stevie was very young, like Johnny's son, but sometimes Johnny was the son, it was a very tender relationship. Anytime Johnny was in the studio, you could never guess how he would be. When everyone else was ready, he wasn't, sometimes he'd fall asleep. He shook your concentration, but maybe that's not such a bad thing, and gave great performances

out of nothing. He had a lot of good ideas. He wanted to sing bits of all the national anthems of the world ... Italy, France, Japan.

What was interesting for Johnny was the fact that we were doing something different. We did three songs. One of them, 'Lydia', was about a girl that Johnny was in love with but she was in a relationship. When he did the song in the studio, he called her and played it over the telephone. The second song had the working title of 'Lullaby': it developed from an improvisation, it's very Sicilian, very surreal, the lyrics are about his daughter, Jamie. The other song is a sort of mazurka, with a European feel, like Kurt Weill. It starts with four accordions. Johnny was thinking about Judy Garland. He says something like, 'One day they all turn away ...'

If Johnny Thunders was indeed thinking about Judy Garland—or even Janis Joplin, who uttered similarly forlorn sentiments in 'Kozmic Blues'—he resorted to the same tactics as the fatal femmes when he returned to his doctor, within days of the last appointment, for a little something extra. Hoping to intervene before the guitarist could pick up yet another prescription for tranquillisers, Alan Hauser called the private practice, but to no avail.

It wasn't really a case of Johnny falling into decline, rather his life finally catching up with him after he separated for good from both Susanne and Christopher. They had provided a lifeline to stability. On February 3, the guitarist flew out to Paris for some dates at the Gibus and a recording session with his old friend Stiv Bators. Only the shows went ahead as planned. Something very bad manifested, and it wasn't Stiv and his girlfriend Caroline's cat, Satan. While the rest of the musicians involved in the project—Sigue Sigue Sputnik's Neal X, The Godfathers' Kris Dollimore, and Vom from Dr. & The Medics—were left to their own devices, Dee Dee Ramone and Thunders ended up staying in Stiv and Caroline's apartment on Rue St Honore.

The sessions themselves—at which Thunders (inaudibly or even allegedly) played guitar on two tracks, 'Two Hearts' and 'Ain't Got Nobody'—were distinctly ill-fated. It had not been a good idea to house the two New Yorkers under the same roof, as Stevie Klasson explained:

> [Johnny] said that Dee Dee accused him and Stiv of stealing some money; they told him they hadn't, but Dee Dee smashed up Johnny's guitar and then poured a bottle of bleach into his suitcase. All Johnny had was his guitar and clothes—he didn't have an apartment. Johnny was so hurt by it, and he took it badly. Much later he did get back at Dee Dee, in a club in New York called the Scrap Bar, which became one of Johnny's favourite haunts. He smacked Dee Dee on the back of the head as hard as he could with a beer pitcher, then the bouncer threw Dee Dee out.

In the immediate aftermath of the Dee Dee incident, Thunders took refuge with one of his oldest friends in Paris, Octavio Cohen-Escali, whom he had known since the days of the Dolls. While Johnny was well below par, in the company of Octavio and his girlfriend Isis he rallied round some, as Octavio would note:

> The night he moved in, he asked Isis to sing, then he suggested we do some more songs. We taped some of it at home, there was one called 'Big Lips', which had French lyrics, then he worked a song around Isis called 'Seduction'—he said he would have liked to have a string section in it. Then there was one called 'Discord Parfait', which means being in tune yet not agreeing.

Despite an arrangement to record the material on May 15, with Neal X acting as producer, the plan never came to fruition. *Mona et moi*, however, premiered at the Odeon cinema in Paris on April 4, scooping the prestigious Jean Vigo prize. Now Johnny truly was a movie star but broke as ever. He played two more gigs at the Gibus to boost his resources.

With a handful of acoustic dates scheduled in Ireland, Johnny looped back to England on April 25, 1990, where he was supposed to catch a plane to Dublin. The timing was crucial, as the Dublin show was to be televised. Retiring to the airport bathroom to powder his face, which he did in the style of Jackson Pollock—liberally and messily—Thunders was brought to the attention of customs officers, who mistook the loose powder for a narcotic substance and frog-marched him off for questioning. In all he was held for twenty-four hours and missed the first show.

After completing what remained of the Irish gigs, accompanied by Jamey Heath, Thunders went to stay with Mick Vayne in Leeds before beginning the English leg of the dates. Mick had first met his hero in '88, when his band, The Vaynes, supported The Oddballs on a six-week European jaunt. In '89, Vayne again met up with Thunders when he was back in town for a British tour. With some prior medical training in his background, he grew increasingly concerned for the guitarist. Mick:

While we were talking, he nodded out. It got worse as the night wore on. I'd never known him to be like that before—he'd always been so lively. I realise now, when I look back, the more time he spent here, the more out of it he got. He was depressed, he'd been put on antidepressants, and they can be really heavy. He'd take far too many and forget how many he'd taken. He'd get into his pyjamas, lie on the sofa, and watch videos night and day. He used get out a lot of films that had something do with drugs, like the John Belushi film *Wired* and that Richard Pryor movie where he's taking cocaine.

One day, he wanted to go and look at a second-hand clothes shop I'd told him about. He was walking down the road with a big spliff when he goes, 'Do you think I'm a bit more retarded than the last time you saw me?' 'You are a bit.' 'I can't remember anything anymore, I can't remember what I'm doing, do you think I'm taking too much?' 'Yes, I'd lay off the antidepressants, they're not good for you, especially in the amounts you're taking them.' 'I'll start cutting them down, one every day.'

He was deteriorating. If you're going to come off heroin or methadone, you need to do it properly. Later that same day, he said, 'I think I'm going to die soon. If I die, I'll leave you my guitars.' If he hadn't have died, I wouldn't have thought anything more about that conversation. It didn't seem to be serious.

Vayne was called upon to play guitar for the remainder of the mini tour after Thunders 'fell asleep' on his hand, trapping a nerve.

On May 11, Johnny flew out to Greece for three shows, returning to England for a further five days before the start of another acoustic tour, in Germany. It seemed as if each goodbye was becoming ever more poignant:

I had to wheel Johnny through Heathrow airport on a luggage trolley—he'd fallen asleep. He gave me this little portrait pendant of Christ, which I always wear around my neck. He said it would keep me safe. He'd been to a Catholic shop with Gerard [Gerard Famous, also formerly of The Vaynes] in Leeds. He had a big box full of crucifixes and rosaries. He used to feel guilty, and he believed that they would somehow protect him. He also gave Gerard and myself a little saint thing representing St Jude, made out of monk's robes. He said his mother made him wear St Jude. St Jude is the patron saint of lost causes.

Before he returned to New York, where a run of gigs had been set up by Amy Koster (a friend of Jamey Heath's who worked for a management agency), Thunders approached Alan Hauser to discuss a studio album. Like an elastic Lazarus, the guitarist had once again bounced back, repaired by the constant distractions of gigging. Although Jungle may have lacked the financial clout that ensures billboard coverage and blanket radio play, they had always shown support to their highest profile artist, especially in times of crisis—which were often. However, Jungle were going through a rough patch, largely due to the slide of their distributor, Rough Trade, into bankruptcy. Sales of *Bootlegging The Bootleggers* had been a little shaky, and Alan Hauser mulled over the pros and cons of taking Johnny Thunders back into the studio:

> A number of things made us hesitant. The new band, even though they were a stabilising influence, were a six-piece from different parts of the world, so logistically it would have meant the cost of flights and apartments for all of them. The situation with our distributor meant that we didn't have the resources to gamble. We also knew that whenever Johnny went into the studio, he seemed to think that the only way he could have a good time, and therefore make good music, was to be out of his head, which led to problems.
>
> However, he was very anxious to prove to us that he was cleaning up his act, and indeed he managed to, albeit only for a period of three or four months. Also, *Copy Cats*, which is an excellent album, had gone way over budget. Seeing that we were worried about finances, they proposed recording at a sixteen-track studio in New York to keep the budget low, but it was more of a demo studio. It wouldn't have done Johnny any favours to have tried that, it didn't make any sense. Much to our regret, we put the project on hold.

On June 3, Stiv Bators was hit by a car. Miraculously, he seemed unhurt, if a little dazed. After taking her spindly little beau home, Caroline wanted to call a doctor, but Stiv shrugged off the suggestion. Aside from an odd sensation that he likened to an out-of-body experience, Bators reckoned that he was okay. Later that night they retired to bed, where Stiv died in his sleep from internal injuries. On his next appearance in Paris, Alice Cooper dedicated 'Under My Wheels' to the former Dead Boy.

Shaken by the news of Bator's sudden departure, Thunders began to get himself in order. The old rock'n'roll resurrection routine was starting to wear as thin as Johnny himself. The bone structure that had made his face a pale canvas for photogenic shadows was becoming a little too pronounced. Initially, the insidious aspect of illness was masked, possibly even to the guitarist, by all the years of drug use. Mariann Bracken:

> I think he was aware that he was sick, but I don't believe he thought it was a medical problem. I feel he thought it was the drugs that were making him ill. If Johnny had a toothache, he'd call me up: 'What am I going to do?' He was like that with everything. Not long before he died, he said, 'I've got a lump on my neck, what should I do?' 'Go to a doctor.' He didn't go to doctors; he didn't believe in them. I think he was scared to go.

When Receiver Records licensed *Live At The Lyceum*, the rights of which had in part reverted back to Thunders, he put the unexpected windfall to good use. On September 3, 1990, he checked into Hazelden, the world-renowned rehabilitation centre in Minnesota. Although there is another branch of Hazelden in New York offering similar services, Thunders sought help far from home. On his own turf, the guitarist had always been at the centre of a vicious circle, unable to resist the 'gifts' of those who got off on making him their drugged deity. Mariann Bracken:

> Johnny went into a rehabilitation centre. He called me one day and said, 'I can't take no more.' He had some friends [Heather and Cathy Boruch] that were talking to him about it. He said that had triggered him off. The day before he went in, he stayed at our house so we could drive him to the airport. He was nervous, scared about what was going to happen, he wanted to start a new life.
>
> He called me from Hazelden the first night. He was in a lot of pain, he told me he knew that it was going to be hard, but he was going to do it. He was in almost a month, and we spoke at least two or three times a day. He took part in these sessions where you talk

to people who have the same problem. He called me before one of them. It seems that they write things down about each other during the session. He was joking with me: 'I wonder what they're going to write?'

After he died, we were going through some of his papers, and we found the letters from the sessions. They all say exactly the same thing: 'You're killing yourself about your children, you're not like your father, it's not your fault about the kids, you can't find them.' He knew Susanne was a good mother. He loved Jamie. Johnny and Susanne had their problems; maybe they couldn't live together, but he knew he never had to worry about his daughter. I know that Susanne loved Johnny and he loved her; it makes it even sadder that they couldn't get it together. At Hazelden, they recommended NA [Narcotics Anonymous] meetings, but Johnny didn't believe in them. He wasn't for talking to a whole bunch of people. When he came out of rehab, he was okay for a little while . . .

Returning to New York, Thunders did his best to keep things together, settling into a one-bedroom apartment at 227 East 21st Street. It was the first time he had lived alone, and the fact that his new abode was in spitting distance of a police station somewhat tickled him. On Friday, November 30, The Heartbreakers got together for a one-off gig at the (New York) Marquee. Billy Rath, who had forsaken rock'n'roll for God, was replaced by Tony Coiro from Walter Lure's band, The Waldos. Above all, the night belonged to Jerry Nolan, who had instigated the idea:

I'd been wanting to do it for a long time. I'd wanted it so bad and it's a good thing it did happen because that was my last time playing with Johnny. I was so happy that night, I played so well. Walter and Tony said, 'Boy, look at Jerry, look how happy he is.' It was great, and Johnny admitted it was too—that's all I wanted him to do, because he could be a scumbag, he could like it and say he hated it. I didn't want him to do that, I wanted him to say he liked it. He told Walter, 'You know, I hate to admit it, but fucking Nigs, what a show.'

As the Christmas lights came on in London, Johnny and The Oddballs regrouped for some European dates, kicking off with a gig at the Marquee on December 21. Thunders was in good spirits, the benefit of his short stay at Hazelden still apparent, as his old pal Gail Higgins Smith recalled:

Because we went through so many formative years together, even though there were a lot of months after the early years when we were apart, every time I saw Johnny, it was just like seeing him the day before. In the later times, it would really depend on the particular night I saw him, how he would be. He would either be the old Johnny or some monster Johnny.

I'm really glad that the last time I saw John was when he did that final show at the Marquee. That night he was exactly the John I knew when he was eighteen. I remember saying, 'I heard about you being off the drugs.' He said, 'Oh Gail, you know me.' 'But you're so like the old John.' 'That's because I'm drunk and coming off the drugs I was on last night.' But it was like seeing a glimpse of John that I hadn't seen in years.

After the London Marquee show, the band travelled to Switzerland for a couple of gigs before Johnny and Jamey Heath headed off to Paris to play a five-night stand at the Gibus. Just as most people were thinking about their new year's resolutions, Thunders gave up on his. Journalist Nick Kent, the NME's former *enfant terrible*, ran into the guitarist as the clocks were striking the final notes of 1990. In his book *The Dark Stuff*, he notes:

The last time I saw him though—Jesus Christ, I could hardly stand to look at John. You know in a bullfight how when the decisive dagger had been plunged into the neck of the bull and basically it's all over for the poor creature and it goes limp and cross-eyed before sinking slowly into the saw-dust. Well, that's how Thunders looked on the night of New Year's Eve just as 1991 was being ushered in: limp and cross-eyed from all the torments he'd been visiting upon himself...

Back in New York, the 'party' continued with all those who wanted to absorb the rarefied air of getting high with Johnny Thunders. Realising that he was going to have get out of town fast if he was to survive, Thunders finalised his long-nurtured plan to go to New Orleans and start over. Stevie Klasson was on standby to join him there, as was Jerry Nolan. The guitarist also got in touch with Barbara Becker, a former artistic collaborator of Christopher Giercke's who was now managing Dr John in New Orleans. First, however, there was a handful of dates in Japan with The Oddballs to take care of, and a recording commitment in Germany with punk band Die Toten Hosen (The Dead Trousers), who were in the process of making a covers album of the spiky classics of their youth entitled *Learning English—Lesson 1.*

Before departing for Tokyo, Johnny met up with Jerry Nolan. Like Thunders, the drummer had left Sweden and returned to New York. With the help of his girlfriend, Phyllis Stein, whom he'd known since the Dolls, Nolan had taken up the fight for self-conquest over old habits, but his pal wasn't faring so well.

A lot of people look at Johnny and me like brothers, but it was more than that. It was more a father/son relationship. It's respect. I take Johnny a hundred percent for what he is, and he takes me a hundred percent. That's based on trust. There were no two people closer. He could come to my house and spill his guts, I'm talking about marriages, pregnancy, disease, his wounds ... help him to heal them so he wouldn't have to go to a doctor, everything. But you know what? I couldn't do that to him. I couldn't spill my guts to him, but I accepted that. Johnny would come to me, show me all his track wounds and know that I wouldn't tell nobody.

It was the day before he was supposed to go to Japan, there were a couple of things that I didn't know what they meant. Odd places for bruises to be—back, chest. I didn't find out until weeks later that was the leukaemia. I started to talk him into forgetting the gig, I tried to tell him we had to go to the hospital. I told him I would have stayed, we would have got a private room that I'd be in the room with him or sitting just outside the door. I almost got him to do it, and then he got scared. He just got scared of needles, doctors, hospitals, the whole bit. You may not realise this, but most junkies are afraid of needles. I told him he was going to die. I said, 'Take care on this tour, you shouldn't be going anyway, you know that.' Johnny had this thing when I would go on about his health: he would thank me for my concern, then he would reach a point where he would say, 'Okay, Jerry, you made your point.' We shook hands. His handshake was very weak. Then I hugged him.

I left Johnny on 14th Street and 3rd Avenue, the exact same corner where I greeted Johnny for the first time after I'd auditioned for the Dolls. As I walked down the street, I'm saying to myself, 'I don't like the idea that I just said goodbye to him in the same place as we said hello.' By the time I got home, I said, 'He's not going to Japan. He'll never live if he don't go in the hospital right now.' That night he was supposed to go to Japan. He never made it. He never made it the next day. He just made it the fourth day. He was going to call me from New Orleans, I was going to go with him; he said, 'Jerry we'll do it fifty-fifty, just like we always did.'

A fragile Johnny Thunders set off to Japan on March 30. Having missed his original flight to London, where he should have picked up his regular prescription prior to the dates, Thunders was taken to a hospital in Tokyo by Mick Webster. Fearing for the guitarist's health, the doctors at the International Clinic told him to pull the shows and return home. The gigs went ahead anyway, Thunders playing to adoring audiences in a country where he had long been venerated. He was even chased down the street by a mob of flower wielding teenage girls.

For Gaku Torii, who had not seen the guitarist in almost three years, it was a chance to catch up:

He was here for seven days, and I was with him for most of that. The first show was in Tokyo, at the Power Station. He looked tired. He was using an ordinary Les Paul Standard, which he'd borrowed from Stevie, but it was too heavy for him. He put it down and just sang. He was very bluesy, rootsy. The second gig was at Club Citta in Kawasaki; the third show was an acoustic with Stevie and Jamey at a club called the Anti Knock in Shinjuku. Steve Berlin, the saxophonist from Los Lobos, joined them onstage.

Then he went into the studio with a punk band called Ebi [Shrimp] to record one track, 'Fucking Police'. Later, me, Johnny, Stevie, and Mick went to see Los Lobos play, but after half an hour Johnny said he was tired, so I went back to the hotel with him. He showed me pictures of Jamie, told me how pretty she was. I remember him saying that he didn't like living with women these days, he preferred drugs. He asked me if I wanted to manage him because I'd sorted out a deal for him.

A Japanese company, Meldac, wanted him to do an album of covers from the 60s, material like Spencer Davis and The Yardbirds, with top Japanese musicians. They were going to call it Johnny Thunders & The Gang Rockers. He'd also asked me if I would organise an acoustic album deal for him. He'd even chosen a photograph for the cover and a title, *Hurt Me More*. He started talking about wanting to make a record in New Orleans with Dr John. I noticed that whenever I was on the tour bus, he was playing

Willy DeVille's *Victory Mixture* album, which was recorded with Dr John. He dreamed about New Orleans, and although I didn't want to manage Johnny, I did talk to the Japanese branch of WEA about his New Orleans idea, and they were interested.

On April 9, accompanied by tour manager Mick Webster, Jamey Heath, and Stevie Klasson, Thunders visited Thailand for a couple of days of rest and recuperation. Aside from picking up some custom-made silk suits, Johnny ventured into Jimmy Wong's tattoo parlour in Bangkok with Stevie Klasson:

> I got a snake and an Indian Chief's skull done, and Johnny got Jesus on the cross on his forearm. He didn't get any colours done on it, except for a little red on the black because he said the pain was too much. He was fascinated by religious symbolism. We were videoed while it was being done. After Thailand, we went back to New York. I got him a ticket to go to London. He gave me the keys to his apartment. His nephew Danny [Bracken] and I were to clean it up and pack his things, so he would be ready to go to New Orleans.

After seeing his doctor in London, Johnny went straight to Germany with Mick Webster, where two acoustic shows had been set up in Braunschweig and Berlin to cover the cost of the flights. After the gigs, they were collected in Cologne by Die Toten Hosen frontman Campi, who explained:

> For the album we decided to do an all-star version of 'Born To Lose' with TV Smith, Cheetah Chrome, Dick Manitoba, and Joey Ramone. When Johnny arrived, he listened to the versions, then put his vocals on it. He was very tired, he didn't look so well, but he really pulled himself together while he was in the studio. We recorded his guitar tracks in the toilet because he liked the sound

in there. When we played it back, we were happy with it, but he wanted to do it again. He tried to do his best. On the other hand, he asked if we could do it tomorrow—he forgot that tomorrow he was leaving. He was pretty confused but aware of it—he even joked about it. After the session, on the way out to the car, he said to Mick, 'Let me drive.' Everybody knew that he was not able to drive anymore. He didn't have a lot of power. He had to concentrate very hard all the time on what he was doing.

Between two guitars, a suitcase, and his saddlebags, Johnny had everything he needed for New Orleans: enough money from his work engagements to tide him over, a reserve of prescription drugs, and those shiny new silk suits. En route to catching his flight, Thunders dished out his loose change to the poor at a railway station in Germany before taking the train to the airport. Staggering with exhaustion, he was turned back from the departure gate by airline staff who wouldn't let him through until he had a medical. Mick Webster:

> After the medical, he was walking round the no-smoking area with the biggest cigar you've ever seen, and he wasn't going to put it out for anybody. 'To hell with them,' he said. 'If they want to get me out of here, they've got to come and get me.' Finally, we got to the gate. Normally, at the end of a tour, it would be, 'See you in a couple of weeks.' This time he held out his hand. He'd never done that before. I got a really strange feeling, but I didn't want to think about it. When I got home, I must admit I was pretty worried.

From the moment Johnny Thunders vanished beyond the departure gate on April 22, 1991, his exacts movements become harder to substantiate. At a stop-off in Chicago, the guitarist called up Mariann Bracken to say he had lost his ticket. The family wired him some money for a new one, but it was never collected. Once he'd arrived in New Orleans, a taxi driver dropped him at the St Peter guesthouse at Burgundy and St Peter Street, between 9:30 and 10pm. The desk clerk on duty, Lesley Carter, later told the *New Orleans Metro* newspaper that Thunders had been 'dressed all in black from head to toe, and he was sweating. At one point, I was afraid he was going to fall on me. He wasn't obnoxious. He looked real white, like a Geisha girl.'

After checking into room 37, the guitarist had a quick mooch around Bourbon Street. Returning to the guesthouse, he called Stevie Klasson, who passed the phone number on to Thunders' sister. Mariann Bracken:

> We talked when he got there. We must have spoken for fifteen minutes or so. He sounded great. He told me how much he loved it there, how there was singing in the streets. He said he'd done well in Japan and Germany and even joked that might have to pay income tax for the year. He never made it. He told me I wasn't going to have to pay a mortgage anymore. All the time he was in the Dolls, he used to say, 'Someday, I'm going to pay your mortgage.'

After talking to Stevie and Mariann, Johnny became disconnected from all that was familiar. What exactly happened in those final fraying hours as he slipped over the horizon will always remain inconclusive. However, it would appear that Thunders' presence in New Orleans triggered a surge of activity in the drug-dealing community. In his weakened state, the guitarist was easy prey for any passing opportunist.

Sometime that evening, Johnny made the acquaintance of brothers Mike and Marc Ricks, who were staying in the neighbouring room. After smoking a couple of joints, all three visited a bar in the French Quarter and then returned to the guesthouse. The brothers apparently crashed out, only to be woken by a series of jolts, like a fight without voices, coming from Thunders' room. Around eight in the morning, the hotel receptionist called Johnny about the noise. He asked if he could come and talk to her. Nothing was ever heard from the guitarist again.

At approximately 3:30 that afternoon, cleaner Mildred Coleman knocked on the door of room 37. When no one replied, she let herself in with her passkey and found Thunders curled up under the dresser amid a scene of disarray. Whether Johnny had been fighting with someone or struggling to stay alive has never been ascertained.

On the street across from his apartment, Willy DeVille happened to be strumming his guitar when a police car ruined the picturesque scenario of an afternoon in the Big Easy, as it pulled to a halt outside the St Peter guesthouse. A resident of New Orleans, DeVille watched the activity with a dispassionate distance until the hotel manager asked him if he knew who Johnny Thunders was. Formerly of New York, DeVille regularly booked business associates into the St Peter and was acquainted with the staff. After officials from the coroner's office left with the body, a nervous hotel employee asked him to accompany her into room 37.

There are more inconsistencies surrounding the death of Johnny Thunders than around the demise of Marilyn Monroe. Without hard fact, the terrible speculation began: Thunders had been spiked with acid, robbed, murdered, left to die by people or persons unknown, New Orleans flotsam that seeped in like a tide and dissipated by daylight. There is no way of assessing what grains of truth may have been lost in a miasma of rumour denser than a Louisiana swamp. What is known is that room 37 was totally trashed, and most of the guitarist's possessions stolen, including his passport, makeup, lyrics, silk suits, and shoes—yet it wasn't treated as a crime scene. His saddlebags were sent home empty. Not only did his family have to come to terms with his death, they also had to deal with an unresolved situation, as Johnny's niece Chrissy Bracken noted:

If it had been in New York, it would have been treated as a homicide case. In New Orleans this was just a Johnny Doe who was doing drugs. They didn't realise how much press and all the hassle they were going to get. There was a syringe in the toilet; the police threw it away, they didn't test it. They said no alcohol was found, but they interviewed a bartender who said that Johnny had a drink with him. Alcohol stays in the body for a long time. We're never going to get the answers. Why were there empty packets of methadone? He'd just come back from London to get it.

Ultimately, Johnny Thunders arrived in New Orleans exhausted and in very poor health; whatever went down sealed his fate in a particularly wretched manner. Like Billy Murcia some eighteen years earlier, many people, including the media, assumed that Thunders died from a suspected (expected) drugs overdose. In its report, the New Orleans Coroner's Office commented upon the 'presence of methadone and cocaine' in Thunders' body, but the quantities found were far from lethal. However, in the terminology of the autopsy, his death was still 'drug-related'.

In a letter to Alan Hauser, clarifying the report, Coroner Frank Minyard noted that, 'Under ideal circumstances, tests for Hepatitis C and HIV would have been performed . . . the doctor performing the autopsy did not feel strongly enough about either condition to order the tests to be performed.' (One wonders what exactly constitutes 'ideal circumstances' for an autopsy?) Concluding his explanation, Minyard also mentioned the advanced spread of malignant lymphoma (a form of leukaemia) and stated, 'I believe he was in a seriously weakened condition as a result of this malignancy and that this contributed very strongly to his death.'

* * *

Johnny Thunders returned home for the very last time, and with his death an era ended. Finally, Johnny's suffering was over, and the outpouring of grief commenced, as Mariann Bracken recalled:

The funeral was unbelievable. The church, St Anastasia's, was packed. There was over a forty-car procession and so many flowers and floral pieces, guitars, hearts. There were more people than anybody can imagine. Steven Tyler was there, Deborah Harry sent flowers, so did Mötley Crüe and Aerosmith. The fans came from all over; they were very nice, respectful. My husband said in one row there was a man with a $500 suit on and at the end of the row there was a girl with an earring in her nose and tattoos. Some of the people left little things next to Johnny in the coffin: a picture, a prayer card, a guitar pick . . . at first we were going to take them out, but then we decided to keep them there. Johnny had so many people that cared.

Somehow, Johnny's partner in crime, Jerry Nolan, made it through the funeral:

I don't remember bits of it, it was very dream-like, I don't know why. I'm usually very clear headed but it didn't flow, it was strange. This is what I thought I would do to my friend; I would kiss him hello, leave the room and talk to everybody, then I would go back and kiss him goodbye. That's what I did.

Johnny Thunders was buried on Monday, April 29, 1991, in St Mary's Cemetery, on the outskirts of Queens. He was thirty-eight years old.

Jerry Nolan took his friend's death extremely hard. After a period of mourning, he slowly began to resurface. He participated in a memorial gig in Thunders' honour at the New York Marquee on June 19 that included Patti Palladin; members of The Oddballs, The Heartbreakers, and the Dolls; and other New York notables. The event raised $19,000 for Johnny's children, Vito, Dino, and Jamie.

As the summer gained momentum, Jerry started restoring a 1972 Triumph motorbike that he had originally discovered in Sweden. With a prior owner who had overcome a drug habit by diligently customising the bike, the Triumph became a talisman of hope.

In August, the drummer visited London, accompanied by Phyllis Stein. The first thing he did when we met up was to show me a copy of the July 16 edition of the *Village Voice* containing an impressive nine-page memoir: 'Beyond The Valley Of The Dolls: A Guided Tour From Elvis To Sid—by Jerry Nolan with Doug Simmons.'

Not always the easiest of people to please, Nolan fixed me with one of his great cute 'n' tricksey grins that fleetingly obliterated all the loss. He hoped that the article would lead to a book or even a movie. The onset of winter put paid to all that, as his constant companion, Phyllis, explained:

When we returned to New York, we started to concentrate on Jerry writing his book. We were given the names of literary agents and we were going to speak to a rock biographer. Jerry had also been working in the studio with his friend Greg Allen. Being in the studio was good for Jerry, as was a role in Rachel Amodeo's movie. He was upbeat and positive about the future. He kept telling me that he was finally really happy.

In the beginning of November we thought he had come down with the flu and migraine headache. He was very sick. The doctors told me he had bacterial pneumonia and meningitis. They were giving him antibiotics and told me he would recover. Jerry was in the hospital about three weeks when he suffered a major stroke which left him in really bad shape, irreparably damaged.

The reality was that he would never be able to leave that hospital alive. He was ill for another eight weeks and died on January 14, 1992, from complications. I had called Mariann that evening to ask her to help me with funeral arrangements. As if by telepathic communication, within two hours of that conversation, Jerry died. When Johnny died, Jerry asked Mariann that if anything happened to him, could he be buried next to Johnny. So, yeah, he's buried right near Johnny. They're close, and that's what Jerry would have wanted.

CHAPTER FIFTEEN

ALCHEMICAL RESOLUTIONS

Time, the silent thief, takes all in its wake, but the memories remain. It's been over thirty years since Johnny Thunders and Jerry Nolan checked out. More recently, they have been joined by their Heartbreakers comrades Billy Rath and Walter Lure, the whole line-up reported to be playing again in the rock'n'roll ballrooms of eternity.

What would they have made of being a 'must buy' on Record Store Day, or being downloaded? In the commercial afterlife, Thunders & co are a tangible presence, due in no little part to the continuing efforts of Jungle Records. Exemplars of hard-bitten rock'n'roll and the life that goes with it, we won't see the likes of The Heartbreakers again, nor their cohorts, Stiv Bators, Willy DeVille, Dee Dee Ramone, et al. Reckless and resolute, they maintained a wayward integrity to the end. Rising from the bad-lands of rock dreams, they became the heirs of a pulp-punk mythology that resonates to this very day.

Perceived as the epitome of outsider chic, Johnny Thunders was always the antidote to the big spectacle of corporate rock, though he could enthral large audiences when the bookings arose. There was something gladiatorial about his gigs that intensified the performance; a certain amount of tension always worked for Thunders, who was cannier than people realised when it came to stagecraft. If he never started a show at the precise time, it was because he knew how to make an audience hungry. A sense of palpable excitement would permeate the venue, the audience like sailors caught in a storm, waiting for the biggest wave to hit them. Electrifying to his fingertips, the guitarist knew how to make the stage his own, and he did what all great performers do, projecting his persona into something magnetizing and mythical. He was witty, too, out-heckling the hecklers. (Someone should release a recording of Johnny's best retorts and rambles.)

Thunders was fond of saying that his purpose was 'to make the kids dance', evoking the rock'n'roll innocence of the 1950s, when Seven Day Weekends lasted all year. Steeped in the songs of his youth, Johnny's creative vision never erred or bowed to fashion. He was his music in the same way that Nico and Marc Bolan were, their core identity in every song, unlike those who butterfly between fads, reinventing themselves in the manner of David Bowie.

Each gifted performer is a dream-weaver, able to utilise a kind of glamour even if the reality of their existence is far from easy. Johnny Thunders appealed to people who wanted to live on their own terms, beyond society's grasp, and he spoke most clearly to the disenfranchised, for whom authenticity is everything. However, he never planned on being an outsider archetype. Options narrow once a person is immersed in drug addiction, one foot in Hades, the other in survival. Today, the term 'drug addict' has been softened to 'substance misuser'—a misleading term that tiptoes around the desperation and desolation of the user's fraught life.

Under such chaotic circumstances, Johnny Thunders nevertheless managed to maintain a career. Possessed of an intense charisma, the guitarist pulled off his finest act—that of being Johnny Thunders—with a gypsy élan. From Ronnie Spector to Bob Dylan, the greats of his era have acknowledged Johnny's work, while his music has appeared on the soundtrack of *The Sopranos* and Scorsese's *Bringing Out The Dead*, among others. Like Ronnie Spector, who covered 'Memory', Johnny possesses one of those attitudinal voices that sing from the heart of a bygone New York, a combo of hard luck, hard love, and hard times.

Johnny Thunders moved seamlessly through the decades, paying little heed to what was considered 'current' in music. Though he was not oblivious to other acts, his approach was an insular one, which suited his self-protective persona. There is a telling clip on YouTube with a rather bombastic interviewer in which Johnny virtually vanishes inside of himself. In his later years, he knew how to match the mood of anyone who tracked him down, like to like. One of Mötley Crüe who shall remain nameless described himself as once having had a 'Johnny Thunders' moment with a model on each arm and a bottle of Jack Daniels. Of course, Johnny was never short of female companions, but he was never gauche. He didn't have to introduce himself in Crude style as Mr Rock'n'roll because he was rock'n'roll.

Unfortunately, Johnny—like myself—was of a generation that believed in music as if it were a religion, with drugs as its unholy sacraments. The Heartbreakers left behind a musical manifesto of the junk life in much the same way as William Burroughs interpreted his experiences of heroin into literature. Unlike The Heartbreakers, however, Burroughs was the scion of a wealthy family and belonged to an intellectual milieu that was one step removed from the daily grift of a street junkie.

Heavy-lidded, stoned cold Keith Richards was the dangerous template for an already wounded kid like Johnny, who didn't have the stabilising factor of a father around as he was growing up. Keith Richards has been fortunate enough to never have to recant for his drug use, although it is very clear that he has left that life behind. His longevity is the stuff of legend, long may he reign, but he never was a street junkie, and he has long enjoyed a cossetted lifestyle.

Johnny Thunders' story was very different. It must have crucified him when his father left: imagine the desolation of a child thinking they may have been the reason for a parent's desertion. Ultimately, Johnny, like many addicts, tried to self-medicate the emotional pain away. His sense of abandonment is apparent in what is considered his signature tune, 'You Can't Put Your Arms Around A Memory', and in many of the songs he chose to cover in the acoustic spots at his live shows.

Those not familiar with Johnny's work might consign him to the 'hard-assed rock'n'roll' corner, but he was so much more. His life was both a blessing and a curse. At the end, he recognised his plight, but he simply wasn't strong or well enough to leave the drugs behind. This doesn't make him a bad person, just a fallible, hurt one. It was his constant, often-losing battle to keep his soul intact that made him forgivable. Not forgetting those beautiful nocturnal eyes. Johnny, like most junkies, had learnt to play everything to his best advantage, but all it bought him was short term, short-change victories.

In order to survive, Johnny Thunders was almost constantly on the road, playing low-budget tours. This also became a trap, as he could not deal with continual gigging without drugs. Despite his once commenting that he could play just as well on drugs as off, his idea of sobriety was a methadone script (an opioid substitute), and he was unable to maintain even that.

Ensnared in a state of perpetual need, junkies go in ever-diminishing circles, chasing the high while all else falls apart. We find his equals in Chet Baker and Nico, each of them supremely talented but afflicted by addiction. Like Johnny Thunders, they too had to carve out a niche on the margins of mainstream culture, which if anything honed their angular brilliance before an audience that existed as a kind of devoted secret society.

* * *

Johnny Thunders: In Cold Blood has been a live document, but this will be the final version. Most books are set in stone after publication, but I have been able to include additional material and mature as an author with each edition. A last interview with Jerry Nolan in the summer of 1991 was also pivotal to the book's development. Visiting with his companion, Phyllis Stein, they noted how, in the time of The New York Dolls and The Heartbreakers, the majority of media interest came from the UK and Europe—a balance that has since changed. America has now accepted both bands as their own, although this is to a discerning rather than a mainstream audience.

This final revision has also given me the opportunity to write with a better understanding of drug use and its consequences, for which I am grateful. With the passing of years, Johnny's motto became 'Do as I say, not as I do', a far cry from his self-proclaimed 'love songs to heroin and girls'. Doctors are rarely sympathetic to junkies, which would have been another barrier toward him getting the medical help he so desperately needed at the end of his life. Jerry Nolan did all that he could to encourage Johnny to go to a hospital. They may have been musically estranged at that point, but the bond between them always ran deep.

The motif of 'heroin chic' has insidiously embedded itself in contemporary culture, from perfumes such as Opium to glossy magazine photo shoots featuring waif like creatures in artful decay. Heroin chic is a serpent's promise, obscuring the truth of addiction and making it appear attractive as well as seductive. The latest hippest ingénue will be cast to play an addict on television or in a film, and so the lie carries to all corners of society. However, in real life, junkies are rarely given a warm welcome. They are society's scapegoats, someone to pin the blame on. In Johnny's time, US president George H. Bush strenuously objected to needle-exchange schemes, which were implemented in the UK to stem the spread of blood-born viruses. Tangentially, Gus Van Sant's 1989 movie *Drugstore Cowboy* avoided reality by setting the scene in a mystical nowheresville of motels, featuring a beautiful cast in designer downbeat clothing. Beyond Hollywood's vision of photogenic junkies, however, addicts were waking up to the horrors of AIDS and hepatitis. (The word 'hipster' originates from the posture of opium smokers, laying on their side as they imbibe from a pipe.)

Johnny Thunders might have sung about playing games but he was far more honest about the toll the junkie life takes. Addiction is relentless, and 'decent' folks would rather turn away from those laid low by junk. Every city has street homeless addicts, crying silently into the void of their own despair. Johnny Thunders, like all users, was somebody's son, partner, and parent, but he was a runaway train, careening toward his own tragic destiny. Johnny's night never ended, but for the reader, the casual observer, the person who has convinced themselves that they alone can dally with heroin and crack every now and again and walk away unscathed, they still have time to turn back, start over, and forget the lie of junkie glamour.

People who do fall for hard drugs are often in the most terrible inner turmoil. It is not a state to be envied or copied but to be avoided at all costs. If they are to escape, those already trapped in addiction must be shown compassion rather than castigated. Addiction is incredibly cunning, the traps unseen and the maze ever more complex. Before a person realises, they are held fast by invisible snares. To sneer at their plight is an admission of ignorance.

Although Johnny died before the age of the internet, his image proliferates, while stories, not all of them true—just as it was when he was still alive—keep his legend alive. One reoccurring theme that blights some of the fan pages dedicated to the guitarist is the idea that he wasn't loved. People project their own fantasies of how they would have 'saved' Johnny, had they been present. No one could have 'saved' Johnny except himself, but he was loved not just by his fans and friends but by his mother and his sister, and in the later years by his Swedish girlfriend, Susanne Blomqvist.

In a relationship with a junkie, the addiction becomes a spectral corrupting presence, an ominous third party that destroys not just the user but those closest to him. Johnny left behind a wife, Julie, with whom he had two sons, as well as a daughter, Jamie, with Susanne. Heroin erodes the fabric of life.

Despite the existence of the 1992 Cherry Red version of *In Cold Blood* as a reference point, some journalists in print and online are happier to fabricate shock stories about the guitarist, ramping up the sleaze factor for their own ends, but the truth is out there. Danny Garcia's documentary *Looking For Johnny* goes the distance in trying to present a balanced view, featuring the likes of Leee Black Childers, Marty Thau, Gail Higgins Smith, Walter Lure, Sylvain Sylvain, Bob Gruen, Neal X, Chris Musto, and Kim Montenegro. An effective collage of the elusive guitarist, Mr Johnny

Thunders, is created. Sections from a Swedish Television documentary about *Drugs And The Artist* that include one of the best interviews ever filmed with the guitarist make *Looking For Johnny* a valid document. It clearly wasn't one of Thunders' best days when the Swedish camera crew descended on him; he is defensive, edgy, probably wanting to go and score with the money they had paid for his participation. The closing sequence of Johnny walking alone through a grey New York that seems to close in around him has the quality of a Scorsese movie. The light is opaque and so is Johnny, aside from his scarlet shirt. The dandification of the Dolls was always inherent in Johnny's style, but here there is no longer a limo, just worn-down heels hitting the pavement. One of the saddest stories in the film comes from former Doll Sylvain Sylvain, who saw Johnny in his last days, carrying all of his possessions in a bin bag.

Johnny Thunders influenced at least five generations of rock'n'roll bands and culture, although the less well informed might not have realised, taking their cues instead from more celebrated groups such as Mötley Crüe or Guns N' Roses or even Duran Duran. Pioneers in any field are almost always overlooked, at least for the first half-century. It is only now that The New York Dolls are cited alongside The MC5 and Iggy & The Stooges as being pivotal in rock'n'roll history, the bridge crossing the chasm of the 1960s to the Fabulous Seventies, to borrow a phrase from Nick Kent.

Fast-forward a year or two, to when The New York Dolls were in full flight, the utmost in trashed glamour and louche guitar licks. No wonder that David Bowie, only recently emerged from his bippity-bobbity bohemian phase, took one look at the Dolls and promptly ran all the way to their favourite shoemaker to get some sling-back mules. This may sound of little import, but it shows that Bowie wanted to walk in the Dolls' shoes—quite literally. From this union of influences we find the roots of *Aladdin Sane*, wherein the Dolls, Billy Murcia especially, are eulogised in 'Time'.

Bowie was just the beginning—an example of how someone as marginalised post-Dolls as Johnny became could still leave an indelible mark that he is as yet not fully credited for. I see his shadow in contemporary 'cutting-edge' fashion, Japanese models in carefully studied gutter-punk poses showing off salon versions of Thunders' raven-wing riot tresses and wearing the kind of fingerless lace mittens that Johnny often sported. As it should be, Thunders is included in a Wikipedia list of notable musicians who played Les Paul Juniors, although it is Green Day's Billy Joe Armstrong who gets his own custom model. Armstrong, however, has made no secret of his admiration for Thunders, having recently covered 'Memory'.

For some, Johnny Thunders has become a secret signature, a touchstone of authenticity and a reminder of the great American myth of the antihero, fallible yet beautiful. It is virtually impossible to quantify his import both musically and stylistically, but for those that know, there was no one better. A diminutive dandy, when Johnny Thunders sauntered down the street, the night held her breath.

Of course, there was a price to pay. There always is. The guitarist anticipated that death would further enhance his legend. Once an artist is set in stone, their work and import can be better assessed, besides which any troublesome ways are more easily forgiven and forgotten. Once upon a long ago, it would have been thought foolish to imagine that Johnny Thunders would be namechecked in numerous celebrity rock memoirs, from Nikki Sixx to Viv Albertine. *Johnny Thunders: In Cold Blood* started a literary genre to which fellow New York Dolls Sylvain Sylvain and Arthur Kane added their voices in autobiographies. Jerry Nolan was also considering writing his memoirs but died before this could be fully realised, while we also have Walter Lure's account, in which he recalls the early antics of The Heartbreakers in London and New York.

Back in the 90s, when I was working on a biography of The New York Dolls entitled *Too Much Too Soon* (Omnibus), I was able to interview one of the band's former managers, the genial Marty Thau. The majority of his comments were pertinent, and it was clear that the belief he'd had in the band was absolute until faced with a conservative industry and unyielding co-managers. With eyes that may have been slightly rheumy or even teary, he said that he feared that no one would be talking or even remembering

The New York Dolls in ten or ten years. There was no malice in his perspective, just a kind of settled resignation. He had all but buried the Dolls along with his youth and marriage, his disappointment still tangible.

Longevity or a posthumous lifespan is utterly unpredictable. The musicians and artists who maintain a presence tend to fill a contemporary need. Antiheroes who appear not to give a damn about society's expectations flourish in conservative times. Johnny Thunders now weaves his way through popular culture. If I was to compare him to anyone, in terms of style and beautiful insouciance, it would be Serge Gainsbourg, cigarette smoke curling into the mists of time.

* * *

Perhaps it is only in death that we can grasp a person's totality. Johnny Thunders has now entered the realm of perpetual mystique, and his reach today is greater than ever. For Johnny, children were a life-affirming experience. Sadly, he never got to see his own grow up or spend time with his grandchildren due to his addiction, which loomed large over his entire existence. Most people are able to keep their shadow side contained, but this does not apply to drug users, no matter how hard they try.

In the depths, though, there is redemption. Even if he lost all else, Johnny still had his soul, which resonates in his music and memory.

NINA ANTONIA, JANUARY 2023

ACKNOWLEDGEMENTS

Thank you to everyone who gave of their time and resources over the years, especially Johnny Thunders, Jerry Nolan, Mariann and Rusty Bracken, Christopher Giercke, Alan Hauser, Leee Black Childers, Walter Lure, Billy Rath, Henri-Paul, Michael Beal, Marcia Resnick, Bob Gruen, Stiv Bators, Gail Higgins Smith, John Perry, Susanne Blomqvist, Patti Palladin, Freddy Lynxx, Pedro Mercedes, Peter and Xena Perrett, Severina Karris, Phyllis Stein, and Danny Garcia.

INDEX